MW01017605

Captured at Kings Mountain

Captured at Kings Mountain

The Journal of Uzal Johnson

A LOYALIST SURGEON

Edited by

Wade S. Kolb III and Robert M. Weir

With the Assistance of Anne H. Weir

THE UNIVERSITY OF SOUTH CAROLINA PRESS

© 2011 University of South Carolina

Published by the University of South Carolina Press
Columbia, South Carolina 29208

www.sc.edu/uscpress

Manufactured in the United States of America

20 19 18 17 16 15 14 13 12 11   10 9 8 7 6 5 4 3 2 1

Library of Congress Cataloging-in-Publication Data

Johnson, Uzal, 1757?–1827.
  Captured at Kings Mountain : the journal of Uzal Johnson, a loyalist
surgeon / edited by Wade S. Kolb III and Robert M. Weir ; with the
assistance of Anne H. Weir.
     p. cm.
  Includes bibliographical references and index.
  ISBN 978-1-57003-961-4 (cloth : alk. paper)
   1. Johnson, Uzal, 1757?–1827—Diaries. 2. American loyalists—New
Jersey—Diaries. 3. New Jersey—Biography. 4. United States—History—
Revolution, 1775–1783—Personal narratives. 5. King's Mountain, Battle of,
S.C., 1780. 6. Ferguson, Patrick, 1744–1780. 7. Southern States—History—
Revolution, 1775–1783—Campaigns. 8. Surgeons—United States—Diaries.
9. United States—History—Revolution, 1775–1783—Medical care. 10. United
States—History—Revolution, 1775–1783—Campaigns. I. Kolb, Wade S., III.
II. Weir, Robert M. III. Weir, Anne H. IV. Title.
  E278.J64A3 2011
  973.3'75—dc22

                          2010035277

This book was printed on Glatfelter Natures, a recycled paper with 30 percent
postconsumer waste content.

Contents

Illustrations

Preface

We first encountered Uzal Johnson's diary of "occurrences" during the American Revolution over a decade ago when one of us was working on another project that involved research in the Thorne Boudinot Collection at Princeton University. An anonymous diary found there—later identified as Johnson's—prompted our curiosity, especially after part of it turned out to be remarkably similar to the journal kept by Lt. Anthony Allaire—another Loyalist who, like Johnson, was captured by American forces at the battle of Kings Mountain on October 7, 1780. Having been published in 1881, Allaire's diary had long been known to historians, who considered it the best account from the British side of the American victory that would prove to be a turning point in the War for Independence. The two journals therefore posed an intriguing textual problem: who was copying whom here? The more we worked on it, the more convinced we became that Johnson was not a plagiarist, that his diary was the more important of the two journals, and that it deserved publication.

Wade Kolb, who was then an undergraduate student, received a grant from the Honors College of the University of South Carolina to assist with the project, and the Department of History and the University Research and Productive Scholarship Fund subsidized the Weirs. In addition the National Endowment for the Humanities provided a Travel to Collections grant that enabled us to enlarge the scope of our research.

Accordingly what we all had envisioned as a relatively short-term project turned out to be more complex and time consuming than we had imagined, and years rolled by. Along the way we accumulated a host of scholarly debts, not only to the above-mentioned institutions, but also to the many individuals and repositories that made their facilities, materials, and expertise available, or scrutinized our work. Princeton University generously granted permission to publish Johnson's journal, and the New Jersey Archives, the New-York Historical Society, the New Brunswick Museum, the North Carolina Archives, the South Carolina Department of Archives and History, and the William L. Clements Library at the University of Michigan as well as the South Caroliniana Library and the Thomas Cooper Library at the University of South Carolina were especially accommodating. The following individuals also deserve our heartfelt thanks: Peter Sederberg, then dean of the University of South Carolina Honors College; Thomas McNally, dean of libraries at the University of South Carolina; Allen Stokes, director of the South Caroliniana Library; Patrick Scott, director of Special Collections, Jeffrey Makala and Zella Hilton of the Rare Book Room, Virginia Weathers, Joshua Garris, and the entire staff of the Reference Department, Robert Amerson and Jo Cottingham of Interlibrary Loan Services, and Ross Taylor of the Map Division, all of the University of South Carolina. Robin Copp and her staff members Lorrey McClure and Beverly Bullock of the Books Division of the South Caroliniana Library supplied patient and knowledgeable assistance.

Theodore Steinke graciously and expertly drew the maps, and William Sudduth, Charles Kovacik, and David Rembert provided welcome assistance with the cartography and illustrations. Tony McLawhorn helped us navigate the rough waters of the technological world. Debbie Rowland of the Calhoun County (South Carolina) Museum and Lois R. Densky-Wolff of the University of Medicine and Dentistry of New Jersey supplied important information. Keith Krawczynski assisted with preliminary research; John Frierson's interest in the project helped to fuel our own; and Bobby Moss's own work on Uzal Johnson and other participants in the American Revolution proved to be very useful. Charles Lesser not only read the manuscript but also called our attention to and provided valuable illustrative material. Robert Calhoon and Cory Stewart also read and made excellent suggestions regarding all or portions of the manuscript. Eric Emerson, now director of the South Carolina Department of Archives and History, provided vital encouragement during the early stages of the project, and the search-room staff of the archives consistently supplied good advice and courteous help. Matthew Lockhart, editor of the *South Carolina Historical Magazine,* and Alex Moore, of the University of South Carolina Press, as well as the anonymous readers for the press, helped to bring the project to completion. Stephen Hoffius prepared the index. We, the editors, thank all who made this edition possible.

Introduction

"Mrs. Mills with a Young Child in her Arms set out all Night in the Rain with her Husbands Corps[e]," a sympathetic observer recorded in his diary on October 14, 1780. Whigs had captured Colonel Ambrose Mills, a prominent North Carolina Loyalist, at the battle of Kings Mountain on October 7. A week later a drumhead court, assembled near what is now Rutherfordton, North Carolina, tried and executed him along with eight others. Dr. Uzal Johnson, another Tory prisoner—hitherto perhaps best known for treating the wounded of both sides after the battle—captured the poignant scene in the diary published here.

Some background information is useful for understanding the significance of Johnson's "Memorandum of Occunces [Occurrences] during the Campaigne [of] 1780." Most important, the American victory at Kings Mountain was a turning point in the Revolution, "the first link in a chain of evils," Sir Henry Clinton, the British commander in chief, would term it, "that followed each other in regular succession until they at last ended in the total loss of America." Because the victory gave hope to the Whigs and greatly dispirited the Loyalists, many commentators have concurred.[1] Among these writers Lyman Draper was perhaps the foremost, and his monumental work *King's Mountain and Its Heroes* (1881) remains very useful, partly because it includes some firsthand accounts of the battle by participants. One of these narratives, Anthony Allaire's "Memorandum of Occurrences during the Campaign in 1780," has long been regarded by historians and bibliographers as perhaps the most informative document generated by the British side.[2]

In his account Allaire occasionally refers to "my friend, Dr. Johnson," who in turn periodically mentions "my friend Allaire" in his diary. Comparison of the two documents suggests that reciprocity went well beyond such courtesies. Extended passages in their respective accounts are identical. Given the duplication of some material long available in Allaire's journal, a reader might fairly question why the present edition of Johnson's diary is necessary, particularly since another version of it has been published.[3] A complete answer is complex and will emerge more fully throughout the present work, but a preliminary response is as follows. First, Johnson's journal covers more time and territory than Allaire's; and second, the similarities between the two accounts raise potentially troubling questions about their authenticity. Furthermore, if such doubts can be resolved, the discrepancies in the two volumes become worth investigating. Accordingly, because neither Draper—who was unaware of Johnson's manuscript—nor its recent editor pursued the subject, the present edition of Johnson's diary seeks to identify the precise relationship between the two journals and thereby provide a basis for reasonable conjectures about the wider implications of their superficial resemblances and more significant differences.

I
THE DIARIES AND THEIR AUTHORS

The question of authenticity is basic, for if these journals are not what they appear to be, all bets are off. Who were the authors, and did they really write the documents attributed to them? Anthony Allaire, who was twenty-five years old in 1780, was born in New Rochelle, New York. A lieutenant in the Loyal American Regiment, a Loyalist regiment raised in New York in late 1776 and early 1777, he and approximately 120 other men detached from several Loyalist battalions served in a special unit under Maj. Patrick Ferguson during the southern campaign of 1780–81. Allaire, who acted as the unit's adjutant, termed them "the American Volunteers." Along with many of his companions, Allaire was captured at the battle of Kings Mountain. About a month later, he escaped and made his way to Charles Town, South Carolina, which the British then held. Continuing with the British army until the end of the war, he, like many other Loyalists, received land in New Brunswick, Canada, where he died in 1838.[4]

Uzal Johnson, who was born in Newark, New Jersey, in April 1751, earned a bachelor of medicine degree from Kings College (now Columbia University) in 1772 and began practicing in his hometown. In 1776 he received a commission as a surgeon in the First Battalion of the Second Regiment of Whig troops, raised in Essex County, New Jersey. But apparently he defected to the British after the Declaration of Independence.[5] Pursuant to legislation passed against Loyalists in 1776, 1777, and 1778, state authorities subsequently confiscated his medicines and other personal property. Meanwhile, Johnson obtained a surgeon's commission in the New Jersey Volunteers. Its several battalions eventually enrolled at least 2,450 men, or approximately one-sixth of the more than 15,000 Loyalists who served in some fifty provincial corps of regular troops raised in America.[6]

As did Allaire, Johnson later served in Ferguson's Corps. Captured at Kings Mountain, he remained a prisoner of war until he was paroled and subsequently freed by an exchange of prisoners sometime before March 2, 1781. A little over a year later, he reentered civilian life, married,[7] and resumed his practice of medicine in Newark. In time he was sufficiently successful to become president of the local medical society and a member of the vestry of Trinity Church. By the 1790s his house was something of a landmark, and well before his death on May 22, 1827, he had become prosperous enough to own several town lots. Whether he stayed in touch with Anthony Allaire after the war is not certain, but he may well have, for he named a son born in 1788 Isaac Allaire.[8]

The provenance of the diaries purportedly kept by these two young men provides clues to their authenticity. The manuscript of Johnson's journal is now among the collection of Boudinot Papers given to Princeton University by Mrs. Langdon K. Thorne in 1954. This Loyalist document was probably not part of the patriotic exhibit at the public opening of the Boudinot mansion in Elizabeth, New Jersey, in 1943, but Johnson's family Bible was displayed there. The house itself belonged at one time to Elias Boudinot, who served as president of the Continental Congress from 1782 to 1783. His more obscure, older brother, John, was a doctor. Someone therefore plausibly but erroneously concluded that he was the author of the anonymous journal. Later another researcher, using internal evidence, correctly identified it as the diary of Uzal Johnson.[9] The crucial question for present purposes is how did this item become part of the Boudinot Papers? One cannot be absolutely sure, but the most likely route was by way of Uzal Johnson's granddaughter, Jane Mary Kip, who married one of Elias Boudinot's nephews, Elias E. Boudinot (1791–1863).[10] Doubtless she contributed her grandfather's diary to the family cache of Revolutionary War documents.

The Allaire diary also remained in the hands of Allaire's descendants until it came to rest in the New Brunswick Museum at Saint John. Allaire's daughter Eliza Maria married John Robinson (1788–1866), the son of another prominent Loyalist, Lt. Col. Beverley Robinson of New York. Their son J. Delancy Robinson furnished Lyman Draper with a transcript of the diary, which became the basis of the published version, "Memorandum of Occurrences during the Campaign in 1780." The original remained in Robinson's hands and eventually became part of the Beverley Robinson Papers housed in the New Brunswick Museum. In the 1970s, however, it went missing for some time until an alert reader recognized the volume and returned it to the museum.[11]

The genealogical routes of both documents are therefore traceable, but they are sufficiently tangled to suggest that a reader should approach these

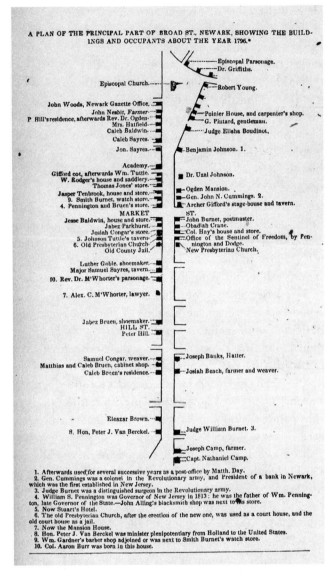

A PLAN OF THE PRINCIPAL PART OF BROAD ST., NEWARK, SHOWING THE BUILD-
INGS AND OCCUPANTS ABOUT THE YEAR 1796.*

·······Episcopal Parsonage.
·······Dr. Griffiths.

Episcopal Church.····

····Robert Young.

John Woods, Newark Gazette Office.
John Nesbit, Farmer·····
P Hill's residence, afterwards Rev. Dr. Ogden·····
Mrs. Hatfield·····
Caleb Baldwin·····
Caleb Sayres.····
Jon. Sayres·····

····Poinier House, and carpenter's shop.
····G. Pintard, gentleman.
·····Judge Elisha Boudinot.

Benjamin Johnson. 1.

Academy.····
Gifford cot, afterwards Wm. Tuttle.····
W. Rodger's house and saddlery.····
Thomas Jones' store.····
Jasper Tenbrook, house and store.····
9. Smith Burnet, watch store.····
4. Pennington and Bruen's store.····

Dr. Uzal Johnson.

Ogden Mansion.
Gen. John N. Cummings. 2.
Archer Gifford's stage-house and tavern.
ST.

MARKET
Jesse Baldwin, house and store.····
Jabez Parkhurst.····
Josiah Congar's store.····
5. Johnson Tuttle's tavern.····
6. Old Presbyterian Church·····
Old County Jail.

John Burnet, postmaster.
Obadiah Crane.
Col. Hay's house and store.
Office of the Sentinel of Freedom, by Pen-
nington and Dodge.
New Presbyterian Church.

Luther Goble, shoemaker.····
Major Samuel Sayres, tavern.····
10. Rev. Dr. M'Whorter's parsonage.····

7. Alex. C. M'Whorter, lawyer.

Jabez Bruen, shoemaker.····
HILL ST.
Peter Hill.····

Samuel Congar, weaver.····
Matthias and Caleb Bruen, cabinet shop.····
Caleb Bruen's residence.····

Joseph Banks, Hatter.

Josiah Bench, farmer and weaver.

Eleazar Brown.····
8. Hon, Peter J. Van Berckel.····

Judge William Burnet. 3.

Joseph Camp, farmer.
Capt. Nathaniel Camp.

1. Afterwards used for several successive years as a post-office by Matth. Day.
2. Gen. Cummings was a colonel in the Revolutionary army, and President of a bank in Newark,
which was the first established in New Jersey.
3. Judge Burnet was a distinguished surgeon in the Revolutionary army.
4. William S. Pennington was Governor of New Jersey in 1813; he was the father of Wm. Pennington, late Governor of the State.—John Alling's blacksmith shop was next to his store.
5. Now Stuart's Hotel.
6. The old Presbyterian Church, after the erection of the new one, was used as a court house, and the
old court house as a jail.
7. Now the Mansion House.
8. Hon. Peter J. Van Berckel was minister plenipotentiary from Holland to the United States.
9. Wm. Gardner's barber shop adjoined or was next to Smith Burnet's watch store.
10. Col. Aaron Burr was born in this house.

Johnson's home on Broad Street was near the center of Newark
during the 1790s. From Frank Urquhart et al., *A History of the
City of Newark, New Jersey, 1666–1913* (New York: Lewis
Historical Publishing Co., 1913)

diaries cautiously. Because a version of Allaire's account was in print more than sixty years before Johnson's journal surfaced, the latter could conceivably be a forgery. But verbatim replication of extensive passages from a readily identifiable original would seem to be a strange way to cobble together a counterfeit document. Moreover, British officers did frequently carry small notebooks in which they kept memoranda and, occasionally, diaries, and Johnson's journal certainly bears the hallmarks of an eighteenth-century document. The paper and ink are appropriate for the period, and the small notebook (4 x 6 inches and 121 pages) in which he wrote would have been readily portable in the field.[12] Absolute proof that Johnson carried it with him is lacking, but some lapses in grammar and spelling suggest that he wrote under less than ideal conditions, and cramped penmanship and crammed pages indicate that in the first part of the diary, at least, the writer tried hard to avoid wasting space. In addition he mentioned numerous incidents—some not included in Allaire's diary—which can be verified from other sources. In short Johnson's journal appears to be genuine.

Allaire's book is only a bit more problematic. Comparison with a letter known to have been written by him suggests that the handwriting in the volume is his. The notebook, like Johnson's, is small enough (3¾ by 5¾ inches and 158 pages) to have been easily carried, and its author took equal pains to waste as little paper as possible. The volume also opens with military matters: standing orders, passwords, and the like, as well as the "Memorandum of Occurrences during the Campaign of 1780." It is also worth noting that Lyman Draper—who apparently never saw the original notebook but whose knowledge of the events surrounding the battle of Kings Mountain was encyclopedic—believed that Allaire's journal was authentic. These facts suggest that his assessment was correct, as far as it went.

But someone was probably copying from someone. At the very least, Allaire and Johnson cooperated in writing their accounts, which frequently appear to be verbatim transcriptions of each other. More significant, perhaps, neither journal contains a labeled entry for one date, May 9, 1780.

Whose version was the primary document and which was secondary therefore becomes an intriguing question. Some characteristics of Allaire's journal suggest an answer. His complete notebook is a hybrid, part journal, part literary commonplace book, and part scrapbook. It contains, in addition to the military section, prose quotations, poetry, and newspaper clippings. Much of its content, in short, is derivative. Does this indicate that he copied his journal of the southern campaign? Of course not, but it does suggest that his pride of authorship was not fiercely exclusive. Moreover the military journal itself contains tantalizing indications that parts of it may have been lifted from Johnson's journal. In otherwise identical passages, Allaire's spelling, grammar, and penmanship are often better than Johnson's. Whatever this difference might suggest about the skills and education of the authors, such refinements would normally characterize not a first but a second draft. Furthermore, comparison of similar sections in the two diaries reveals that Allaire sometimes placed a word or two later in a sentence than Johnson did, as if in copying he first omitted and later inserted them. In addition Johnson often enumerated dates in a string of consecutive uneventful days that failed to warrant substantive entries. Allaire, on the other hand, frequently gave only the opening and closing dates of such periods.[13] Johnson's practice was compatible with an attempt to maintain an ongoing daily record; Allaire's with that of someone writing later. Finally Allaire ended his diary in November 1780, but Johnson continued his record until March 1781, a difference that might indicate the persistence of a more methodical habit. Obviously these clues are not conclusive, but they suggest that occasionally, at least, Allaire copied from Johnson's journal.

The duties and circumstances of the two men during the periods covered reinforce this inference. Allaire was the group's adjutant and, as such, was responsible for the paperwork of the unit, including reports of captured materials and the like. Thus he had an official as well as a personal interest in some of the information contained in these diaries. But he was also a line— as well as a staff—officer, and this entailed other duties. These put him in the field with the soldiers, and wearing the two hats made him a busy man. In short one suspects that he had the motivation but frequently not the time to record the events of the day. Johnson, on the other hand, was a medical officer. Thus, except after significant battles when he was caring for the wounded, he seems to have enjoyed considerable leisure. Keeping a journal would have been a constructive way to occupy his time. Their respective circumstances therefore probably helped to make Johnson the more faithful recorder of the days' events. The men frequently shared quarters, however, and many similar entries may have been collaborative compositions in which each individual contributed information that the other lacked. Johnson may also have occasionally copied from Allaire. But if either document deserves to be termed the primary source, it is undoubtedly Johnson's.

Obviously credit belongs where credit is due, and if Johnson was indeed the primary diarist, he should be recognized for what his journal made him— namely, the most important Loyalist chronicler of the events surrounding the battle of Kings Mountain. That two such similar accounts contain significant discrepancies raises a fundamental question about reliability, however. Which is the better version? The answer depends on how one wishes to use the material. Allaire, who probably had access to his commander's maps, was often more accurate in providing verifiable names and locations.[14] At times he also provided information that Johnson omitted (although the opposite was more frequently the case). On October 29, 1780, for example, Allaire recorded that most of the prisoners at Salem, North Carolina, were marched "to a height about half a mile from the town. Here we heard a Presbyterian sermon, truly adapted to their principles and the times; or, rather, stuffed as full of Republicanism as their camp is of horse thieves." Johnson, who was ill that day, did not attend the service, nor did he mention it. But the records of the local Moravian community support Allaire's facts, if not his sentiments.[15] Indeed his journal, which is replete with caustic comments, reveals that he was considerably more hostile than Johnson toward rebel Americans.

Not surprisingly the different attitudes of the two men sometimes produced strikingly different journal entries. While they were at Ninety Six, a small hamlet in South Carolina, their observations varied significantly. On June 22 Johnson was more specific about this "flourishing part of the Country, the Land round about it in General is good. Natural Growth is Oaks, Black Walnut, Hickery, &c which are very large & thrifty, the Land is cleared for a Mile Round the Town, it produces Wheat, Indian Corn, Oats, Hemp, Flax, Cotton, & Indigo." Allaire, on the other hand, noted on the twenty-fourth that his quarters in town were "opposite the jail, where I have the constant view of the Rebels peeping through the grates, which affords some satisfaction to see them suffer for their folly. Some of them are magistrates; one the executioner of the five that were hanged here some time in April, 1779."[16]

Allaire was also more careful about military proprieties. On August 28, for example, Johnson observed that "Coll. Ferguson . . . had promised to do his best to get us all relieved from the disagreeable service in the back Woods." On the following day, however, part of the unit received orders that "greatly mortified us, for now we began to see our destiny was fixed to do duty in the back Woods seperate from the Main Army, with the Militia." Allaire, ever the good soldier, merely noted that their orders were "disagreeable." He also tended to omit material that might reflect adversely on British conduct. In August 1780 Whig forces under Elijah Clarke laid siege to Augusta, Georgia. Eventually a relief force from Ninety Six and the local garrison compelled Clarke's withdrawal, capturing many prisoners in the process. "Twenty seven of them," according to Johnson, "were hanged at Augusta, & twenty seven brought to Ninety-Six to share the same fate." Allaire's account on the twenty-fourth gave some detail about the battle but did not mention the hangings.[17]

The diaries also reveal significant differences in their attitudes toward women. Take, for instance, their respective diary entries for July 9, when they spent the night at a farmhouse near Ninety Six. There, Allaire noted, "we found two women, and spent the night, though not to our satisfaction. It afforded some merry scenes with those two modest country women."[18] Johnson omitted not only the sexual innuendo but all mention of the encounter. Fancying himself as something of a ladies' man, Allaire tended to regard women as objects. Johnson, on the other hand, approached them with the compassion of a good physician. Allaire's silence on the matter and Johnson's sympathy for Mrs. Mills after the execution of her husband, in the scene described at the beginning of this introduction, provides a case in point. So too does Johnson's observation that the people on the border of North and South Carolina had "always been kept in ignorance, & told of the Cruelty of the English, one Poor Woman expressed great surprize at seeing our Men so mild, she asked if there was not Heathens in our Army that eat Children, she had been told there was." Allaire made no comparable observation; he simply did not appear to have been very interested in women as people. In contrast Johnson often put them at center stage. Their descriptions of the Coleman household accordingly typify the subtle but substantial difference in their attitudes. On September 5, not far from the Pacolet River in present-day Union County, South Carolina, Johnson wrote, "I took quarters at Mr Colemans. . . . Mrs. Coleman is a very warm Tory, she has two Sons in Coll. Innes's Corps. She has a family of small Children & has been Mother of five in two Years, they have been greatly distressed by the Rebels for their Loyalty, the House strip'd of all the Beds & other furniture, & the Children of all their Cloaths." Allaire's version reduced this description to the observation that they lodged at "one Coleman's, who is a very warm Tory. His wife and all her children have been stripped of all their clothes, bedding, and other furniture. She was mother of five children in two years."[19]

In short the two diaries complement each other and are therefore useful for different purposes. Surprisingly—although understandably because of their respective duties at the time—Johnson recorded more detail about the actual battle of Kings Mountain than Allaire did. In addition Johnson's work includes more about the fate of prisoners and their relationship with the local populace in North Carolina than Allaire's because he was there nearly four months longer. Most important, perhaps, Johnson also tells us more about not only women but also Americans in general than does Allaire, whose attitudes restricted his vision.

That Johnson stayed in the United States after the war and his friend Allaire took refuge in Canada thus seems almost predictable from their journal entries. But precisely how Johnson reentered the good graces of his neighbors is obscure. Scattered evidence, nevertheless, provides some hints. The leaders of the Revolution in Newark and its surroundings were disproportionately Presbyterians; Johnson—at least in later life—was an Episcopalian. Accordingly one does not have to be a cynic to suspect that his contribution to the building fund for the First Presbyterian Church in 1786 was more than an act of unadulterated altruism. Nevertheless his usefulness as a physician was probably crucial, and it was scarcely coincidental that doctors were among the Loyalists most apt to return to their original communities at the end of the war. Johnson's diary might also have helped. For if Whig authorities scrutinized it before deciding what to do about him, they would have found that it revealed an honorable and compassionate man whose presence might benefit the community.[20]

II

THE BRITISH CAMPAIGN AGAINST CHARLES TOWN

Because the American Revolution erupted in April 1775 with the battles of Lexington and Concord, British authorities naturally assumed that Massachusetts was the militant center of the rebellion. Meanwhile royal governors in the southern colonies from Virginia to Georgia repeatedly assured them that a large part of the population in those areas was loyal. Only a few ships and soldiers, they maintained, could deal with matters there. As a result British strategy during the first three years of the war concentrated on subduing the northern colonies. The South remained a sideshow, although in February 1776 a substantial expedition sailed for North Carolina to test and bolster southern support. In South Carolina, however, British sympathizers had shown their hand prematurely. In November 1775 a skirmish during which about 1,900 men surrounded Whig militia at a makeshift fort near Ninety Six prompted retaliation, and a patriot force of more than 2,500 soldiers captured 130 Loyalists encamped on the Reedy River and intimidated many more throughout the backcountry. Meanwhile bad weather and logistical problems delayed the arrival of the British force, and impatient Highland Scots, who constituted the most cohesive group of zealous Loyalists in North Carolina, also jumped the gun. Whigs then routed them at Moore's Creek Bridge in February 1776. Thus, when the British fleet arrived, there were few organized Loyalists to support. Reluctant to leave the area without accomplishing something but unprepared to lay siege to Charles Town, the British commanders headed south, intending if possible to capture and hold Sullivans Island at the entrance to the harbor. A base there might close the chief port in the southern colonies to the Americans.[21]

The resulting battle occurred on June 28, 1776. South Carolinians had been working on a fort at the southern end of Sullivans Island. Looking at its still unfinished walls of palmetto logs and sand, the Continental army commander in the south, Gen. Charles Lee, termed it a slaughterhouse and recommended its abandonment. But South Carolina troops under the command of Gen. William Moultrie occupied the fort, and neither he nor the president of the state, John Rutledge, was willing to give it up. Riflemen posted at the north end of the island protected the rear of the installation. Any British troops who tried to cross the inlet there, one Carolinian accurately observed, "would be pretty well melted down." Attacking the fort therefore proved to be mainly the task of the Royal Navy. But the spongy palmetto walls absorbed cannonballs like sandbags and the fort held up well, and the provincial troops acquitted themselves, Lee admitted, more bravely than he had expected. As a result the British suffered the loss of one ship, substantial damage to several others, and nearly two hundred killed and wounded. Seventeen defenders died and twenty suffered wounds.[22]

After the British fleet sailed away, North Carolina, South Carolina, and Virginia dealt with threats from the west. Largely because of white encroachment on their lands, the Cherokee Indians began attacking frontier settlements during July 1776. Virginians retaliated farther north, and the two Carolinas responded with a joint expedition. The South Carolinians, whose arms and supplies were the envy of the North Carolinians, fielded about twelve hundred men, who devastated the Indian towns and cornfields. While the Native American inhabitants starved, the victorious Whigs suppressed the remaining Loyalists, who had always been most numerous in the backcountry, particularly between the Broad and Saluda rivers in South Carolina. But many of the men most committed to the British cause had already fled to Florida, where they would form military units such as the East Florida Rangers and the South Carolina Royalists. Those that remained could not counter the relatively well-organized patriot militia. The irregular warfare that followed accordingly weakened British support in the area and trained Whigs for partisan operations later in the war.[23]

British authorities' assumptions about the soft underbelly of the rebels were probably never correct, and such thinking was certainly out of date by the time they decided that a southern strategy was in order. But the secretary of state for the American colonies, Lord George Germain, had long believed that British forces only needed to show up in the southern colonies and the Loyalists would turn out to support them. Early on the British believed that such aid was superfluous, but after France and Spain entered the war (in February 1778 and June 1779, respectively), Great Britain faced formidable enemies that could threaten its West Indian possessions and even England itself. Such dangers presaged greater costs and sacrifices, which would be politically unpalatable. The ministry therefore needed all the help it could get, and the Loyalists became a more important consideration. Consequently Germain ordered Sir Henry Clinton, the commander in chief in America, to detach eight thousand troops from his main force in New York for service in Florida and the West Indies; Clinton himself was then to capitalize on the presumed strength of the Loyalists in the southern colonies by a campaign designed to conquer everything from Georgia northward to Virginia.[24] If all went according to plan, the British army would sweep through an area, organize the Loyalists as an effective militia, and move on. Meanwhile the Loyalists would maintain British control.

Some delay ensued, but in the late autumn of 1778 Clinton sent three thousand soldiers under the command of Lt. Col. Archibald Campbell to take Georgia, and the British southern strategy appeared to meet with quick success. In late December, Savannah fell, and Augusta followed shortly thereafter. So many individuals appeared to welcome the change that British authorities reestablished the old royal government, making Georgia the only reconquered colony under civilian control. Although the British were overextended and unable to hold Augusta, South Carolina seemed to be ripe for plucking. True, a small force sent toward Beaufort met defeat at the battle of Port Royal Island in February 1779, but the British assumed that many erstwhile rebels had become disillusioned with their new government and the war. Thus when American forces under Gen. Benjamin Lincoln threatened the Georgia backcountry, Gen. Augustine Prevost countered by a rapid thrust near the coast toward Charles Town. Patriot resistance was minimal, and by May 11 he was able to demand the surrender of the city.[25]

Gov. John Rutledge, acting with the advice of his council, agreed to capitulate, provided that South Carolina be allowed to remain neutral until the end of the war, when it would share the fate of the other colonies. Rutledge's actions have been the subject of considerable controversy among historians. Some argue that he merely sought to buy time with deceptive negotiations while awaiting aid from General Lincoln. Other scholars maintain that the offer was genuine and that it reflected resentment against the Continental

Congress for providing South Carolinians with inadequate protection and recommending that they defend themselves by arming slaves. These interpretations may both be partially correct but incomplete. What may have made neutrality seem like a viable option were prevailing practices in the West Indies and, in particular, the conditions under which French Guadeloupe surrendered to British forces in 1759. The terms of that capitulation, which were well publicized in the English press while Rutledge was a student in London, were not only strikingly similar to what he proposed for South Carolina in 1779 but also remarkably successful from the French point of view. The inhabitants of the island were allowed to keep their property, and most prospered under British rule before the Peace of Paris returned Guadeloupe to France in 1763.[26]

Perhaps aware of this history, Prevost—who had served in the West Indies during the Seven Years' War—rejected Rutledge's proposal and demanded unconditional surrender, which the Carolinians refused. Prevost then retreated to escape, being trapped by Lincoln, who was hurrying to the defense of Charles Town. An inconclusive battle at Stono a month later allowed British forces to withdraw to Georgia without further serious opposition, but they left a small garrison at Beaufort to control the best deepwater port on the southern coast. Inadvertently, because of widespread plundering—which Prevost tried but failed to control—this expedition also left a legacy of increased hostility among Americans along Prevost's route.[27] Nevertheless the negotiations at Charles Town did nothing to dispel British notions that South Carolina would be an easy conquest.

In September 1779 General Lincoln and a French fleet under Admiral d'Estaing laid siege to Savannah, but the final assault on October 9 failed, and Clinton was therefore free to mount a full-scale campaign in the southern colonies. On December 26, 1779, he set sail from New York with approximately ninety transports, fourteen armed naval vessels, eighty-five hundred men, and four hundred horses, in addition to much equipment. Storms pounded them on the voyage, blowing one vessel all the way back to England, sinking others, and killing almost all of the horses. By the end of January 1780, most of the ships had reached Savannah, where the fleet regrouped and refitted. The British fleet then sailed for the North Edisto River, and during the second week of February troops began landing on Simmons (now Seabrook) Island, South Carolina. Some units, including fourteen hundred men under Gen. James Paterson, remained behind in Georgia to divert the attention of the American defenders.[28]

Paterson's force included the American Volunteers, commanded by Maj. Patrick Ferguson. Known to his friends and family as Pate, Ferguson was a thirty-five-year-old Scottish officer who had first entered the army in 1759. Impressed by the marksmanship of German and American riflemen, he later invented a rapid-fire breech-loading rifle that, unlike its muzzle-loading counterparts or the more common musket, was reliable in wet weather. With such a weapon, one of his facetious friends claimed to be able to hit a flea at eight paces.[29] More significantly, during the battle of Brandywine on the road to Philadelphia in September 1777, Ferguson commanded a small unit equipped with these weapons when an enemy horseman came within easy range. Ferguson ordered him to halt, but the man ignored him and rode slowly on. Unwilling to shoot someone in the back who was "very coolly" doing his duty, Ferguson held his fire. Later he came to believe that the officer was George Washington—something, the Scotsman added, he was glad that he did not know at the time. Although he may have been mistaken about the American's identity, Ferguson's reaction speaks well for him. Nevertheless no one should mistake his sense of fair play for squeamishness because he had no qualms about harsh measures when he considered them appropriate. The destruction of New Haven, a sweep up the west side of the Connecticut River with fire and sword to Springfield, its destruction, and an equally devastating return down the east side of the river would be most useful, he believed, because the British could thereby "in a fortnight ruin the Granary of New England."[30]

Despite a wound suffered at Brandywine that crippled his right arm, Ferguson continued in the service and thirteen months later was able to implement some of his more draconian ideas when he led a successful attack on Little Egg Harbor, New Jersey. Among his soldiers in this foray were some from the New Jersey Volunteers; later a number of men picked from this and other Loyalist regiments formed the American Volunteers. One of them was Uzal Johnson, who served as the group's surgeon.[31]

Theoretically each British regiment—nominally about eight hundred men—had one surgeon and one surgeon's mate. Surgeons were military doctors, whose designation reflected their most conspicuous duty—namely, operating on the wounded. Theirs was a grim business that, in Europe at least, affected their social status even in civilian life, where sharp distinctions prevailed in the medical professions. Doctors, who reigned supreme, performed the intellectual labor; surgeons, who were called mister, did the dirty work. These distinctions broke down in the colonies, and most of the approximately thirty-five hundred physicians practicing in 1775 functioned as apothecaries and surgeons as well as doctors. Unlike Johnson, who graduated from college, most received their training under the apprenticeship system rather than in one of the two colonial medical schools at Philadelphia and New York. Nevertheless American practitioners appear to have enjoyed higher social status than their European counterparts, although some of the stigma attached to surgery remained. In South Carolina, for example, surgeons, like butchers, were reputed to be disqualified as jurors because they were deemed "less compassionate" than other men.[32]

Such invidious distinctions prevailed well into the nineteenth century in the British army, where surgeons often had middle-class backgrounds, whereas regular officers usually came from the upper classes. The result, through most of the eighteenth century, was that military surgeons ranked below the most junior ensigns and were generally ignored on ceremonial occasions. Johnson nevertheless enjoyed the privileges of a commissioned officer, and his experience seems to suggest that more egalitarian American attitudes permeated the British Loyalist units. Certainly he had the respect of his fellow officers, who, in the words of one, considered him to be "a very good Surgeon." But whether this judgment was based on his education, his skill, or his personal qualities is hard to say. Unfortunately the patient whose care prompted this assessment died. Significantly, however, the patient's death does not appear to have diminished Johnson's reputation, for everyone recognized that doctors were quite limited in what they could then accomplish. One sick patient doubtlessly spoke for many others when, after being tormented by ineffectual treatments, he observed that the doctor's failure to call one day seemed to have relieved him "from half of my ailment."[33]

Still, Johnson's role was considered important. Because the causes of infections and diseases were not yet understood, alleviating visible symptoms—which was no small matter—remained the focus of medical attention. Thus bleeding was an all-purpose remedy, and a standard manual for military surgeons published in 1776 noted that wounds of the chest and abdomen, being "serious," required that the patient "be bled all he will bear, bleeding to be repeated at intervals." This procedure usually involved taking sixteen to twenty-four ounces of blood from an arm. Surgical operations proceeded under anything but antiseptic conditions, and mortality was correspondingly high, perhaps 50 percent among amputees. Nevertheless, by the late seventeenth century, Dutch and Prussian military men had recognized that cleanliness had its virtues, if only as an adjunct to military discipline. When William of Orange became king of England in 1688, he had accordingly introduced Dutch practices. Historians have therefore surmised that the better-disciplined British army maintained cleaner camps and consequently suffered less from disease during the Revolution than the Americans. Perhaps so, but Johnson had surprisingly little to say about hygiene even though the subject was within his purview and coastal South Carolina was a notoriously

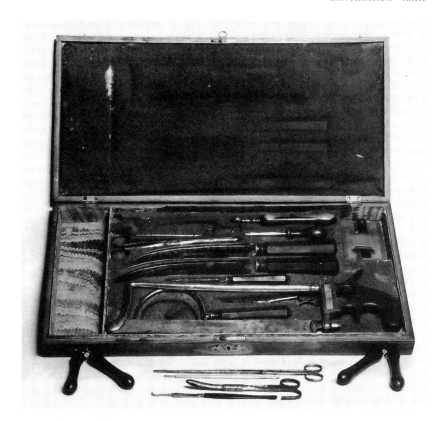

Surgeon's portable instrument case. Guidance to the use of these instruments could be found in *Plain Concise Practical Remarks, on the Treatment of Wounds and Fractures; to which is Added an Appendix on Camp and Military Hospitals . . .* (Philadelphia: printed by Robert Bell, 1776) by John Jones, who was Johnson's professor of surgery at Kings College. AFIP Accession Number 22-8691-2. Courtesy of the Armed Forces Institute of Pathology and Armed Forces Histopathology Center, Department of Defense, Washington, D.C.

unhealthy place. Perhaps because his detachment moved frequently and reached the healthier upcountry before autumn, when malaria and other illnesses were most prevalent, such concerns were relatively superfluous. Nevertheless Johnson recorded several instances when he himself was seriously ill.[34]

He was healthy, however, and just outside of Savannah on Sunday, March 5, when he began his "Memorandum of Occunces [Occurrences] during the Campaigne of 1780." As a matter of record, the campaign commenced for him that day, but several Loyalist battalions had been in the Savannah area for some time reviewing signals, training, and awaiting marching orders. Being "form'd from different Regts" and therefore not "Uniform in their Practice," these units needed to work out the kinks to "be able to Act together at their Landing" and thereafter. Noting that punishments were to be "as few as is . . . Consistent with the Support of Military Discipline," officers reminded their men that they were all picked volunteers who should try to bring honor on their units and "Justify the Generals [*sic*] good Opinion" of them. Company commanders accordingly hoped to treat the men as "Fellow Soldiers Fighting in one cause for their King For Liberty [and] For Their Familys & Property." Encouraged to make "a free Choice of comrades," small groups of soldiers would "Sleep & Mess together," care for "each other in Sickness," and "Share in hardships as well as in Danger." Such a buddy system, commanders believed, would please the men and "much increase their Confidence in Action."[35]

This reasonable assumption was yet to be thoroughly tested when the American Volunteers began their march toward Charles Town. But combat lay ahead, for Clinton had decided after surveying the situation that the city was more strongly defended than he had expected and he would need more troops then he had first thought. He therefore ordered Gen. James Paterson, whose corps had been left behind in Georgia to create a diversion, to join the main army. Paterson's second in command, Alexander Innes, was to bring along all the cattle he could round up. But, mindful of the counterproductive effects of the plundering on Prevost's expedition a year earlier, Clinton quickly added, "for God's sake no irregularities."[36]

By the tenth of March, some of the American Volunteers had crossed the Savannah River; Johnson and the remainder followed the next day. As Paterson's corps moved northward by the main coastal road, Clinton's soldiers consolidated their positions on James Island and the south side of the Ashley River. By the end of March, Paterson's troops had joined Clinton's, and on the twenty-ninth, advance units crossed the Ashley River at John Drayton's plantation several miles upstream from Charles Town. They then swung south between the Ashley and the Cooper rivers, and on April 1 began entrenching themselves some eight hundred yards north of the fortifications at Charles Town, which ran across the peninsula from the Ashley River on one side to the Cooper River on the other.[37]

The siege continued for six weeks. Although superior British naval forces maintained an effective blockade, Benjamin Lincoln's army could still have escaped overland. But, given local authorities' flirtation with neutrality the year before, abandoning the most important city in the south would have been politically disastrous. Thus, as a British observer noted, the Americans had caged themselves and, he surmised, would soon sing, "I can't get out, I can't get out." His hopes were justified, for on April 12 Clinton dispatched Lt. Col. James Webster with fourteen hundred men to seize a key bridge across the headwaters of the Cooper River. Two days later Webster's men under the immediate command of Ferguson and Lt. Col. Banastre Tarleton attacked and routed American forces at Moncks Corner. And on the twenty-sixth of April, Charles, Earl Cornwallis captured Mount Pleasant across the harbor from Charles Town. These actions cut communications between the city and the rest of the state. Gen. Benjamin Lincoln and the defenders of Charles Town held out for nearly three more weeks, but the British shelled the town heavily, soon setting it afire. When an officer lamented that the Americans had been able to put out the flames, Clinton privately observed that it would be "absurd, impolitic, and inhuman to burn a town you mean to occupy." On May 12, 1780, the defenders surrendered. The British capture of the city, with more than five thousand troops and militia in it, was—until the fall of Bataan to the Japanese in 1942—the largest single defeat inflicted on the United States by a foreign enemy.[38]

III
WAR IN THE BACKCOUNTRY

The capitulation of Charles Town temporarily seemed to extinguish most resistance in South Carolina. So many individuals "took protection," or swore allegiance to the Crown, that on May 25, British commanders believed that the Carolinas had been "conquered in Charles Town." Because this supposition would lead Clinton—who was not prone to political mistakes—to make a major blunder, more explanation of his overconfidence may be useful. First, as previously discussed, southern governors had long assured British authorities that most of the inhabitants of the lower south, especially in the backcountry, were loyal to the Crown, and expectations in London were high that Clinton would find this assessment to be accurate. He in turn was accordingly predisposed to do so. Equally important, perhaps, Clinton's trusted adviser on local matters was James Simpson, who had been a longtime resident of South Carolina, a considerable property holder in the backcountry near the town of Ninety Six, and, briefly before the war, attorney general of South Carolina. In the spring of 1779 Secretary of State Lord George Germain had sent him to Georgia to gather intelligence about political sentiment there and in the Carolinas. His findings turned out to be highly favorable: many individuals, he reported, were disenchanted with their new governments and tired of the privations of war. Hindsight suggests that these assessments were too rosy, but Simpson was undoubtedly an able man, and he clearly knew more about the local situation than anyone else in Clinton's entourage. Clinton therefore relied heavily upon him, and Simpson quickly became the chief liaison between local residents and the British command. He was *the* man to see if one had problems. And supplicants naturally tended to exaggerate the warmth of their feelings toward the British. In fact Simpson made it clear that he did not talk to inveterate rebels unless they initiated the contact.[39] The information that he gathered and relayed to Clinton was therefore inherently biased. But the readiness with which scattered American forces were surrendering seemed to confirm Simpson's reports.

As a result Clinton misjudged the local situation. Under the terms of the surrender agreement, Continental army troops became prisoners of war. The enlisted men were destined for close confinement, most of them eventually on prison ships. At first the officers were restricted to Haddrell's Point (across the Cooper River from Charles Town) and its environs. Militiamen and civilians, on the other hand, were paroled—that is, upon swearing not to aid their rebellious former comrades and to turn themselves in when demanded by British authorities, they were permitted to return home. Those who surrendered outside of Charles Town received similar treatment. Thus much of the population looked forward to an extended period of neutrality. But this expectation conflicted with British plans to use local manpower to pacify South Carolina and aid with the invasion of North Carolina. Confronted with the prospect of being conscripted for this purpose, erstwhile rebels, Clinton reported, "seemed at first to boggle at the idea of arming against the [Continental] Congress, but with respect to the French and Spanish they seem to say they are willing to join most heartily against them." But, reflecting British assumptions about the strength of the rebellion in different areas of the country, Clinton continued, "in the northern provinces this is all I would ask; but we seem so totally masters here that I insisted on their being ready on the first call."[40]

Having ordered the distribution of handbills throughout the backcountry that outlined his general plans for the new militia, Clinton on June 3 issued a fateful proclamation. Recapitulating the conditions under which paroles had been granted, it announced that following the surrender of Charles Town and the defeat of the rebels, "it is become unnecessary that such paroles should be any longer observed." Rather it was now "proper that all persons should take an active part in settling and securing His Majesty's government, and delivering the country" from anarchy. After the twentieth of June, most of the inhabitants of South Carolina were to be "freed and exempted from all such paroles, and may hold themselves restored to all the rights and duties belonging to citizens and inhabitants." These duties of course included service in the British militia. Most historians believed—as did several British officers at the time—that this proclamation was a mistake.[41] Not surprisingly many South Carolinians concluded that if they were going to have to fight on one side or the other, better it be on the American. Others joined the British militia unwillingly and soon proved unreliable.

Implementing Clinton's plan was Maj. Patrick Ferguson's responsibility; in fact Major Ferguson had suggested much of it. Like many of his contemporaries, he had long been a student of the militia and its role in society. Scotsmen in particular had a special interest in the subject because England had disarmed Scotland after putting down the Scottish rebellion of 1745. That Scotland therefore had no militia in the middle of the eighteenth century became a cause for concern during the Seven Years' War. Moreover a number of intellectuals—including Patrick's distinguished philosopher cousin, Adam Ferguson—believed that a society without a militia lost not only a means of defense but, equally important, a source of internal cohesion. Among pamphleteers who accordingly called for the establishment of a Scottish militia, Patrick Ferguson was perhaps the most professionally knowledgeable. But these calls went unanswered, and in 1780 Scotland still lacked such a force.[42]

South Carolina, however, allowed Ferguson to develop his ideas about militias in a different context. On May 16, four days after the fall of Charles Town, Ferguson submitted the "Plan for Securing [the] Province of South Carolina." Loyalists, he predicted, would be quite willing to serve on active duty for eight months of the ensuing year, provided their service was restricted to South Carolina and adjoining provinces and this service would exempt them from further military duties except as members of a home defense force. Militia battalions, Ferguson believed, should include two field officers, one adjutant, and one quartermaster from the British army. Each company would be commanded by a lieutenant, chosen by the rank and file, but his immediate subordinate should be an appointed ensign drawn from the noncommissioned officers of the regular army. Professionals were, he thought, necessary to "establish some degree of discipline and regularity." Having accomplished its mission, this cadre could then move on to other areas. Most of the populace, Ferguson erroneously assumed, would cooperate if given the opportunity, and local routes of communication were sufficiently limited that four or five strategically located forts would enable a very few troops to control the countryside. "Negroes" could build these blockhouses in a few days; thereafter, he assumed, thirty invalided soldiers with an equal number of militia and two small cannon would be sufficient to man them. Putting all of these recommendations into practice was more than the British could manage as they came under increasing Whig pressure later in the year, but they clearly tried to follow Ferguson's blueprint, right down to the use of regular sergeants to train the militia.[43]

Ferguson had also impressed Clinton, who appointed him inspector of militia, with instructions that embodied the main points of his own plan. However, active service in the field was to be limited to six months rather than eight. Ferguson was to provide each man with ammunition and cloth for "a rifle shirt, and when practicable supply those with arms who have none." Anyone unwilling to serve on foot might bring a horse at his own expense. "You will," Clinton continued, "pay particular attention to restrain the militia from offering violence to innocent and inoffensive people, and by all means in your power protect the aged, the infirm, the women and children of every denomination from insult and outrage." In addition to the units that were to accompany the army in offensive operations, Ferguson was to establish a domestic militia to maintain order at home. Older men with families would compose these units, which should assemble periodically under their own officers. Handbills outlining the arrangements for the militia were distributed throughout the backcountry; these flyers, it should be noted, were explicit about the maximum term of active service to be required of younger men. Interestingly enough, in making Ferguson responsible for these arrangements, Clinton ignored the advice of one of his subordinates, Lt. Col. Nisbet Balfour, who told him that his prospective inspector of militia was "*generally*" reputed to be "violent tempered" and excessively harsh with his troops.[44]

Whether a hot temper contributed to Ferguson's ultimate downfall is debatable, but his handling of the South Carolina backcountry men suggests that he was more judicious than Balfour indicated. The "country people," Ferguson soon found, were "unaccustomed to military restraints & become so soon homesick" that keeping them in the field was difficult. He tried to make examples of a few recalcitrant individuals by cropping their hair and drumming them out of camp, but he was aware that if he repeated this with "every lad who left camp when the whim struck him," the ranks of his militia "would become very thin." In many ways Ferguson was an excellent commander, and mutual respect seems to have governed his relations with most of his men, whom he deemed, when they were properly officered and disciplined, "very fit for rough & irregular war, being all excellent woodsmen, unerring shots, careful to a degree to prevent waste or damage to their ammunition," and inured to hardship.[45]

A general order issued in Charles Town on June 28 commanding everyone to show respect to the Loyalist militia suggests that not every British soldier thought as highly of American provincials as Ferguson did. "Almost every

British Officer [except Ferguson] regarded with contempt and indifference the establishment of a militia among people differing so much in customs & manners from themselves," a militia colonel recorded later. Another Loyalist officer recalled an incident in which Carolina militiamen replaced exhausted horses to haul heavy supply wagons up a steep river bank that was "slippery as ice," only to be beaten and cursed by British officers. Not surprisingly these particular men soon deserted.[46]

The contempt of the British galled Loyalists, and an apparent change in policy may also have produced pervasive resentment. After Clinton left South Carolina, Cornwallis stipulated that the active militia service to which men might be subject was six months in "each" twelve, not merely six months in the year following enlistment. Whether he thereby merely clarified an ambiguity or actually increased the requirement, his action was justified insofar as he quickly discovered that South Carolina was nowhere near as pacified as Clinton had assumed. But reneging on what seemed to be an implied promise was scarcely the way to promote the loyalty of lukewarm Tories. No wonder a Loyalist from Pennsylvania would later observe that the South Carolina militia was "in general faithless and altogether dissatisfied in the British Service."[47]

This dissatisfaction would escalate after Ferguson and the American Volunteers left the environs of Charles Town on the way to Ninety Six. Before departing from South Carolina for New York on June 8, Clinton had dispatched three columns toward the backcountry. One was to move northwest along the Savannah River to Augusta; another under Cornwallis had started up the northeast side of the Santee River toward Camden even before the fall of Charles Town. And at the end of May, Lt. Col. Balfour led a third group that passed through Moncks Corner with six hundred to eight hundred men, including Ferguson, Uzal Johnson, and the American Volunteers. Proceeding up the south side of the Santee River, they soon reached Orangeburg, where they began organizing a Loyalist militia. Leaving one hundred regulars there, the troops continued on to the confluence of the Broad and Saluda rivers, where Balfour split the force, sending part up the western side of the Broad while he and the others continued up the north side of the Saluda—which they forded—to reach the town of Ninety Six. The area north of the Saluda River proved to be the center of Loyalist strength in the backcountry, and Balfour was generally pleased at his reception, although he soon reported that the "friends" of the British were not as "numerous as expected."[48]

A considerable number of Loyalists did live in the northern portion of the Ninety Six District, however, and the British were eventually able to raise seven regiments totaling about four thousand men from the area, which was the only one in which Ferguson personally supervised the training. Perhaps partly because no more than fifteen hundred of these men were available for six months' service in the field, Balfour scornfully implied that Ferguson wasted his time marching the men around to the sound of his silver whistle, but British commanders generally considered these units to be the best of the Loyalist militia in South Carolina.[49] Although Uzal Johnson rarely mentioned specifics about training this militia, his journal does provide a fairly complete account of where his unit was on any particular day.

During the late spring of 1780, Ferguson's duties with the militia largely dictated the location of the American Volunteers; later, enemy activities became a more significant determinant. The fall of Charles Town stunned South Carolinians, and for a brief time a deceptive calm prevailed. But it was inherently unstable. The shock of the defeat wore off quickly, and in trying to capitalize on their ascendancy, the British inadvertently hastened their opponents' recovery. In short, calculated severity backfired, and Lt. Col. Banastre Tarleton's actions in particular became a rallying cry for Whigs. Pursuing a unit of retreating Continental troops from Virginia under Col. Abraham Buford that failed to reach Charles Town before its fall, Tarleton's dragoons moved fast enough to cover more than one hundred miles in slightly over two days. Along the way they paused long enough to burn plantation buildings belonging to Thomas Sumter, an ex-Continental army officer who had been inactive for some time. Sumter escaped to become one of the most energetic Whig partisans. On May 29 Tarleton caught the Virginians at the Waxhaws, a small settlement on the North Carolina–South Carolina border. Although outnumbered, Tarleton attacked and quickly overwhelmed the Virginians. What exactly happened next remains debatable, but some men were probably killed while trying to surrender. Despite later Whig mythology, a careful recent analysis of the engagement by historian Jim Piecuch suggests that the British neither planned nor perpetrated a systematic massacre. But Tarleton's horse had been killed under him, and he would later claim that he lost control of his troops because they believed that he too had been shot. Nonetheless the American countersign at the battle of Kings Mountain would be "Buford," and the Americans would shoot down prisoners to shouts of "Buford's play."

Tarleton's claim may have been true, but his summary of the action and subsequent praise by Clinton and Cornwallis suggest that British commanders welcomed the opportunity to make an example of anyone who resisted British rule.[50] Thus, after William Hill's iron works on Allison Creek became the scene of a Whig gathering early in June, the British destroyed it. When a Presbyterian minister in the vicinity of Rocky Mount preached a fiery sermon advocating resistance, the British response was to imprison him and burn his church. Indeed, Maj. James Wemyss, who commanded men from the Sixty-third Regiment, termed all Presbyterian churches "sedition shops" and treated them accordingly as he devastated the area around the Pee Dee River in northeastern South Carolina.[51]

Attempts to terrorize men who could escape were relatively futile, however. Moreover gratuitous severity was scarcely the best way to legitimize the reimposition of British rule; governments are supposed to protect, not oppress, people. As a result of its soldiers' actions, one Carolinian observed, "Great Britain" created "a hundred enemies, where it had one before."[52]

By no means were all of these enemies in the backcountry. A landlady in Charles Town forced a British soldier out of her house with an ax, and Francis Marion, whose partisan exploits became legendary, operated around the port of Georgetown. But the comparatively large and widely scattered population in the interior of the state made that area particularly difficult to control. Partisan leaders such as Andrew Pickens from the vicinity of Ninety Six and dozens of others could move around almost at will; of some thirty-five battles fought during the last six months of 1780, almost thirty occurred in the South Carolina upcountry. One of them, the battle of Camden on August 16, in which the main British army under Cornwallis defeated the southern Continental army commanded by Horatio Gates, probably resulted in more than a thousand Americans killed and wounded. But even this resounding victory did not entirely reassure British commanders, because the Continental army's approach had revealed an incredible "fund of disaffection," which Cornwallis tried to counter by executing prisoners of war who had deserted the British militia to join the enemy. Whig partisans were able, nevertheless, to wage an increasingly successful guerrilla war. Most of the engagements were small militia skirmishes, but the American rebels won the overwhelming majority of them, decimating scattered British units and disrupting vulnerable lines of communication.[53] Realizing that they could be "beat in detail" despite their ability to win major victories such as those at Charles Town and Camden, British commanders made vigorous, if largely futile, efforts to suppress these partisans. Instead of training the Loyalist militia, Ferguson and his troops increasingly spent their time trying to deal with elusive rebels.

Four small, relatively unheralded battles turned out to be crucial steps on the road to Kings Mountain: the battle of Thicketty Fort (July 30), the second battle of Cedar Springs (August 7–8), Musgrove's Mill (August 19), and first Augusta (September 14). Thicketty Fort, on the Pacolet River, was a sturdy wooden outpost manned by South Carolina Loyalists and a British sergeant. On Sunday, July 30, a mixed force of about six hundred American militia captured the fort and its outnumbered defenders without firing a shot.[54]

Isaac Shelby commanded the immediate attackers, but two other colonels—namely, Clarke and McDowell—were also active in the area. Elijah Clarke was a North Carolinian who had moved to South Carolina and then to Georgia sometime before the Revolution. Probably in his thirties or forties at the time, he was the quintessential frontiersman: illiterate, energetic, and a born fighter whose comrades were tempted to pause during battles just to watch him in action. He was in charge of the contingent from Georgia. Charles McDowell was born in Virginia but grew up in western North Carolina, where he became a militia commander and acquired experience fighting Indians. At age twenty-nine, Isaac Shelby was younger and somewhat better educated than the other colonels; he lived in an area that was first considered to be part of Virginia, then western North Carolina, and now Tennessee. He too was an experienced Indian fighter.[55] McDowell and Shelby led militia from North Carolina, many of whom lived over the Appalachian Mountains. The paths of these men would cross Ferguson's several times before his came to an abrupt end at Kings Mountain.

Clarke, Shelby, and their men camped on Fair Forest Creek near Cedar Springs on the night of August 7. Tories sent after them by Ferguson approached before dawn, and the Whigs fell back a few miles to the iron works at Lawson's Ford on the Pacolet River. A sharp engagement followed, the Americans won, and the victors were in pursuit of their adversaries when they almost ran into Ferguson's main force. Retreating in good order, most of the rebels escaped. Estimates of the size of the groups involved and the losses on each side differ, but Allaire believed that the Americans had about twenty-six killed or wounded; the British twenty to thirty.[56]

The battle at Musgrove's Mill was bigger and more significant. After escaping from Ferguson, Clarke, Shelby, and their men withdrew toward North Carolina, regrouped, and planned their next attack, which they decided should be against a Tory outpost at Musgrove's Mill on the Enoree River. Some South Carolinians joined the mountain men, and during the night of August 17 about two hundred horsemen rode hard enough to cover forty miles before daybreak. But instead of encountering a small Loyalist garrison, as they had expected, they discovered that their opponents had been reinforced and currently numbered about five hundred men, including provincial troops from New York, New Jersey, and South Carolina. Unable to retreat on their exhausted horses, the Americans took up defensive positions. Then sending a small party forward to lure the British into a trap, they waited. The plan worked perfectly. As the advance party fell back in good order, the British, thinking they had routed the Americans, rushed forward into a hail of deadly fire. Having killed or wounded more than 150 at the cost of 4 dead and 7 wounded, the Whigs withdrew with 70 prisoners.[57] At this point the American commanders planned an attack on Ninety Six, but upon learning of the overwhelming British victory at Camden on the sixteenth, thought better of it and retreated toward North Carolina. Before the leaders separated, Shelby suggested that they plan to field another army drawn from the backcountry militias and over-mountain men, who lived on the cusp of the frontier in and beyond the southern Appalachian Mountains. Designating several individuals to keep the various commanders informed of Ferguson's doings, the men then dispersed.[58]

On September 2, 1780, Ferguson, the American Volunteers, and hundreds of Tory militia from the Ninety Six District headed north toward Gilbert Town (now Rutherfordton, North Carolina). Six days later and approximately sixty miles to the east, the main British army under Cornwallis marched toward Charlotte. His intended destination was Hillsborough, where he planned to establish a supply depot and raise Loyalist militia units. Ferguson's job was to protect the army's left flank. Accordingly he is supposed to have sent a verbal message to Shelby and the over-mountain men to the effect that if they gave the British any further trouble, he would cross the mountains, execute their leaders, and devastate their country.[59]

Meanwhile Elijah Clarke rode south, gathering South Carolinians and Georgians for an attack on Augusta, which was a key British outpost on the Savannah River. On September 14 Clarke and about six hundred men descended on the town. They quickly captured much of it, including a strong stone building, the Mackay House. But their hold on this miniature fortress was fleeting; the Tory who commanded at Augusta, Thomas Brown, led an attack that immediately retook it. Using captured cannon, Clarke then besieged the house for four days. But Brown had been able to send word of his predicament to Ninety Six, and on the eighteenth, British reinforcements arrived. Clarke and his men who had stuck it out through the siege (many had not) retreated quickly, but the British captured and hanged some of them. More executions followed as Tories and Indians scoured the countryside in search of rebels. By this time official policy had become to hang "every man that has taken protection and is found acting against us." How personally responsible Brown was for the atrocities that occurred at this time is debatable, but his reputation has yet to recover from them.[60]

IV

The Battle of Kings Mountain and Its Aftermath

This first battle of Augusta was the proximate cause of Maj. Patrick Ferguson's downfall. Lt. Col. Elijah Clarke, as he withdrew, headed for Gilbert Town and the over-mountain men; and Major Ferguson, who knew about the outcome of the siege at Augusta, tried to cut off his retreat.[61] As a result the American Volunteers and the Loyalist militia remained too far west too long, and they—not Clarke and his men—were the ones cut off.

The story of Kings Mountain has been told well many times. Uzal Johnson's account will therefore provide most of the present version, but a brief outline of events may be useful here. Upon receiving Ferguson's threat to cross the mountains and lay waste to the country, Colonels Shelby and John Sevier called for the over-mountain men to meet at Sycamore Shoals on the Wautauga River (in present-day eastern Tennessee). Accordingly as many as one thousand mounted riflemen assembled there on September 25. Samuel Doak, a Presbyterian minister, sped them on their way with a rousing sermon assuring them that they wielded "the sword of the Lord and of Gideon." While they were en route, men from the two Carolinas and Georgia joined them. By October 6 they had reached an area of extensive cowpens about thirty miles west of Kings Mountain, where they had learned the enemy was going to camp.[62]

Why Ferguson chose to make a stand there is puzzling. He knew he was being pursued and was probably outnumbered. The main British army was close enough that he doubtless could have reached safety with it had he tried. But if his messages to Cornwallis had gotten through in time, he could reasonably have expected to receive reinforcements. More to the point, perhaps, to cut and run would have damaged the British cause politically and undermined his own career. Moreover such a course would have been most mortifying to pride. In all respects "we live on victory" was the relevant maxim.[63] Besides, reaching Kings Mountain first would enable him to occupy the high ground, which normally would have been advantageous. (It is easier to charge downhill, especially when wielding a bayonet, which was what Ferguson expected his men to do.) That he did not erect breastworks or other defensive measures suggests that he overrated the natural strength of his position and may have believed that the rebels would not dare to attack him there. At any rate he was willing, probably even eager, to risk a fight.

The over-mountain men were also ready for a showdown. Having chosen a Virginian, Col. William Campbell (who was known for his ruthless suppression of Tories), as their temporary commander, they sent some 900 horsemen ahead on the strongest mounts; the rest came on behind. The vanguard rode all night and much of the next day through rain until they reached the base of the mountain, which they encircled without being discovered. Alexander Chesney, one of Ferguson's officers, was dismounting to report "all quiet" when the shooting began. Working their way uphill from boulder to boulder and tree to tree, the attackers had excellent cover in the dimly lit woods, while, higher up, Ferguson's men made good targets. Also, as is common when firing downhill, Ferguson's men frequently overshot their targets. All the while the over-mountain men followed Campbell's injunction to "shout like hell and fight like devils." Accompanied by a handful of men, Ferguson charged the enemy for the last time. Several rifles cracked and he fell from his white horse, dead before or soon after he hit the ground. Capt. Abraham DePeyster assumed command and tried to surrender, but the firing continued sporadically for some time. In a battle that, by Johnson's account, lasted only an hour and five minutes, a British major and more than 150 Tories died; approximately 160 were wounded too severely to travel, and nearly 700 became prisoners of war. As an independent fighting unit, Ferguson's command and the American Volunteers ceased to exist on October 7, 1780.[64]

Ostensibly because Tarleton had been sick, Cornwallis failed to send reinforcements in time to save Ferguson, but the Americans assumed that the British would immediately try to avenge the defeat. Encumbered by their prisoners, Campbell and his men accordingly retreated northward as rapidly as possible. Near Gilbert Town, North Carolina, they paused long enough to convene an irregular court and condemn thirty prisoners to death for alleged war crimes. Nine of them—including, as Johnson recorded, Col. Ambrose Mills—died before their captors had second thoughts about the proceedings and resumed the march. Along the way most of the over-mountain men went home, while the prisoners and their guards continued on to Salem. Johnson remained there and in the surrounding Moravian settlements for nearly a month, during which, he noted, many of the enlisted prisoners of war joined the Continental army rather than remain in close confinement. The rest proceeded to Hillsborough, where their captors jailed the rank and file but allowed the officers freedom within prescribed boundaries.[65] Thomas Jefferson, then governor of Virginia, made preparations for receiving the remaining prisoners of war, and some of them eventually reached the state. But many—including Anthony Allaire—escaped, and American authorities soon paroled some of the officers, among them Johnson, to Charles Town, where they were later exchanged. Of the hundreds of prisoners taken at Kings Mountain a year earlier, only sixty were still in custody by October 1781.[66]

Meanwhile the British command tried to counter the effects of Ferguson's defeat. To keep the over-mountain men busy at home and off his back, Cornwallis encouraged the Cherokee Indians to attack the Wautauga settlements. He also called for reinforcements from British units operating in the Chesapeake Bay area and postponed his plans for an immediate invasion of North Carolina. Instead he fell back from Charlotte to the little hamlet of Winnsboro, South Carolina, where he established his winter headquarters. Early in January 1781 he marched north again with a small army of about thirteen hundred men. Reinforcements from Virginia were scheduled to join him; a force from Charles Town captured the port of Wilmington, North Carolina, to use for transshipping supplies; and Francis, Lord Rawdon remained behind with about five thousand men to protect South Carolina and Georgia.[67]

Two American generals and their troops were chiefly responsible for upsetting these arrangements. Nathanael Greene, who had replaced Gates as the Continental commander in the south after the disastrous American defeat at Camden, arrived in South Carolina in December. Greene was probably the ablest American general after Washington, innovative, resourceful, and persistent. One of his senior officers, Brig. Gen. Daniel Morgan, was essentially a Virginia backwoodsman whose military experience stretched back to the Seven Years' War, when he had been a teamster with the British forces in western Maryland. His presumed insubordination there earned him a court-martial and a flogging, which scarred his back and seared his memory. Greene, who realized that his army was outnumbered but that the British were spread too thinly for their own good, boldly divided his already small force. While he remained in the northeastern part of South Carolina with some troops, he sent a smaller detachment under Henry Lee toward the coast to cooperate with Francis Marion. Morgan and about seven hundred men went west into the area where Ferguson had been; their mission was to test the security of British outposts and collect sorely needed supplies.[68]

Aware of Morgan's general whereabouts, Cornwallis sent Tarleton with eleven hundred troops after him. They met at Hannah's Cowpens, thirty miles west of Kings Mountain. All night long before the battle, Morgan—in a scene reminiscent of Shakespeare's Henry V of England preparing for the battle of Agincourt—circulated through the camp, rallying his men. The next morning, he posted his Continentals toward the rear and his least reliable troops, the militia, in the front lines with orders to fire twice and withdraw. As Morgan expected, the British attacked; the militia fired and moved back, and Tarleton, believing that the Americans were in full retreat, charged ahead right into the withering fire of the Continentals. Tarleton escaped with his life, but more than eight hundred of his men remained on the field, dead, dying, or prisoners of war.[69] Tarleton's reputation for invincibility lay somewhere among the corpses.

Given the large number of lukewarm Whigs and Loyalists whose zeal for either cause varied in proportion to its victories, Cornwallis *had* to do something to reverse this defeat. He accordingly burned his excess baggage and set off in pursuit of both Morgan and Greene, who had rejoined and were rapidly retreating northward. At times their rear guard and the British advance parties were within sight of each other, but, luckily for the Americans, it was a wet winter, and they had the advantage of knowing the country and its many large rivers. Greene's officers arranged to have boats available at the rain-swollen crossings; Cornwallis's troops frequently had to wait until the high waters receded. On February 13 and 14, Greene's tired men crossed the Dan River to Virginia, and the equally exhausted British gave up the chase.[70]

Cornwallis then withdrew southward. Reaching Hillsborough, he issued a proclamation: "Whereas it is His Majesty's most gracious wish to rescue his faithful and loyal subjects from the cruel tyranny under which they have groaned for many years, I have thought proper to . . . invite all such faithful and loyal subjects to repair, without loss of time, with their arms and ten days provisions, to the royal standard now erected at Hillsborough." Tarleton recalled the results: "Many hundred inhabitants of the surrounding districts rode into the British camp, to talk over the proclamation, inquire the news of the day, and take a view of the King's troops." Scarcely one hundred Tory militiamen actually joined the British at any one time. On paper, however, the recruiting effort produced seven companies.[71]

Lest this nominal British success become more tangible, Greene recrossed the Dan River, and the pursued became the pursuer. Cornwallis retreated further, and Greene followed. On March 15 they met at Guilford Court House (now a suburb of Greensboro) in one of the bloodiest battles of the war. At one point, advancing Americans and retreating Redcoats became entangled in hand-to-hand combat. Firing grapeshot, Cornwallis's cannon cut down friend and foe alike to break the momentum of the American charge. Such tactics worked insofar as the Americans withdrew first, but, as one Englishman observed, "another such victory would ruin the British army." Greene could replace his losses; Cornwallis could not. Putting their wounded in wagons that bounced along over rutted roads, the British made an agonizing retreat to Wilmington.[72]

There Cornwallis convinced himself that he should proceed to Virginia. British commanders had long planned operations around Chesapeake Bay and already had a substantial number of troops in the area. Moreover Cornwallis believed that Virginia supplied Greene with men and materiel. Thus the way to save the Carolinas would be to attack Virginia. On April 25 Cornwallis's troops began the long march from Wilmington to Yorktown. It was a fatal move. For a few brief days in September, French naval forces commanded adjacent waters, while French and American troops under Washington and the Count de Rochambeau prepared to lay siege to the British fortifications. Outnumbered and cut off from reinforcements and retreat, Cornwallis surrendered on October 19, 1781. Receiving the news in London, the British prime minister observed, "It is all over." Parliament decided that Britain had wasted enough resources trying to keep the colonies in the empire. It was time to let them go.[73]

Winding down the war took time, however. After the battle of Guilford Court House, Greene had headed almost straight south instead of following Cornwallis to Wilmington or Yorktown. At the second battle of Camden, or Hobkirk's Hill, on April 25, Rawdon, who commanded in the Carolinas in Cornwallis's absence, surprised and drove the Americans from the ridge north of Camden on which they had encamped preparatory to attacking the town. Greene's comment afterward was, "We fight get beat rise and fight again. The whole Country is one continued scene of blood and slaughter."[74]

Greene never won a pitched battle, but the presence of his regular troops—coupled with the operations of Sumter, Marion, Pickens, and other Whig partisans—jeopardized British control of the countryside sufficiently that they could not maintain their outposts. Rawdon evacuated Camden on May 10. In June, Greene laid siege to Ninety Six. Rawdon brought reinforcements, and Greene had to retreat. But the British themselves withdrew a few days later, accompanied by hundreds of Loyalists and their families. Upon reaching the comparative safety of Charles Town, the refugees from Camden and Ninety Six established themselves outside the fortifications in a squalid little settlement known as Rawdon Town, whose population rapidly increased as the British abandoned one post after another. The last substantial engagement between Continental forces and British regulars occurred at Eutaw Springs on September 8, 1781. Again the British held the field at the end of the day, only to relinquish it shortly thereafter. By early December, Greene's enemies had retreated to the immediate environs of Charles Town, and he could justifiably gloat, "Thus the conquerors of the Southern World are pent up with little more than ground enough to encamp on."[75]

Still, diplomatic talks in Paris went slowly. Another year elapsed before negotiators signed the preliminary treaty of peace on November 30, 1782. And the final, formal recognition of American independence and the end of the war did not come until September 3, 1783. Preparations for a complete British withdrawal from the south proceeded more rapidly. In April 1782 a new prime minister ordered Sir Guy Carleton (who had replaced Clinton as commander in chief) to evacuate Savannah, Charles Town, and New York. The British withdrawal from Savannah in July confirmed the Loyalists' worst fears, summed up in their plaintive question to Carleton, "Where are the friends of Government . . . to fly for succour?" The answer was, in all directions. In December more than 100 ships sailed from Charles Town for East Florida and the West Indies, another 25 to England, and about 50 for New York. Altogether at least 129 ships evacuated more than nine thousand refugees, both black and white, plus the thirty-five hundred regular British troops that remained in the province. Gen. Alexander Leslie, who presided over the frustrating final arrangements for the withdrawal from South Carolina, remarked that he "would not undertake this business again for any earthly consideration."[76]

Uzal Johnson left South Carolina before the final British evacuation, and his attendant frustrations were doubtless fewer than General Leslie's. Tracking his every step after the end of his diary on March 7, 1781, has not been feasible, but he left some prominent footprints in the record, and they make it possible to locate him at particular points. On the seventh of March, according to his diary, Johnson was on the way to the British post at Nelson's Ferry. How long he was stationed there remains unclear; but the British had evacuated this post by May 23, when General Greene recorded the fact.[77] Whether Johnson was merely visiting Charles Town or had left Nelson's Ferry permanently by the twenty-fourth of March is also unknown, but he was clearly in town that day.

For on that Saturday afternoon, he watched his friend Anthony Allaire pick up his pistols and walk down Meeting Street to face Ensign Robert Keating of the Prince of Wales Regiment. Their quarrel had begun a week earlier when a number of Loyalist officers (not, apparently, including Johnson) had spent the afternoon and evening drinking at York's Tavern. When a fifer from another unit came in, Allaire and some others decided to take him with them to go "serenade some Ladies." Somehow Keating got the idea that Allaire was trying to inveigle the fifer into accompanying him on a solo venture rather than with the group as planned. Words passed between them, and then blows. Others soon broke up the fight, and for awhile it appeared that the two men would be able to smooth things over. Allaire realized that his own actions had been the result "of liquor" and that the whole affair had begun in "a Drunken Frolick." When mediators suggested that he apologize, he agreed to do so, provided that Keating would do the same. But Keating refused, and the quarrel escalated. Early Saturday afternoon they encountered each other at Hick's store, and Keating attacked Allaire with a cane. Allaire attempted to defend himself, but Keating hit him over the head hard enough that had it not been for his "Hatt and Feathers," Allaire testified, the blows would have felled him. Keating then lunged at Allaire with a sword. Parrying the thrusts with his own cane, Allaire refused to duel with swords—with which he was not as proficient as Keating—but demanded "immediate satisfaction" with weapons that would level the playing field.[78]

He then retreated and, having asked an associate to remit the proceeds from his personal effects to his brother in New York in the event he were killed, put two loaded pistols in his pocket—one of which, he later claimed, he intended to give to Keating—and strode out into the street. Johnson and some others followed at a distance. The affair ended on Meeting Street, almost in front of Keating's quarters. Before Allaire could give him the second pistol, Keating again attacked with a cane; Allaire "told him twice or thrice to stand off" or he would "blow his Brains out," and then he fired. The shot struck Keating in the abdomen, and he died that night. Allaire was immediately court-martialed for "Willful Murder." Testifying in his own behalf, he claimed self-defense, while Johnson and several other witnesses corroborated much of his testimony. The court then acquitted him, and General Clinton approved its findings. His honor having survived the altercation and the court-martial, Allaire, along with nearly three thousand officers, men, and dependents of some of the Loyalist regiments—part of a group that would ultimately total more than twenty-two thousand men, women, and children—eventually sailed from New York for Nova Scotia and New Brunswick, where their units disbanded in the autumn of 1783.[79]

Meanwhile, by the fall of 1781, Uzal Johnson had returned to the New York area and rejoined the First Battalion of the New Jersey Volunteers on Staten Island, where it had been during much of the war. Approximately six months later, on April 23, 1782, he retired from the army, and on January 3, 1783, Jane Wilmot and he took out a marriage license in New York. Their wedding there occurred on February 4, 1783.[80]

NOTES

1. Johnson's journal is in the Thorne Boudinot Collection, Manuscripts Division, Department of Rare Books and Special Collections, Princeton University

Library, Princeton, New Jersey. Henry Clinton, *The American Rebellion: Sir Henry Clinton's Narrative of His Campaigns, 1775–1782, with an Appendix of Original Documents,* ed. William B. Willcox (New Haven, Conn.: Yale University Press, 1954), 226. See, for example, Stephen Conway, *The War of American Independence, 1775–1783* (New York: St. Martin's Press, 1995), 119; Henry Lumpkin, *From Savannah to Yorktown: The American Revolution in the South* (Columbia: University of South Carolina Press, 1981), 91; Christopher Ward, *The War of the Revolution* (New York: Macmillan, 1952), 2:741; Harold E. Selesky, ed., *Encyclopedia of the American Revolution,* 2nd ed. (Detroit, Mich.: Charles Scribner's Sons, 2006), 1:869; Tom Wicker, "Turning Point in the Wilderness," *Military History Quarterly* 11 (Fall 1998): 62–71.

2. Lyman C. Draper, *King's Mountain and Its Heroes: History of the Battle of King's Mountain, October 7th, 1780, and the Events Which Led to It* (1881; repr., Spartanburg, S.C.: Reprint Co., 1967); Laura Arksey, Nancy Pries, and Marcia Reed, *American Diaries: An Annotated Bibliography of Published American Diaries and Journals* (Detroit, Mich.: Gale Research, 1983), 1:116; Josephine L. Harper, *Guide to the Draper Manuscripts* (Madison: State Historical Society of Wisconsin, 1983), 151; Lumpkin, *From Savannah to Yorktown,* 55; Hank Messick, *King's Mountain: The Epic of the Blue Ridge "Mountain Men" in the American Revolution* (Boston: Little, Brown, 1976), 121.

3. Draper, *King's Mountain,* 512; Uzal Johnson, *Uzal Johnson, Loyalist Surgeon: A Revolutionary War Diary,* ed. Bobby G. Moss (Blacksburg, S.C.: Scotia Hibernia Press, 2000).

4. Draper, *King's Mountain,* 480, 513–15; Paul H. Smith, *Loyalists and Redcoats: A Study in British Revolutionary Policy* (Chapel Hill: University of North Carolina Press, 1964), 49; Jonas Howe, "Major Ferguson's Riflemen—the American Volunteers," *Acadiensis* 6 (October 1906): 241, 246.

5. Genealogy of the Johnson–Kip–Burnet–Van Wagenen families (Newark, N.J.), transcribed by Lewis D. Cook in 1960 from the Universal Family Bible, New Jersey Historical Society, Newark (Draper—apparently erroneously—indicates that Johnson was born in 1757); *Columbia University Alumni Register, 1754–1931* (New York: Columbia University Press, 1932), 448; William H. Shaw, *History of Essex and Hudson Counties, New Jersey* (Philadelphia: Everts and Peck, 1884), 1:303; *Minutes of the Provincial Congress and the Council of Safety of the State of New Jersey, 1775–1776* (Trenton, N.J.: Naar, Day & Naar, 1879), 375; William S. Stryker, *"The New Jersey Volunteers" (Loyalists) in the Revolutionary War* (Trenton, N.J.: Naar, Day & Naar, 1887), 25.

6. Richard P. McCormick, *Experiment in Independence: New Jersey in the Critical Period, 1781–1789* (New Brunswick, N.J.: Rutgers University Press, 1950), 31; Adrian C. Leiby, *The Revolutionary War in the Hackensack Valley: The Jersey Dutch and the Neutral Ground, 1775–1783* (New Brunswick, N.J.: Rutgers University Press, 1962), 205–6; Records of the Commissioners of Forfeited Estates, Essex County, Account Book of Sales, Box 2, February 5, 1779, New Jersey Archives,

Trenton; Stryker, *"New Jersey Volunteers,"* 5; Paul H. Smith, "New Jersey Loyalists and the British 'Provincial' Corps in the War for Independence," *New Jersey History* 87 (Summer 1969): 75; P. H. Smith, *Loyalists and Redcoats*, 60–61.

Raised by Brig. Gen. Courtland Skinner after September 4, 1776, the New Jersey Volunteers had a complicated history that involved several reorganizations over its seven-year existence. Nominally six battalions at the beginning, it was reduced to four in 1778, and then to three later in the war (P. H. Smith, "New Jersey Loyalists and the British 'Provincial' Corps," 72). In 1778 Johnson was listed in the fifth battalion; by 1779 he had become part of the first battalion (Stryker, *"New Jersey Volunteers,"* 5, 8, 12).

7. Card Index, "Loyalists in the King's Army, 1776–1783," New Jersey Archives, Trenton; Edward Alfred Jones, *The Loyalists of New Jersey: Their Memorials, Petitions, Claims, etc., from English Records* (Boston: Gregg Press, 1972), 106.

8. In 1816 he was elected vice president of the Essex County Medical Society; in May 1819 he became president and served until March 1825. (Lois Densky-Wolff, Head of Special Collections, University Libraries, University of Medicine & Dentistry of New Jersey, George F. Smith Library of the Health Sciences, Newark, citing The Minute Book of the Essex County Medical Society for 1816–1865, p. 1, kindly supplied this information.)

In addition, the Medical Society of New Jersey, which was founded in 1766, successfully petitioned the colonial legislature for a law to regulate the practice of medicine. The resulting act, passed in 1772, which was the first of its kind in the colonies, established a licensing system for physicians that required applicants to pass a professional examination (David L. Cowen, *Medicine and Health in New Jersey* [Princeton, N.J.: D. Van Nostrand, 1964], 10–14). On May 12, 1818, the society appointed Johnson one of five examiners for Essex County (Minutes of the Medical Society of New Jersey, vol. 3, New Jersey Historical Society, Newark).

Johnson as vestry member certified by Dr. Uzal Ogden, Rector, April 2, 1804, Trinity Cathedral Miscellaneous Documents, New Jersey Historical Society, Newark; Frank J. Urquhart et al., "A Plan of the Principal Part of Broad Street" in *A History of the City of Newark, New Jersey, 1666–1913* (New York: Lewis Historical Publishing Co., 1913), 1:106; Obituary in the *Newark Intelligencer*, May 31, 1827; Newark Township, Essex County, 1790 Tax Ratables, New Jersey Archives, Trenton; Lewis D. Cook transcript, 1960, New Jersey Historical Society, Newark. Johnson may have acted as a spiritual godfather for a boy of the extended Allaire family in 1791. Glenna See Hill, "The Allaire Family of LaRochelle, France, and Westchester County, New York," *New York Genealogical and Biographical Record* 126 (January 1995): 57.

9. Margaret M. Sherry, Reference Librarian/Archivist, Rare Books and Special Collections, Princeton University Library, to Robert Weir, August 30, 1999; *New York Times*, March 28, 1943; Lewis D. Cook transcript, 1960, New Jersey Historical Society, Newark; George A. Boyd, *Elias Boudinot: Patriot and Statesman, 1740–1821* (Princeton, N.J.: Princeton University Press, 1952), 6, 18, 19n1, 106, 136, 289;

Mrs. James B. Harris to Mrs. Robert L. Mann, Manuscripts Division, Princeton University Library, March 27, 1967.

10. Lewis D. Cook transcript, 1960, and Elias Boudinot Stockton Genealogical Collection, both at New Jersey Historical Society, Newark.

11. Julia Jarvis, *Three Centuries of Robinsons: The Story of a Family* (Don Mills, Ontario: T. H. Best Printing Co., 1967), 83–84; G. S. Hill, "The Allaire Family," 58–59; Draper, *King's Mountain,* 299n; Information from the staff of the New Brunswick Museum, Saint John, New Brunswick, Canada.

12. John Peebles, *John Peebles' American War: The Diary of a Scottish Grenadier, 1776–1782,* ed. Ira D. Gruber (Mechanicsburg, Pa.: Stackpole Books, 1998), 1, and for a convenient list of published diaries and journals by British officers, see pp. 561–62; Verbal opinion of Don C. Skemer, Curator of Manuscripts, Princeton University Library, July 9, 1992.

13. See, for example, subsequent notes to Johnson's entries of May 18–20, June 12, 25, July 2–8, 28, and August 21, 1780.

14. Generally, existing maps were better than no maps, but, as one British commander complained, "all the maps of the country which I have are so very inaccurate" that estimating distances was difficult. And, indeed, a modern computer analysis of one of the best maps of South Carolina (the one published in 1773 by James Cook) misplaced settlements in relation to each other by an average of 15 degrees and 6.9 miles. A contemporary map of New Jersey—admittedly a smaller state—erred by only 3.25 miles. Douglas W. Marshall and Howard H. Peckham, *Campaigns of the American Revolution: An Atlas of Manuscript Maps* (Ann Arbor: University of Michigan Press, 1976), 99.

15. "Diary of Allaire," in Draper, *King's Mountain,* 512; Adelaide L. Fries, ed., *Records of the Moravians in North Carolina,* vol. 4, *1780–1783* (Raleigh, N.C.: Edwards & Broughton, 1930), 1632.

16. "Diary of Allaire," in Draper, *King's Mountain,* 499.

17. "Diary of Allaire," in Draper, *King's Mountain,* entry for Sept. 1, p. 505, and for Sept. 24, pp. 508–9; Johnson's entry for Sept. 25, 1780.

18. Allaire's entry for July 9, in Draper, *King's Mountain,* 499.

19. Johnson's entry for Sept. 14, 1780; "Diary of Allaire," in Draper, *King's Mountain,* 506.

20. Dennis P. Ryan, "Six Towns: Continuity and Change in Revolutionary New Jersey, 1770–1792" (Ph.D. diss., New York University, 1974), 152, 219; Joseph Atkinson, *The History of Newark, New Jersey, . . . from 1666 . . . to the Present Time* (Newark, N.J.: William B. Guild, 1878), 333; David E. Maas, "The Massachusetts Loyalists and the Problem of Amnesty, 1775–1790," in *Loyalists and Community in North America,* ed. Robert M. Calhoon, Timothy M. Barnes, and George A. Rawlyk (Westport, Conn.: Greenwood Press, 1994), 69.

21. P. H. Smith, *Loyalists and Redcoats,* 18–19; Ira D. Gruber, "Britain's Southern Strategy," in *The Revolutionary War in the South: Power, Conflict, and Leadership,* ed. W. Robert Higgins (Durham, N.C.: Duke University Press, 1979), 205–10;

John W. Gordon, *South Carolina and the American Revolution: A Battlefield History* (Columbia: University of South Carolina Press, 2003), 29–32; C. Ward, *War of the Revolution*, 2:662–66, 669–70; William B. Willcox, *Portrait of a General: Sir Henry Clinton in the War of Independence* (New York: Knopf, 1964), 81, 85.

22. Conway, *War of American Independence*, 81–82; C. Ward, *War of the Revolution*, 2:671–78; Robert M. Weir, *Colonial South Carolina: A History* (1983; repr., Columbia: University of South Carolina Press, 1997), 330; Ebenezer Hazard, "A View of Coastal South Carolina in 1778: The Journal of Ebenezer Hazard," ed. H. Roy Merrens, *South Carolina Historical Magazine* 73 (October 1972): 177–93. Encouraging his men the day after the battle, an American officer told them that those who died at Fort Moultrie "are now in heaven, riding in their coaches like hell, by G-d" (Hazard, "View of Coastal South Carolina in 1778, 193).

23. Robert L. Ganyard, "Threat from the West: North Carolina and the Cherokee, 1776–1778," *North Carolina Historical Review* 45 (Winter 1968): 47–66; Journal of William Dells, 1776, Filson Library of the Filson Historical Society, Louisville, Ky.; Clyde R. Ferguson, "Functions of the Partisan-Militia in the South during the American Revolution: An Interpretation," in *The Revolutionary War in the South: Power, Conflict and Leadership*, ed. W. Robert Higgins (Durham, N.C.: Duke University Press), 241, 249, 251–52; Robert S. Lambert, *South Carolina Loyalists in the American Revolution* (Columbia: University of South Carolina Press, 1987), 68–69, 105.

24. Alan C. Valentine, *Lord George Germain* (Oxford: Clarendon Press, 1962), 366; Conway, *War of American Independence*, 103; P. H. Smith, *Loyalists and Redcoats*, 77, 170–71; Gruber, "Britain's Southern Strategy," 217.

25. Conway, *War of American Independence*, 108, 109; C. Ward, *War of the Revolution*, 2:680–81, 685; Lawrence S. Rowland, Alex Moore, and George C. Rogers Jr., *The History of Beaufort County, South Carolina* (Columbia: University of South Carolina Press, 1996), 217–19; Edward McCrady, *The History of South Carolina in the Revolution, 1780–1783* (1902; repr., New York: Russell & Russell, 1969), 361.

26. McCrady, *South Carolina in the Revolution, 1780–1783*, which gives the most detailed early account of the negotiations over neutrality in 1779, defends South Carolina authorities but bogs down in the question of whether they were dishonorably surrendering the fate of the state to others (pp. 360–81). James Haw, "A Broken Compact: Insecurity, Union, and the Proposed Surrender of Charleston, 1779," *South Carolina Historical Magazine* 96 (January 1995): 30–53, is an extensive, judicious, modern discussion of the incident that emphasizes the degree to which South Carolinians felt abandoned and unprotected by the Continental Congress.

See also Geoffrey Best's *Humanity in Warfare* (New York: Columbia University Press, 1980), p. 61, which provides relevant background in noting that capitulations of besieged places during the eighteenth century were not normally surrenders in the modern sense but agreements that gave one side occupation and unconfined the other. Such arrangements often bound those who capitulated to future neutrality. British military commanders in Florida—including Augustine Prevost himself—advocated such terms when the Americans threatened East Florida early in the war, but the governor overruled them (Martha C. Searcy, *The Georgia-Florida Contest in the American Revolution, 1776–1778* [University: University of Alabama Press, 1985], 59). Later the American James Willing accepted the surrender of planters around Natchez, West Florida, under such conditions (J. Barton Starr, *Tories, Dons, and Rebels: The American Revolution in British West Florida* [Gainesville: University Press of Florida, 1976], 86–87; J. Leitch Wright, *Florida in the American Revolution* [Gainesville: University Press of Florida, 1975], 48). And in 1782 most of the British inhabitants of the West Indian islands of St. Christopher and Nevis surrendered to the French under similar conditions (Jacob Nagle, *A Diary of the Life of Jacob Nagle, Sailor, from the Year 1775 to 1841,* ed. John C. Dann [New York: Weidenfeld & Nicolson, 1988], 39). In short the South Carolinians' offer of neutrality was not as anomalous as it might appear in the twenty-first century.

For British coverage of the treaty covering Guadeloupe, see the *Gentleman's Magazine,* June 1759, 272–78, with material from the *London Gazette, Extraordinary,* June 14, 1759; criticism of the arrangement appears in William Mathew Burt to the Earl of Bute, January 30, 1762 (folio 137), enclosing "Narrative of the Expedition against Martinique and Guadeloupe in 1758 . . ." as well as elsewhere in the North Papers, Transcripts of Documents Relating to Colonial Policy, Chiefly with Reference to the West Indies, 1670–1879 (Rhodes House, Oxford, United Kingdom). For the way the Guadeloupe agreement benefited the British military, see Fred Anderson, *Crucible of War: The Seven Years' War and the Fate of Empire in British North America, 1754–1766* (New York: Alfred A. Knopf, 2000), 315.

27. J. L. Wright, *Florida in the American Revolution,* 40; Gregory De Van Massey, *John Laurens and the American Revolution* (Columbia: University of South Carolina Press, 2000), 136–39; Rowland, Moore, and Rogers, *History of Beaufort County,* 222–27; Weir, *Colonial South Carolina,* 36. For attempts to control plundering, see British Orderly Books, 1779, Coit Papers, Dallas Historical Society, Dallas, Texas.

28. C. Ward, *War of the Revolution,* 2:688–96; Willcox, *Portrait of a General,* 301–2; Mark M. Boatner III, *Encyclopedia of the American Revolution* (New York: David McKay, 1966), 206 (figures for Clinton's force given by different authorities differ slightly); Clinton, *American Rebellion,* 160.

29. James Murray, *Letters from America, 1773 to 1780, Being the Letters of a Scots Officer, Sir James Murray, to His Home during the War of American Independence,* ed. Eric Robson (Manchester, U.K.: Manchester University Press, 1951), 45; Patrick Ferguson, "An Officer Out of His Time: Correspondence of Major Patrick Ferguson, 1779–1780," ed. Hugh F. Rankin, in *Sources of American Independence: Selected Manuscripts from the Collections of the William L. Clements Library,* ed. Howard H. Peckham (Chicago: University of Chicago Press, 1978), 2:287–88; Lumpkin, *From Savannah to Yorktown,* 140–42; George Hanger, 4th Baron Coleraine, *The Life, Adventures, and Opinions of Col. George Hanger Written by Himself* (London:

J. Debrett, 1801), 2:419. For a more critical but judicious evaluation of the Ferguson rifle, see John Buchanan, *The Road to Guilford Courthouse: The American Revolution in the Carolinas* (New York: John Wiley & Sons, 1997), 196–99.

30. P. Ferguson, "An Officer Out of His Time," 2:288–89, 299–300, 308.

31. Ibid., 2:289–90; C. Ward, *War of the Revolution*, 2:617–18; P. H. Smith, *Loyalists and Redcoats*, 48–49; Draper, *King's Mountain*, 57, 61. Draper states that Ferguson was to have 300 men, but a muster roll taken as the corps embarked from New York lists 123 men (Howe, "Major Ferguson's Riflemen," 237–46).

32. Robert K. Wright, *The Continental Army* (Washington, D.C.: Center of Military History, U.S. Army, 1984), 48–49; Matthew H. Kaufman, *Surgeons at War: Medical Arrangements for the Treatment of the Sick and Wounded in the British Army during the Late 18th and 19th Centuries* (Westport, Conn.: Greenwood Press, 2001), 5–6; Philip Cash, *Medical Men at the Siege of Boston, April, 1775–April, 1776: Problems of the Massachusetts and Continental Armies* (Philadelphia: American Philosophical Society, 1973), 1–3; Whitfield J. Bell Jr., "Medical Practice in Colonial America," in *Symposium on Colonial Medicine in Commemoration of the 350th Anniversary of the Settlement of Virginia* (Williamsburg, Va.: Jamestown-Williamsburg-Yorktown Celebration Commission and the Virginia 350th Anniversary Commission, 1957), 59, 61; John Gerard William DeBrahm, *DeBrahm's Report of the General Survey in the Southern District of North America*, ed. Louis DeVorsey Jr. (Columbia: University of South Carolina Press, 1971), 99.

33. Kaufman, *Surgeons at War*, 7; Louis C. Duncan, *Medical Men in the American Revolution, 1775–1783* (1931; repr., New York: Augustus M. Kelley, 1970), 19; Larry R. Gerlach, ed., *New Jersey in the American Revolution, 1763–1783: A Documentary History* (Trenton: New Jersey Historical Commission, 1975), 260–61; Kenneth R. Bowling and Helen E. Veit, eds., *The Diary of William Maclay and Other Notes on Senate Debates* (Baltimore: Johns Hopkins University Press, 1972), 148. For a similar assessment of the ministrations of naval surgeons in 1759, see Stephen Brumwell, *Redcoats: The British Soldier and War in the Americas, 1755–1763* (Cambridge: Cambridge University Press, 2002).

34. Duncan, *Medical Men in the American Revolution*, 10–11; Kaufman, *Surgeons at War*, 10; Cash, *Medical Men at the Siege of Boston*, 8; Mark Harrison, "Medicine and the Management of Modern Warfare," *Journal of the History of Science* 34 (December 1996): 382–85; Weir, *Colonial South Carolina*, 40–41; H. Roy Merrens and George D. Terry, "Dying in Paradise: Malaria, Mortality, and the Perceptual Environment in Colonial South Carolina," *Journal of Southern History* 50 (October 1984): 533–50.

35. January 17, 23, 1780, Capt. F. DePeyster's Orderly Book, January–August 1780 and February–June 1782, New-York Historical Society, New York, New York.

36. Clinton to Germain, March 9, 1780, in K. G. Davies, ed., *Documents of the American Revolution, 1770–1783*, vol. 18, *Transcripts 1780* (Shannon: Irish University Press, 1972), 54; Clinton to Alexander Innes, February 19, 1780, in Royal

Commission on Historical Manuscripts, *Report on American Manuscripts in the Royal Institution of Great Britain* (London: His Majesty's Stationery Office, 1906), 2:92–93.

37. Clinton, *American Rebellion*, 161–63.

38. Clinton to Lord George Germain, May 13, 1780, in Davies, *Documents of the American Revolution*, 18:86–89; Daniel Coxe to John Andrae, March 28, 1780, Henry Clinton Papers, William L. Clements Library, University of Michigan, Ann Arbor; Willcox, *Portrait of a General*, 307; Franklin B. Wickwire and Mary Wickwire, *Cornwallis: The American Adventure* (Boston: Houghton Mifflin, 1970), 130; Henry Clinton, "Sir Henry Clinton's 'Journal of the Siege of Charleston, 1780,'" ed. William T. Bulger, *South Carolina Historical Magazine* 66 (July 1965): 160.

39. Clinton's comment quoted in Wickwire and Wickwire, *Cornwallis,* 132. Valentine, *Lord George Germain,* 366–67; James Simpson, "James Simpson's Reports on the Carolina Loyalists, 1779–1780," ed. Alan S. Brown, *Journal of Southern History* 21 (November 1955): 513–14, James Simpson to Germain, August 28, 1779, p. 516, Simpson to Clinton, May 15, 1780, p. 518; James R. Hill III, "An Exercise in Futility: The Pre-Revolutionary Career and Influence of Loyalist James Simpson" (master's thesis, University of South Carolina, 1992), 74, 99; Simpson to Germain, June 9, 1780, in Davies, *Documents of the American Revolution,* 18:105.

40. Banastre Tarleton, *A History of the Campaigns of 1780 and 1781, in the Southern Provinces of North America* (1787; repr., Spartanburg, S.C.: Reprint Co., 1967), 61–64, reprints the articles of capitulation; William Moultrie to Lt. Col. Balfour, Oct. 16, 1780, and Clinton and Marriot Arbuthnot to Benjamin Lincoln, May 12, 1780, in William Moultrie, *Memoirs of the American Revolution, So Far as It Related to the States of North and South Carolina, and Georgia. . . .* 2 vols. (1802; repr., New York: New York Times and Arno Press, 1968), 2:140, 104–5; George S. McCowen, *The British Occupation of Charleston, 1780–82* (Columbia: University of South Carolina Press, 1972), 9; Clinton, *American Rebellion,* 174–75. Later British success in recruiting American prisoners of war for service in the West Indies seems to support what Clinton was hearing about a willingness to fight against the Spanish and French. See Robert Scott Davis Jr., "Lord Montagu's Mission to South Carolina in 1781: American POWS for the King's Service in Jamaica," *South Carolina Historical Magazine* 84 (April 1983): 89–109.

41. Clinton, *American Rebellion,* 174–75, 440–41; Tarleton, *History of the Campaigns of 1780 and 1781,* 73–74; Lambert, *South Carolina Loyalists,* 97–98, 102n7, 127; Wickwire and Wickwire, *Cornwallis,* 183.

42. John Robertson, *The Scottish Enlightenment and the Militia Issue* (Edinburgh: John Donald, 1985), 7, 117, 150–51, 241.

43. The text of Ferguson's plan, dated May 16, 1780, can be found in the Clinton Papers, William L. Clements Library, University of Michigan, Ann Arbor. Whigs captured a British sergeant major, for example, at Thicketty Fort, where he had been stationed to train the militia (J. B .O. Landrum, *Colonial and Revolutionary*

History of Upper South Carolina . . . [1897; repr., Spartanburg, S.C.: Reprint Co., 1977], 133).

44. Clinton, *American Rebellion,* 175–76; "Extracts from the instructions given to Major Ferguson as inspector of militia [May 22, 1780]" and "Extracts from the handbill distributed by Sir Henry Clinton's orders among the inhabitants of the upper parts of South Carolina and Georgia," in Clinton, *American Rebellion,* 440–41. This undated handbill is filed under May 12 in the Clinton Papers. Almost certainly, however, Ferguson's proposal of May 16 preceded Clinton's announcement of the plan. Ferguson's plan not only reads like a preliminary position paper, but it is also highly unlikely that he would advocate a term of active service different from one that his commander had publicly announced. Furthermore Ferguson apparently drafted Clinton's proclamations on the subject (Adam Ferguson, *Biographical Sketch or Memoir of Lieutenant-Colonel Patrick Ferguson: Originally Intended for the British Encyclopaedia* [Edinburgh: John Moir, 1817], 28). Clinton included a copy of this handbill in a letter to Germain of June 3, 1780 (Tarleton, *History of the Campaigns of 1780 and 1781,* 68–70). Clinton, "Siege of Charleston," 172.

Miscellaneous printing for the British appears to have been done initially aboard ship; later the Charles Town firm of Robert Wells and Son handled much of it (Christopher Gould and Richard P. Morgan, *South Carolina Imprints, 1731–1800: A Descriptive Bibliography* [Santa Barbara, Calif.: ABC-CLIO, 1985], 132). See record of the Paymaster General, Army Establishment, Miscellaneaous Books, PMG 14/72, f. 483, National Archives, Kew, Richmond, Surrey, United Kingdom, for payments to Wells from January 21 to November 14, 1781, which totaled £213,9,0.

45. Lambert, *South Carolina Loyalists,* 133, 134.

46. June 28, 1780, Orderly Books, George Wray Papers, 1770–1848, William L. Clements Library, University of Michigan, Ann Arbor; Robert Gray, "Colonel Robert Gray's Observations on the War in Carolina," *South Carolina Historical and Genealogical Magazine* 11 (July 1910): 144; Charles Stedman, *The History of the Origin, Progress, and Termination of the American War* (London: J. Murray, 1794), 2:225.

47. Cornwallis to Clinton, June 30, 1780, in Charles Cornwallis, *Correspondence of Charles, First Marquis Cornwallis,* ed. Charles Ross (London: John Murray, 1859), 1:499; Stedman, *History of the American War,* 2:206.

48. Clinton to Germain, June 4, 1780, in Royal Commission on Historical Manuscripts, *Report on the Manuscripts of Mrs. Stopford-Sackville, of Drayton House, Northhamptonshire* (Boston: Gregg Press, 1972), 2:167; Lambert, *South Carolina Loyalists,* 104–5, 107; Clinton to William Eden, May 30, 1780, Clinton Papers, William L. Clements Library, indicates that Balfour had eight hundred men; Uzal Johnson estimated them to be about six hundred on May 26.

49. Lambert, *South Carolina Loyalists,* 112; Cornwallis to Germain, August 20, 1780, in Cornwallis, *Correspondence,* 1:503; Robert D. Bass, *Ninety Six: The Struggle for the South Carolina Back Country* (Lexington, S.C.: Sandlapper Store, 1978),

208–9; Cornwallis to Clinton, December 3, 1780, in Cornwallis, *Correspondence,* 1:71. Standard "Signals for the Drum Bugle or Whistle" appear in Lieutenant Anthony Allaire's Order Book, New Brunswick Museum, as well as that of Captain F. DePeyster, New-York Historical Society.

50. J. Tracy Power, "'The Virtue of Humanity Was Totally Forgot': Buford's Massacre, May 29, 1780," *South Carolina Historical Magazine* 93 (January 1992): 5–14; James Piecuch, "Massacre or Myth? Banastre Tarleton at the Waxhaws, May 29, 1780," *Southern Campaigns of the American Revolution* 1 (October 2004): 3–17, available at www.southerncampaign.org; Tarleton to Cornwallis, n.d., in Tarleton, *History of the Campaigns of 1780 and 1781,* 83; McCrady, *South Carolina in the Revolution, 1780–1783,* 565; Tarleton, *History of the Campaigns of 1780 and 1781,* 30–31; Anthony J. Scotti Jr., *Brutal Virtue: The Myth and Reality of Banastre Tarleton* (1995; repr., Bowie, Md.: Heritage Books, 2002), 176–78.

51. Walter B. Edgar, *Partisans and Redcoats: The Southern Conflict That Turned the Tide of the American Revolution* (New York: William Morrow, 2001), 39, 57–59, 63–65; Edward McCrady, *The History of South Carolina in the Revolution, 1775–1780* (1901; New York: Russell & Russell, 1969), 641, 747.

52. Draper, *King's Mountain,* 282; Francis Kinloch to Thomas Boone, October 1, 1782, in Francis Kinloch, "Letters of Francis Kinloch to Thomas Boone, 1782–1788," ed. Felix Gilbert, *Journal of Southern History* 8 (February 1942): 92.

53. Stephen Jarvis, "The Narrative of Colonel Stephen Jarvis," in *Loyalist Narratives from Upper Canada,* ed. James J. Talman (1946; repr., New York: Greenwood Press, 1969), 198; Edgar, *Partisans and Redcoats,* 143; Howard H. Peckham, ed., *The Toll of Independence: Engagements and Battle Casualties of the American Revolution* (Chicago: University of Chicago Press, 1974), 75; Cornwallis to Lt. Col. J. Harris Cruger, August 18, 1780, in Cornwallis, *Correspondence,* 1:56–57; Col. Lord Rawdon to Maj.-General Alexander Leslie, October 24, 1780, in Davies, *Documents of the American Revolution, 1770–1783,* 18:189. (See also Gov. Josiah Martin to Germain, August 18, 1780, in this volume of documents, p. 139.) McCrady, *South Carolina in the Revolution, 1775–1780,* 853.

54. McCrady, *South Carolina in the Revolution, 1775–1780,* 634–35.

55. Ibid., 634; Kenneth Coleman and Charles S. Gurr, eds., *Dictionary of Georgia Biography* (Athens: University of Georgia Press, 1983), 1:190–92; William S. Powell, ed., *Dictionary of North Carolina Biography* (Chapel Hill: University of North Carolina Press, 1991), 4:142, 5:326–27.

56. McCrady, *South Carolina in the Revolution, 1775–1780,* 636–40; Draper, *King's Mountain,* 503. Johnson's estimate was lower for both groups.

57. McCrady, *South Carolina in the Revolution, 1775–1780,* 686–98; Peckham, *Toll of Independence,* 74.

58. Buchanan, *Road to Guilford Courthouse,* 179–80.

59. Ibid., 204, 208; Wickwire and Wickwire, Cornwallis, 195.

60. Edward J. Cashin, *The King's Ranger: Thomas Brown and the American Revolution on the Southern Frontier* (Athens: University of Georgia Press, 1989), 114–20.

61. Ibid., 120–21.

62. Buchanan, *Road to Guilford Courthouse,* 210–15; Draper, *King's Mountain,* 170–71, 223–25.

63. The maxim comes from Clinton's instructions to Lt. Col. James Webster during the siege of Charles Town (Willcox, *Portrait of a General,* 307). In this case, it is worth noting, Clinton used it in a cautionary sense.

64. Draper, *King's Mountain,* 186–88; Buchanan, *Road to Guilford Courthouse,* 223, 228–29, 231–33, 235–36; Lumpkin, *From Savannah to Yorktown,* 97–99. Samuel C. Williams printed portions of Chesney's journal in "The Battle of King's Mountain: As Seen by the British Officers," *Tennessee Historical Magazine* 7 (April 1921): 58. Additional American commanders included Cols. Benjamin Cleveland, Edward Lacey, William Hill, Frederick Hambright, James Hawthorne, Joseph Graham, and James Williams plus Majs. Joseph Winston, William Candler, and William Chronicle. The entire group thus included men from Virginia and North and South Carolina as well as the over-mountain men.

65. Messick, *King's Mountain,* 122–23; Buchanan, *Road to Guilford Courthouse,* 237; Draper, *King's Mountain,* 349, 350.

66. Horatio Gates informed Jefferson that he had ordered the prisoners then at "the Moravian Town" in North Carolina to be marched to Fincastle Court House, Virginia (Gates to Jefferson, November 1, 1780, in Thomas Jefferson, *The Papers of Thomas Jefferson,* vol. 4, *1 October 1780 to 24 February 1781,* ed. Julian P. Boyd [Princeton, N.J.: Princeton University Press, 1951], 86–87). Jefferson recommended that they be sent farther north (Jefferson to Samuel Huntington, November 7, 1780, in Jefferson, *Papers,* 4:98–99). For further arrangements and toing and froing over their fate, see Jefferson to Patrick Lockhart, November 8, 1780, pp. 103–4 and pp. 102, 108–9, 135, 177–78, and 238–39, all in volume 4 of the *Papers of Thomas Jefferson.* Ensign Richard Boyle to Nathanael Greene, February 17, 1781, in Nathanael Greene, *The Papers of General Nathanael Greene,* vol. 7, *26 December 1780–29 March 1781,* ed. Dennis M. Conrad (Chapel Hill: University of North Carolina Press, 1994), 305; Greene to Col. Francis Lock, October 11, 1781, in Nathanael Greene, *The Papers of General Nathanael Greene,* vol. 9, *11 July 1781–2 December 1781,* ed. Dennis M. Conrad (Chapel Hill: University of North Carolina Press, 1997), 441–42 and n1; and the extended discussion in the notes to Johnson's diary for November 4, 1780.

67. James H. O'Donnell III, *Southern Indians in the American Revolution* (Knoxville: University of Tennessee Press, 1973), 106; Conway, *War of American Independence,* 119, 122; Gregory De Van Massey, "The British Expedition to Wilmington, January–November, 1781," *North Carolina Historical Review* 66 (October 1989): 387–411.

68. Greene to Samuel Huntington, December 28, 1780, in Greene, *Papers,* 7:7; Don Higginbotham, *Daniel Morgan, Revolutionary Rifleman* (Chapel Hill: University of North Carolina Press, 1961), 4; Conway, *War of American Independence,* 123.

69. Conway, *War of American Independence,* 123; Higginbotham, *Daniel Morgan,* 133–55.

70. Wickwire and Wickwire, *Cornwallis,* 276; M. F. Treacy, *Prelude to Yorktown: The Southern Campaign of Nathanael Greene, 1780–1781* (Chapel Hill: University of North Carolina Press, 1963), 128–53.

71. Tarleton, *History of the Campaigns of 1780 and 1781,* 256–57, 230; Conway, *War of American Independence,* 123; Greene to George Washington, February 28, 1781, in Greene, *Papers,* 7:369–71.

72. Greene to Washington, February 28, 1781, in Greene, *Papers,* 7:369–71; Wickwire and Wickwire, *Cornwallis,* 274–310, 311 (quote), 314, 316.

73. Wickwire and Wickwire, *Cornwallis,* 318–21; Cornwallis to Germain, April 18, 1781, in Cornwallis, *Correspondence,* 90–91; Conway, *War of American Independence,* 125; John A. Tilley, *The British Navy and the American Revolution* (Columbia: University of South Carolina Press, 1987), 263; C. Ward, *War of the Revolution,* 2:886–96 (quote 895).

74. C. Ward, *War of the Revolution,* 2:802–8; Greene to the Chevalier de La Luzerne, April, 28, 1781, in Nathanael Greene, *The Papers of General Nathanael Greene,* vol. 8, *30 March–10 July 1781,* ed. Dennis M. Conrad (Chapel Hill: University of North Carolina Press, 1995), 167–68.

75. C. Ward, *War of the Revolution,* 2:811, 820–34; Otho Holland Williams to Elie Williams, June 23, 1781, in *Calendar of the General Otho Holland Williams Papers in the Maryland Historical Society* (Baltimore: Maryland Historical Records Survey Project, 1940), 47; McCrady, *South Carolina in the Revolution, 1780–1783,* 228; David Ramsay, *The History of the Revolution of South Carolina, from a British Province to an Independent State* (Trenton, N.J.: Isaac Collins, 1785), 2:232–33; Greene to Richard Henry Lee, December 9, 1781, in Nathanael Greene, *The Papers of General Nathanael Greene,* vol. 10, *3 December 1781–6 April 1782,* ed. Dennis M. Conrad (Chapel Hill: University of North Carolina Press, 1998), 17. For a good, more recent account of the battle of Eutaw Springs, see Hugh F. Rankin, *The North Carolina Continentals* (Chapel Hill: University of North Carolina Press, 1971), 341–61.

76. Earl of Shelburne to General Sir Guy Carleton, April 4, 1782, in K. G. Davies, ed., *Documents of the American Revolution, 1770–1783,* vol. 19, *Calendar 1781–1783 and Addenda 1770–1780* (Shannon: Irish University Press, 1978), 279; Lt. Governor William Bull to Thomas Townshend, January 19, 1783, in K. G. Davies, ed., *Documents of the American Revolution, 1770–1783,* vol. 21, *Transcripts 1782–1783* (Shannon: Irish University Press, 1981), 148–49; Donald M. Londahl-Smidt, "After Eutaw Springs: The Last Campaign in South Carolina" (master's thesis, University of Delaware, 1972), 82, 104; Carleton to Thomas Townshend, January 18, 1783, in Davies, *Documents of the American Revolution,* 19:365; Leslie to Carleton, November 18, 1782, in Davies, *Documents of the American Revolution,* 19:359. The Loyalists' question to Carleton is quoted in McCowen, *British Occupation of Charleston,* 149.

77. Greene to Marquis de Lafayette, May 23, 1781, Greene, *Papers,* 8:299–300.

78. The details of this whole incident can be found in the records of the General Court Martial of Anthony Allaire, in the National Archives, Kew, Richmond, Surry, United Kingdom, War Office, Judge Advocate General's Office, Courts Martial, Proceedings, WO 71, 93: 287–311.

79. Clinton to Lieut. Col. Nisbet Balfour, May 24, 1781, Royal Commission on Historical Manuscripts, *Report on American Manuscripts,* 2:283; Esther C. Wright, *The Loyalists of New Brunswick* (Hantsport, N.S.: Lancelot Press, 1955), 63–67, 98; Paul H. Smith, "The American Loyalists: Notes on Their Organization and Numerical Strength," *William and Mary Quarterly* 25 (April 1968): 268–69n23. Owing to the Loyalist influx, New Brunswick became a separate province in 1784.

80. Because Johnson had been on detached duty, the notation by his name on the muster rolls from the winter of 1779–80 had been "on Command with Capt. Ferguson," or words to that effect. By October 1781 the column "For What Reason Absent" no longer included such explanations, indicating that he had returned to his primary duty station (March 20, September ?, December 2, 1780, October 15, November 23, 1781, Loyalist Regiment Muster Rolls, RG-8-1, C Series, vols. 1851–1860 [*sic*], Microfilm Reels C-3873, C 3874, C-4216, C 4217, Public Archives of Canada, Ottawa, Canada).

Card Index, "Loyalists in the King's Army, 1776–1783," New Jersey Archives, Trenton; E. B. O'Callaghan, *Names of Persons for Whom Marriage Licenses Were Issued by the Secretary of the Province of New York Previous to 1784* (Albany, N.Y.: Weed, Parsons & Co., 1860), 206; E. A. Jones, *Loyalists of New Jersey,* 106.

Editorial Method

We have presented the text of Johnson's journal as literally as possible, retaining his spelling, capitalization, and punctuation. These are sometimes unorthodox and variable. What is thereby lost in readability is offset, we believe, by clearer indications of the circumstances under which he wrote and the originality of his work. Omitted words have been supplied within brackets; bracketed question marks are used to mark difficult to decipher words that have been inferred from the context; completely illegible words and phrases are marked as such. Johnson often omitted both punctuation at the end of lines that appear to complete a sentence and capitalization at the beginning of the next. In these cases we have inserted a bracketed period but not adjusted the capitalization. The pagination in brackets represents Johnson's through page 107; thereafter we have supplied it.

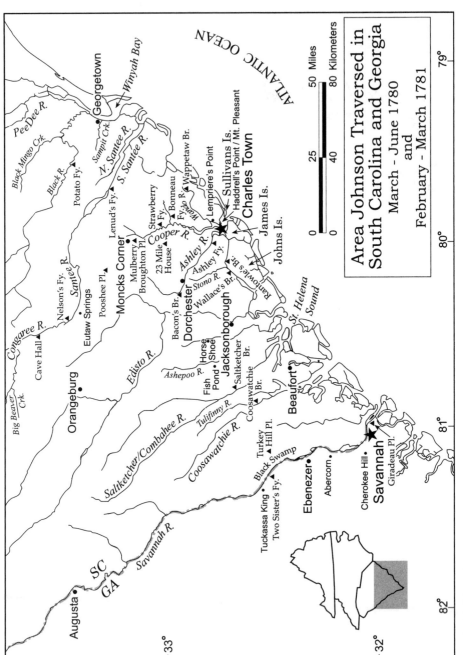

Area Johnson Traversed in
South Carolina and Georgia
March - June 1780
and
February - March 1781

ATLANTIC OCEAN

Map by Ted Steinke

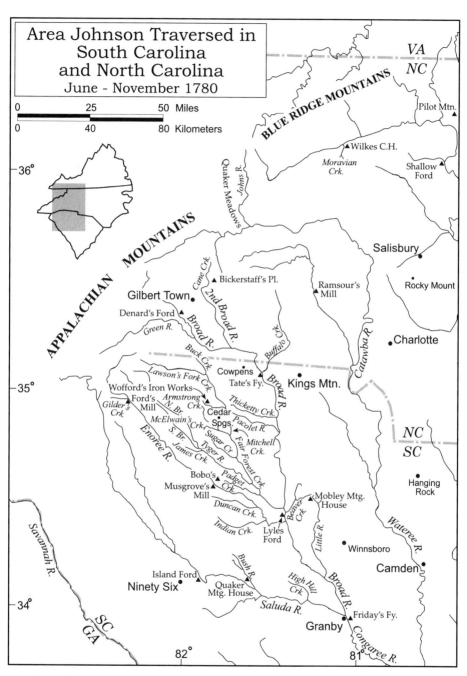

Area Johnson Traversed in South Carolina and North Carolina
June - November 1780

0	25	50	Miles
0	40	80	Kilometers

36°

VA
NC

BLUE RIDGE MOUNTAINS

Pilot Mtn.

▲ Wilkes C.H.

Moravian Crk.

Shallow ▲ Ford

Quaker Meadows

John's R.

APPALACHIAN MOUNTAINS

35°

Cane Crk.

▲ Bickerstaff's Pl.

Gilbert Town●

Ramsour's Mill ▲

Salisbury ●

●Rocky Mount

Denard's Ford ▲

Green R.

Broad R.

2nd Broad R.

Buffalo Crk.

Catawba R.

●Charlotte

Buck Crk.

Cowpens ●
Tate's Fy. ▲

Broad R.

Kings Mtn.

Lawson's Fork Crk.

Wofford's Iron Works ▲
Ford's ▲ Mill
Armstrong N. Br. Crk.
Cedar Spgs. ▲

Thicketty Crk.

Pacolet R.

Gilder's Crk.

McElwain's Crk.
S. Br. James Crk.
Sugar Cr.
Tyger R.

Mitchell Crk.

Fair Forest Crk.

NC
SC

Enoree R.

Bobo's ▲
Musgrove's ▲ Mill

Padget Crk.

Hanging Rock ●

Duncan Crk.

Indian Crk.

Mobley Mtg. ▲ House

Beaver Crk.

Little R.

Winnsboro ●

Lyles Ford

Wateree R.

Camden ●

Savannah R.

Island Ford ▲
Ninety Six ●

Quaker Mtg. House

Bush R.

High Hill Crk.

Saluda R.

Broad R.

Friday's Fy. ▲

Granby

Congaree R.

34°

SC
GA

82°

81°

Map by Ted Steinke

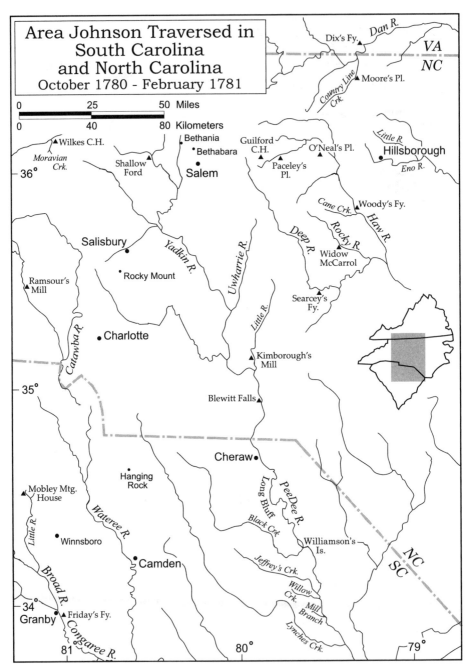

Area Johnson Traversed in
South Carolina
and North Carolina
October 1780 - February 1781

0   25   50 Miles
0   40   80 Kilometers

Dix's Fy.   Dan R.

VA
NC

Country Line Crk.   Moore's Pl.

Wilkes C.H.   Bethania   Little R.   Hillsborough
Moravian Crk.   Bethabara   Guilford C.H.   O'Neal's Pl.
Shallow Ford   Salem   Paceley's Pl.   Eno R.
36°

Cane Crk.   Woody's Fy.
Salisbury   Yadkin R.   Deep R.   Rocky R.   Haw R.
Rocky Mount   Uwharrie R.   Widow McCarrol
Ramsour's Mill   Little R.   Searcey's Fy.
Catawba R.
Charlotte
35°   Kimborough's Mill
Blewitt Falls
Cheraw
Hanging Rock   Long Bluff   PeeDee R.
Mobley Mtg. House   Wateree R.   Black Crk.
Little R.   Winnsboro   Williamson's Is.
Broad R.   Camden   Jeffrey's Crk.   NC
34°   Willow Crk.   SC
Granby   Friday's Fy.   Mill Branch
81   Congaree R.   Lynches Crk.   79°
80°

Map by Ted Steinke

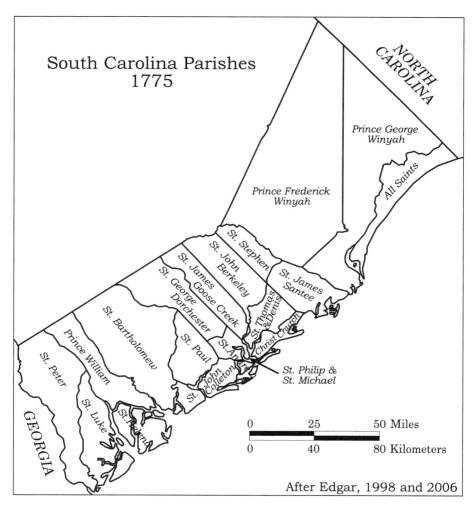

South Carolina Parishes
1775

NORTH CAROLINA

Prince George
Winyah

Prince Frederick
Winyah

All Saints

St. Stephen

St. John
Berkeley

St. James
Goose Creek

St. George
Dorchester

St. James
Santee

St. Thomas
& Denis

Christ Church

St. Bartholomew

St. Paul

St. And

St. John
Colleton

St. Philip &
St. Michael

Prince William

St. Peter

St. Luke

St. Helena

GEORGIA

| 0 | 25 | 50 Miles |
| 0 | 40 | 80 Kilometers |

After Edgar, 1998 and 2006

Map by Ted Steinki; adapted from Walter Edgar, *South Carolina: A History* (Columbia: University of South Carolina Press, 1998), and Walter Edgar, ed., *The South Carolina Encyclopedia* (Columbia: University of South Carolina Press, 2006). Courtesy of the Humanities Council[SC]

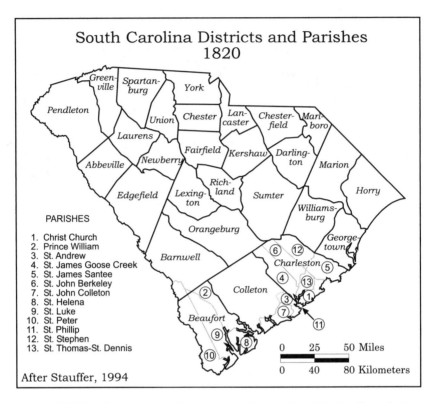

South Carolina Districts and Parishes 1820

Greenville

Spartanburg

York

Pendleton

Union

Chester

Lancaster

Chesterfield

Marlboro

Laurens

Fairfield

Kershaw

Darlington

Marion

Abbeville

Newberry

Rich-land

Richland

Lexington

Sumter

Horry

Edgefield

Williamsburg

PARISHES

1. Christ Church
2. Prince William
3. St. Andrew
4. St. James Goose Creek
5. St. James Santee
6. St. John Berkeley
7. St. John Colleton
8. St. Helena
9. St. Luke
10. St. Peter
11. St. Phillip
12. St. Stephen
13. St. Thomas-St. Dennis

Orangeburg

Georgetown

Barnwell

Charleston

Colleton

Beaufort

0   25   50 Miles

0   40   80 Kilometers

After Stauffer, 1994

Map by Ted Steinke; adapted with permission from Michael E. Stauffer, *The Formation of Counties in South Carolina* (Columbia: South Carolina Department of Archives and History, 1994)

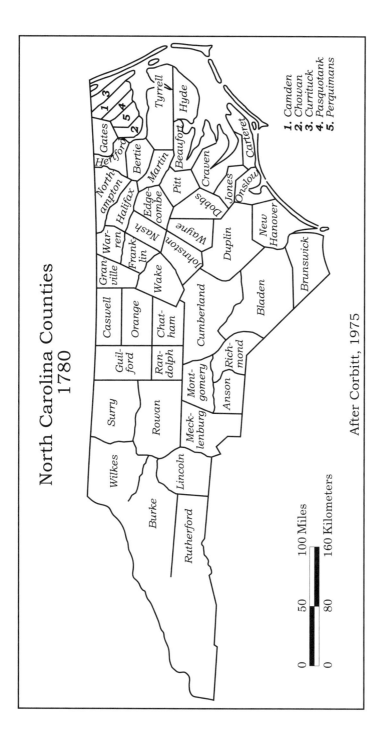

North Carolina Counties
1780

1. Camden
2. Chowan
3. Currituck
4. Pasquotank
5. Perquimans

After Corbitt, 1975

100 Miles
0   50
160 Kilometers
0   80

Map by Ted Steinke; adapted with permission from David Leroy Corbitt, *The Formation of the North Carolina Counties, 1663–1943* (Raleigh, N.C.: State Department of Archives and History, 1975)

The Journal

Memorandum of Occunces [Occurrences] during the Campaigne [of] 1780.

Sunday March 5th[.] The following Regmiments got in motion at Six oClock in the morning under command of Genl. Paterson viz Light Infty comd. by Major Graham, 71st Regt. by Major McArthur. N. York Volunteers Lt. Coll. Turnbull American Vols. Lt. Coll. Ferguson, North Carolinan Lt. Coll. Hamilton, S. Cars. Lt. Coll. Innes, Legion Infantry Major Cochran, a Compy of Dragoons Capt. Campbel[.] in Number about fifteen hundred, we marchd from Geridous Plantation to Cherokee hill Nine Miles where we halted to refresh, at three oClock in the afternoon got in motion & Marchd eight Miles to Abicorn, where we encamped and lay all Night disagreable wet Weather.

Monday 6th [March.] Got in motion at eight in the [p. 2] Morning & marched eight Miles to Ebenezer, a little Village on Savannah River[.] it contains about twenty Houses & a Church. The Inhabitants are high Dutch, it is Garrisoned by our Troops. There are five Redoubts, but no Cannon in any of them.

Tuesday 7th March[.] Remaind at Ebenezer[.] Pleasant Morning, Showery Evening & very Warm. Spent part of the Evening with two Indian Captains. John & James, Smoakd Tobacco & drank Grog with those Devils Incarnate; Coll. Ferguson joind us.

Wednesday 8th [March.] Still at Ebenezer[.] Orders to draw two Days provisions & be ready to March at Revallie beating. Several Men taken suddenly ill with pain & swelling of the Extremities occasioned by a Weed that poisons where it touches the naked Skin when the Dew is on it.

Thursday 9th [March.] Got in motion at Revallie [p. 3] beating[.] passd a Causway three Quaters of a Mile in length-overflowed with Water from two to three feet deep. we Marchd ten miles to a Plantation called two Sister's. There was formerly a ferry here across Savannah River, the Houses are now destroyed & the Place deserted.

Friday 10th [March.] Amn. Vls. & British Legion Marchd three Miles up the Augusta Road to Tuckaseeking, encamped & took breakfast at ten oClock in the Morning. About [illegible] OClock this Morning a Rebel

Lieut. Johnson with twenty Men surrounded a Poor Man's House, having hear'd we were in motion they came to find out the certainty of it. They did no damage to the family neither did they tarry long, being informed we were in possession of the Sisters they thought proper to take [p. 4] themselves off, this is the first Rebel Party we have heard of, Orderd at three oClock in the afternoon to take the Ground we left in the Morning. Coll. Ferguson with one division of Amn. Vols. cross'd the River, Capt. DePeyster with the remainder of the Detachment to cross as expeditiously as possible.

Saturday March 11th[.] cross'd Savannah River such a fresh that the Boats were brought thro Woods a Mile & half, the Water from four to ten feet deep where in a Dry time we might have marched dry, the Horses were swam the River, the Current sets down very rapid.

South Carolina Sunday 12th [March.] Lay encamped a quarter of a Mile from the River in the field where Genl. Moultrie was encamp'd last Summer when our Troops were retreating from Charles Town. Foraging Party [p. 5] of our Dragoons fell in with some Rebel light Horse, Lieut Campbel got slightly wounded.

Monday 13th [March.] Amn. Vs & Legion were ordered forward 26 Miles to secure the passes of Bee Creek, Coosawhatchee & Tylifinny Bridges, which we affected[.] a Pleasant cool Day for marching[.] passed several Country Seats one belonging to Wm. Middleton at Turkey hill, the Roadway level & good, took up our Ground at Dusk at Coosawhatchee Bridge where the Rebels oppos'd our Troops last May & got defeated.

Tuesday 14th [March.] found several Horses and a quantity of Furniture, Continental Stores & ammunition hid in a Swamp by one John Stafford a Sort of Rebel Commissary, he lives at Coosawhatchee Bridge & is by the by a Cursed fool which alone prevents his being a damnd Rogue, at four oClock in the Afternoon Coll. Ferguson, a part of the [p. 6] American Vs. & twenty men of the Legion proceeded Nine Miles to McPherson's Plantation, we got to Isaac McPhersons at Nine oClock[.] fifty Rebels on horse back, had just left this and gone to John McPhersons[.] a Party of ours pursued them but could not overtake them. Major Cochran with Part of the Legion were in pursuit of another party, another Road, but being led wrong by the Guide he arrived just before break of Day in front of our Picket[.] He immediately conjectured it was the Party he had been in pursuit of all Night, he halted and made a position to attack as soon as light but the alertness of our Centinels obliged them to come on sooner than they intended, upon their firing he immediately rushed on the Picket[.] they gave the Alarm & were soon drove to the House, where our detachment were ready [p. 7] for the attack expecting it was Rebels[.] a smart Skirmish ensued. The Melancholy mistake was soon discovered, tho unfortunately two brave Soldiers of the Amn. Vs. and one of the Legion were killed, several on both Sides wounded. Coll. Ferguson got wounded in the Arm by a Bayonet. Lt. McPherson of the Legion in the Arm & hand. Capt. DePeyster with Sixty Amn. Vols. & twenty of the Legion remaind at Coosawhatchee Bridge to secure the Pass till Genl. Patterson came on with the remainder of the Army.

Wednesday March 15th. Still at McPhersons Plantation. Foraging Parties get every thing that is Necessary for the Army.

Thursday 16th [March.] Lay at McPhersons living on the fat of the Land. the Soldiers every Side of us roasting Turkeys, Geese, Fowls, Ducks, Piggs &c, [p. 8] every thing in great plenty[.] this McPherson is a great Rebel, a Man of Property and at present is in Charles Town.

Friday 17th March 1780[.] Still at McPhersons[.] Capt. Depeyster Ordered out in pursuit of a Party a bout six miles in front, they got intelligence & made off[.] he made three Prisoners, & brought in several Horses, this Night Orders were rec'd to March to morrow morning.

Saturday 18th [March.] Got in motion at eight oClock in the morning, & marchd, ten miles to Saltketcher, Major Ladson with eighty Militiamen placed themselves on the N. Side of the River to oppose our crossing[.] they were amused by aCompany of the Legion returning their fire at the place where the Bridge formerly stood, while the Lt. Infty. and remainder of the Legion crossed [p. 9] the River below, and came in their rear before they knew of it. here the Bayonet was introduced, a Capt. Mills & sixteen Privates of the Rebels were kill'd, four badly wounded & one made Prisoner that luckily escaped the Bayonet. Major Graham of the Lt. Infty. & Major Wright of the Georgia Loyalists slightly wounded[.] the former continued his command the latter his march. two Privates of the Lt Infty were also slightly wounded. we remained all Night at Ogilvies Plantation Indian Land, this Days march very tedious, a disagreable rainy cold Day, and through a Swamp, from two to three feet deep of Water.

Sunday 19th [March.] Passed Saltketcher River, at the place where the Bridge [p. 10] formerly stood, (but has been destroyed since the Rebellion) in Boats, and swam the Horses[.] the Causeway on both Sides of the River overflowed with Water from two to three feet deep at the Ferry House about a quarter of a mile from the River. I dressed the Wounds of the four men that were bayoneted yesterday, we mov'd one mile to a Tavern kept by Mr Gipson who is at present prisoner in Ch. Town for not taking up Arms, as they say when his Country so loudly called for assistance.

Monday March 20th[.] Got in motion at eight oClock in the morning, marchd. about two miles ordered to halt the rear Guard were fired on, it provd. to be the York Vols. were getting the Boats on the Carriages, were fired on by a skulking party of Rascals from the other side of the [p. 11] River. three poor lads of the York Vs were killd. what damage was done to the Rebels is not known. detained by this and repairing of Bridges we only marchd seven miles this Day to Godfrey's Savannah.

Tuesday 21st [March.] Moved at eight in the Morning, marchd Sixteen miles to Fish Pond, here we were detained to repair the Bridge till Evening before we crossd; we movd on abt. three Miles through a Swamp and over an exceeding bad Causeway, this Day Coll. Tarleton with his Dragoons joind us from Beaufort where he had been to Mount his Men having lost all his Horses on the passage from N. York, we took up our Ground about ten oClock at Night.

Wednesday 22d [March.] Got in motion at ten oClock [p. 12] in the morning, and marchd ten miles to Horse Shoe, where we were again detained to repair the Bridge[.] after crossing continued our march four miles to Jacksonburgh, a Village containg about sixty Houses, situate on Ponpon River. the most of these Houses are very good[.] the People tolerable well to live, some large Store Houses for Rice, from which they convey it by Water to Chas. Town Market. in short it is a Pleasant little Place, well situate for trade, the Inhabitants are all violent Rebels not a man remaining at Home except two, one of whom was so sick, he could not get out of Bed, the other a Doctor who had got the name of a Friend to Government, the Women were treated with tenderness and the utmost civility. [p. 13]

Thursday 23d March 1780[.] All the Army (except 71st Regt.) and greatest part of the Baggage cross'd Ponpon River in Boats and Flats, the Bridge being destroyed. I remain'd in Town with Coll. Ferguson to dress his wound, & being unwell myself. Coll. Tarleton came up with a Party of Rebel Dragoons soon after crossing the River at Govr. Bees Plantation, he killd ten of them & took four Prisoners. Govr. Bee was formerly Lt. Govr. of South Carolina, is now a member of Congress.

Friday 24 [March.] Remainder of the Baggage and 71st Regt. crossed the River. the Army moved at one oClock in the afternoon, marched seven Miles to Ferguson's Plantation & halted all Night. A Flagg of Truce consisting of a Capt. Saunders, Capt. Wilkinson one Private & a Servant came in at the rear of our Army just as we halted. they were very [p. 14] severely reprimanded by Genl. Patterson for their unmilitary conduct, he told them they were ignorant of the profession they follow'd and in consequence of their behaviour he must detain them all Night, as to their request it could not be granted, which was also very unmilitary, it being to speak to the Prisoners and give them some Necessaries, the Gentlemen of the Flagg were led blindfold to their lodgings.—This Day Coll. Ferguson got the rear Guard in Order to do his King and Country justice by protecting Friends, Widows &c. and destroying R. Property. also to collect live Stock for the use of the Army all of which we Effected by taking Cattle, Sheep &c. and their Negroes to drive them. This Night very disagreable & rainy with very heavy Thunder & lightning.

Saturday 25th [March.] We got in motion at Revalie beating & marchd ten miles to Stono, or Wallace's Bridge. [p. 15] we took up our Ground at three oClock in the afternoon & remain all Night. Lt. Infty. and part of the Dragoons crossed the River.

Sunday 26th March 1780. Took up the whole Day in getting the Baggage and live stock over the River. the Bridge that formerly stood here being destroyed and the one just made very bad, we took up our Ground as soon as we crossd the River on a Neck of Land that runs down between Stono & Rantoll. This Day the Commander in Chief paid us a Visit from James Island, (which is only six miles distance) and narrowly escaped being taken by the Rebels who got intelligence of his visit, and were in close pursuit of him.

Monday 27th [March.] Two Companies of Lt. Infty. Amern. Vols. & one Company of Dragoons, crossed Rantoll Ferry in Scows[.] [p. 16] the rest of the Army crossed Yesterday. Coll. Hamilton of the North Carolinians, and Doctr. Smith of the Hospital proceeding a mile & half in front of the Army to Govr. Rutlidge's House[.] it was immediately surrounded by three hundred, Continental light Horse and they consequently made prisoners,[.] the British Dragoons fell in with them soon after, and had a Skirmish[.] the Rebels soon gave way & shewed them the Road as is customary on such occasions, several of our Dragoons got wounded, how many of the Rebels got hurt we cant say, they did not keep up the combat long enough for many to recieve damage[.] this Morning Capt. Saunders that came in with a Flagg the 24th was sent out, his attendant Capt. Wilkinson not being mentioned [p. 17] in the body of the Flagg is detained as a Prisoner of War. we took up our Ground on Govr. Rutlidges Plantation one mile from his House where we remained all Night.

Tuesday March 28th 1780[.] Moved at Nine oClock in the Morning, March'd eight Miles to Ashly Ferry, where we met the British Hessian Grenideers, Lt. Infty. & Jagers, under commd. of Sir H. Clinton, we, continued our March down the River six Miles to Linings Plantation situate on Ashly River nearly opposite Chs. Town, it commands a very pretty prospect towards the Sea. The part of Georgia, & South Carolina that we have marchd through coming from Savannah is a low flat Country[.] Sandy Soil not a

Stone to be seen, the Roads [p. 18] levil and Good. the Natural produce of the Land along the Sea Coast of Georgia is chiefly Pine scarcely a Stick of other Timber to be seen. when cleared and cultivated, Corn, Cotton & Indigo are raised on the upland, the low swamps laid out in Rice Plantations. Along the Sea Coast much the same Land in South Carolina some Oaks & Hickery intermixed with the Pines; this part of S. Carolina thick settled the most of the Planters very Wealthy, by manufacturing Indigo, Cotton & Rice; very bad Water in this low Country.

Wednesday 29th March[.] Sir H. Clinton with the British & Hessian Grenideers, Lt. Infty. & Jagers passed over Ashly River to Chas. Town Neck early in the Morning. Spent the Day in viewing C. Town, found it not a little like N. York. Ashly & Cowper River form [p. 19] a Bay exactly like East & North River.

Thursday March 30th 1780[.] An Incessant firing of Musketry on the Neck, Cannon at Short intervals[.] this firing was at the Commander in Chief and his attendants reconnoitring, he forbid the British return the fire. Lord Cathness standing by the side of Genl. Clinton was shot through the Body by a Musket Ball, one Jager killd.

Friday 31st [March.] Engineers Tools &c carried over from Linnings Landing, and began to break Ground without molestation under direction of Major Moncrieffe. this afternoon rode two Miles to see two Redoubts, (one of which has four, the other two thirty two Pounders mounted) at the mouth of Wapoocut, a River that runs from Stono to Ashly & seperates from the mainland[?] what's cal'd James Island. [p. 20]

Saturday April 1st 1780[.] Some Cannon and Mortars moved over Ashly River from Linnings Landing.

Sunday 2d [April.] Rode down to view our Fleet at Stono.

Monday 3d [April.] American Volunrs. marchd to Ashly Ferry to cover the Dragoons of the Legion while crossing the River, after they had cross'd we marchd up the River six Miles to Henry Middletons Plantation, passed several famous Country Seats, one called Drayton Hall belonging to the Heirs of Willm. Henry Drayton deceas'd[.] he was a Member of Congress & died at Philadelphia last Winter. it is truly an Elegant Place. Constant firing at our People at Work on the Neck.

Tuesday 4th [April.] Constant Canonade from the Rebels both from their Batteries and Shipping; one of their Ships, endeavouring to move up Cowper River, was [p. 21] fired on from our Works & drove back.

Wednesday 5th April[.] Constant Canonade from the Rebels at our Works on the Neck, in the Evening our Batteries at the Mouth of Wapoocut opened and kept up a warm fire for a few Minutes, then the firing ceas'd on both sides.

Thursday 6th [April.] Canonade from the Rebels at intervals all Day; in the Evening our Batteries on the Neck, & at Wapoocut opened[.] fired all Night at intervals.

Friday 7th [April.] Cannonade at intervals as usual.

Saturday 8th [April.] But little firing from the Rebels; Disagreable rainy morning. Last Night a reinforcement arriv'd at Chs. Town of thirteen hundred commanded by Genl. Scott. They rang [p. 22] all the Bells in Town on the occasion and fired a feu d. Joy. This afternoon abt. four oClock our Fleet hove in sight coming up under full sail with a fresh breeze at South West, and pass'd Fort Moultrie. Rebels strong Post on Sullivan's Island which they boasted no Fleet could ever pass, they were but a Short time passing, what damage is sustained we have not yet learn'd; The Richmond lost her fore topmast, a Cutter lay opposite the Fort all the time the Fleet were passing with a Flagg hoisted to point out the Channel, a heavy Cannonade from the Rebel Battery which each Ship returned, as they passed with a Spirit becoming Brittons.

Sunday 9th [April.] Admiral Arbuthnot [p. 23] came on Shore and went over to Head Quarters on the Neck. by him we were informed there were only seven men killed & fifteen wounded in passing Fort Moultrie, the Shipping damage so trifling twas not worth mentioning[.]

Monday Aprl 10th. Nothing extraordinary[.] Cannonade from our Batteries during the Night to cover the Working parties[.]

Friday [*sic*] 11th [April.] Coll. Ferguson returnd from head Quarters, informs us that the Town was summoned to surrender to his Britannic Majesty, Answer was returnd. that they thought Necessary as well as their Duty to defend it to the last extremity which they meant to do.

Wednesday 12th [April.] Recd. Orders to March, North Carolinians Ordered to join Coll. Ferguson. [p. 24] we left Linnings Plantation at seven oClock in the Evening, & march'd twenty two miles to Beacon's Bridge, where we arrived at five oClock Thursday Morning very much fatigued[.] we halted to refresh till seven. a Cold Morning.

Thursday 13th Apl 1780[.] We got in Motion at seven in the Morning and marchd through a Small Village called Dorchester, it contains about forty Houses & a Church; continued our March to Middletons Plantation, at Goose Creek, (about fifteen Miles from Beacon Bridge & ten from Dorchester) where we met the Legion at one oClock in the afternoon. we then halted till ten oClock at Night, when in company with them we got in motion & Marchd. eighteen miles to Monk's Corner, this forc'd March was in consequence of our being informed that [p. 25] Coll. Washington's, Polaski's, Bland & Owree's Lt. Horse lay here, we arrived an hour before Day break

Friday morning & found the above Enemy here in Numbers about four hundred including some Militia that arrived the Day before commanded by Genl. Huger[.] lucky for them they were under marching orders which made them more alert than usual when the alarm was given, which alone prevented their, being all compleatly taken by surprise[.] they made off with great expedition, we pursued overtook, & killed Polaski's Major Verner, wounded a French Lt. Beaulac, one more officer was taken, & about sixty Privates fifteen of whom were wounded. we had only one Man Wounded & he very slightly. We took thirty Waggons with four Horses to each, fifty very excellent Horses belonging to their [p. 26] Troop. These we converted to British light Horse, Coll. Washington & all his Officers very narrowly escaped, their Baggage Letters, and some of their Commissions were taken.

Friday 14th Aprl 1780[.] Remaind at Monks Corner collecting the Stores &c. at five in the Afternoon two Negroes came in and informed the Commanding Officer of a Party of twenty Lt. Horse being in a Swamp, Capt. DePeyster with twenty Amn. Vs. was Orderd in pursuit of them. he discovered them about three Miles from Camp, killed two, the others ran to a Creek & swam across by which means they made their escape, he took five very fine Horses, Saddles &c all compleat[.] he then returnd to Camp, took one Prisoner; about eleven oClock at Night accidentally a Store House caught fire in which were two Barrels of Powder, were very much alarmed [p. 27] at the explosion, & got under Arms; this confusion was scarcely over when three Ladies came to our Camp, in great distress (Lady Colliton Ms. Betsy Giles, & Ms. Jane Russel). they had been shockingly abused by a Plundering Villain, Lady Colliton badly cut in the Hand by a Broad Sword, and bruised very much, after I dressed her wounds, I went with an officer and twelve men, to the Plantation a mile from Camp to Protect Mrs. Fasseaux who this Villain had likewise abused in like manner, here I found a most accomplished amiable Lady in the greatest distress imaginable. after taking a little Blood from her & giving her an Anodyne she was more composed, and came next morning to Camp to testify against the Villains that abused them in this horrid manner, he was secured and sent to Head Quarters.

Saturday 15th [April.] We left Monks Corner at twelve oClock. My Friend A. Allaire & I had the happiness [p. 28] of escorting the Ladies Home. we were met by a Servant with the News that there was a Villain then Plundering the House, a Party was sent to the House[.] they catchd the Thiefe who was well rewarded for his knavery. The Ladies chose our protection, rather than stay at Home, & begg'd we would conduct them a few Miles to a Plantation called Mulberry Broughton, where we bid adieu to those Ladies with some regret, tho pleas'd in some measure that they thought themselves free from any farther insults, we continued countermarching to twenty three mile House, where we halted all Night.

Sunday 16 April[.] Movd at Nine oClock in the Morning to Strawberry Ferry, a Branch of Cowper River[.] took up the Day in passing the Army & Baggage over the River, continued our March four Miles to Bono Ferry another branch of Cowper River[.] here we came up with the Baggage of the thirty third, Sixty fourth, & Legion, we lay here all Night, as it took up the Night to get over this Baggage[.] [p. 29] a Capts. Guard from our Detachment was sent over to take Charge of a Store of Household furniture sent out of Town and deposited at a Major Butlers for safety, the Store House was full of very Rich Furniture of all kinds.

Monday 17th April 1780[.] Cross'd Bono Ferry at seven oClock in the Morning. March'd Sixteen Miles to Miller's Bridge over a branch of Wando River where we took up our Ground at Nine oClock in the Evening. we came up with the thirty third Regt. at St. Thomas's Church.

Tuesday 18th [April.] Began to fortify at the Bridge, & make a block House in order to keep a post here with few Men.

Wednesday 19th [April.] Coll. Ferguson with fifty Amn. Vols. & part of the North Carolinians moved to join the thirty third sixty fourth Regts. & Ligion which had gone forward to attack a Rebel Post at Lampriers point. The British were coming back, they had march'd up to the Fort, and found it so strong that it was not [p. 30] prudent to Storm it with so few men.

Thursday 20th April 1780[.] Remaind at Millers Bridge finishing the block House[.] News that Coll. Tarleton had taken Nine Sloops, with Good Stores &c &c. some Cannon.

Friday 21st [April.] A Party left under commd. of Capt. Ryerse to defend Millers Bridge, the remainder of the thirty third, sixty fourth, Amn. Vs. & B. Legion, countermarched twelve Miles, to St. Thos. Church.

Saturday 22d [April.] Took quarters at the Parish House; under the disagreable necessity of detaining a Lady from Chs. Town on suspicion of her being a Spy.

Sunday 23d [April.] Moved from the House to the Wood for convenience of Shade.—very warm Weather.

Monday 24th [April.] Lord Cornwallis joind us & took command[.] about ten oClock in the Evening a very heavy Cannonade, & incessant fire of Musketry[.] the Rebels sallied out took eight of the [p. 31] Light Infanty. upon which the whole line got under Arms. some in the hurry turnd out without putting on their Coats, were by the others mistaken for Rebels, & fired on, which unluckily occasioned warm work for a few Minutes. Sixty odd of ours got killed & wounded by our own Men, the Rebels were repulsed,

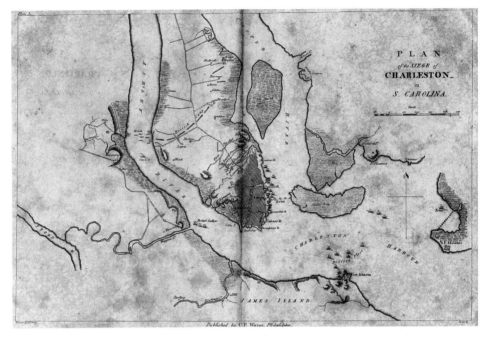

This plan of the Siege of Charles Town, 1780, locates several points mentioned by Johnson, including the shipyard on Charles Town Neck and Gadsden's Bridge to Sullivans Island. John Marshall, *The Life of George Washington, Maps and Subscribers' Names* (Philadelphia: C. P. Wayne, 1807). Courtesy of Rare Books and Special Collections, University of South Carolina Libraries

& in the hurry of retreat finding their Muskets rather an incumbrance, threw thirty odd of them away.

Tuesday 25th [April.] Got in motion at eight oClock in the morning, we were joind by the twenty third Regt. we passed over Millers, & Wapeta Bridges continued our march four miles farther to Wapeta Meeting House where we remain'd till two in the morning.

Wednesday 26th [April.] Moved at two oClock in the Morning[.] marchd. seventeen Miles to Mount Pleasant, opposite Chs. Town, where we took possession of the Ground on which the Rebels had one eighteen Pounder [p. 32] There is a Ferry from Mt. Pleasant to Chs. Town calld Hibben's Ferry. Here are very good Barracks if finished that were begun before the Rebellion. they were used for an Hospital in which we took some invalids and a Doctor. Sullivan's Island is about half a mile from the Point. There is a Bridge or rather Causeway from Huxdrells Point to Sullivan's Island, built at a vast expense under direction of Mr Gadsden, it has four

Arches left for the Tide to flow through, this expense was laid out to procure a safe retreat from Fort Moultrie. About six Miles from the Point stands Christ Church. this Night I might properly sing content with our hard fate on the cold Ground, for I wrapt myself in my great Coat and lay down on the Ground with my Saddle for a Pillow. A blustering cold Night. [p. 33]

Thursday 27th April[.] 1780 Got in Motion at one oClock in the morning & countermarched to Wapeta meeting House, cold North East Wind.

Friday 28th [April.] Fortified the small House by the side of the Meeting House, ten oClock at Night intelligence was brought to Lord Cornwallis that the Rebels had left Fort Lamprie & were gone to Chs. Town, or were penetrating into the Country[.] American Vols. were ordered to march down and discover the fact, we arrived about four in the Morning and found the Fort occupied by the Navy. a Lieut. of the Navy commanding Officer[.] the Rebels had abandoned it & gone to Chs. Town[.]

Saturday 29th [April.] Countermarched to Wapeta Meeting House.

Sunday 30th [April.] We were joind by the N. York Vols. at three oClock in the Morning in company with them marched to Lampriers Point to take post there, took up our Ground [p. 34] at seven oClock in the Evening, the Rebels left in the Fort, four Eighteen, two four Pounders, & five Swivels; it is a very disagreable post being nothing but a bank of Sand, and in a windy Day you must keep your Eyes shut or have them filld with Sand, there is a Ferry from this to Town called Lamprie Ferry[.]

Monday May 1st 1780[.] Bathed in Wando River with my Friend Allaire.

Tuesday 2d [May.] Began to fortify Lampries Point the old Works being destroyed, about Eleven oClock in the Morning Coll. Ferguson, Capt. DePeyster. Capt. Doyle. Lieuts. Taylor & Wilson with sixty Men marched to Hurdrells Point to attack a small Fort that stands on the Causeway about a hundred and fifty Yards from the Main Land; the Tide was so low that they were able to march dry on the right where Coll. Ferguson with thirty Men stormed, Capt. DePeyster Marchd down the Causeway, & soon got possession of the Fort, they [p. 35] met with much less opposition than they expected, seeing it cuts off all communication between Fort Moultrie & the Mainland and keeps them upon proper allowance, besides tis so strongly situate that twenty British Troops would defend against a Thousand, after taking possession of it they were entirely exposed to the Cannon from Fort Moultrie, the part facing it being open and on a level, the Rebils from Ft. Moultrie kept a constant fire with four pieces of Cannon at our Men, till Dark, after which it was made secure from any farther Danger.

Wednesday 3d May[.] Still Fortifying Fort Lamprie, in the Evening a Cannonade began on the Neck, which continued very heavy all Night, with an incessant fire of Musketry, the Cannon chiefly from the Rebels [p. 36] small Arms from us, this Night their Hospital Ship that lay opposite the Town was taken.

Thursday May 4th 1780[.] Continued fortifying the Point.

Friday 5th [May.] Very Windy, in danger of losing ones Eyes by the blowing of Sand, very cold blustering Night.

Saturday 6th [May.] Very disagreable windy Day[.] Still at Lampries Point. News just recievd from Lord Cornwallis that a Patrolling party consisting of Lieut. Nash & Eleven Dragoons were taken by Coll. Washington & Orie's Light Horse near Santee River, Coll. Tarleton was immediately ordered to pursue them. he overtook them at the River, charged & killed a few, took a Major & thirty Privates, our Patrolling party that had been taken were in a Boat rowing over the River, upon seeing Coll. Tarleton they immediately siezed the Guard threw them overboard, rowed themselves back, & joined their respective Regiments again. Coll. Washington [p. 37] and Orie took to the River & Swam over.

Sunday 7th May[.] Orders to draw two Days Provision, & be ready to march at Minutes notice; Coll. Ferguson had obtained permission to attack Fort Moultrie, he rode forward to reconnoitre, we were to remain at our Post till we rec'd Orders to March, the first News was that the Fort was in possession of the British[.] the Rebels surrendered Prisoners of War; Capitulation was as follows. Capt. Hudson of the Navy summoned the Fort on Friday[.] Coll. Scott who commanded sent for Answer[.] Tol, lol. derol, lol, Fort Moultrie will be defended till the last extremity, on Saturday he sent another flagg & demanded a surrender, acquainting Coll. Scott that the Lieut. with the Flagg would stay a quarter of an Hour for his Answer[.] if the Fort was not given up he would immediately storm it & put all the Garrison to the Sword [p. 38] at this Coll. Scott changed the Tune of his Song. he begged there might be a cessation of Hostilities, that the Fort would be given up on the following conditions, that the Officers both Continental & Militia should march out with the honours of War and be allowed to wear their side Arms, the Officers & Soldiers of the Militia to be parolled to their respective Homes and remain peacable till exchanged; the Continental Soldiers to be treated tenderly. Granted by Capt. Hudson. Sunday Morning at eight oClock Coll. Scott with a hundred & twenty Men Marched out of the Fort piled their Arms. Capt. Hudson marched in took possession of Fort Moultrie, the key to Chas. Town Harbour, & puts it in our power to keep out any Enemy that would wish to give the Rebels any assistance. Taken in the Fort fifty Barrels of Powder, forty four pieces of Cannon, one brass ten Inch Mortar three thousand Cannon Cartridges, five hundred [p. 39] live ten Inch shells, forty thousand Musket Cartridges, a vast quantity of Lunt, three Months Salt provision, for two hundred Men, eighteen Tierces of Rice, forty Head of black Cattle, Sixty Sheep twenty Goats, forty fat Hoggs, Six Waggons two Stand of Colours, and many other Articles Necessary in a Fort too tedious to Mention.

Monday 8th May 1780[.] At six oClock in the morning Sir Henry Clinton sent in a Flagg and demanded Charles Town, Genl. Lincoln requested cessation of Hostilities till eight, from eight to twelve oClock, &c. The Truce continued till four oClock Tuesday Afternoon when Sir Henry Clinton recieving a very insolent request, sent in word he saw plainly that Genl. Lincoln did not mean to give up the Town, that the firing should commence at eight oClock in the Evening, at which time began a most tremendous Cannonade throwing of Carcases & Shells into the Town, and incessant fire of Musketry all Night. [p. 40]

Wednesday May 10th 1780[.] Firing still continued all Day, and very brisk all Night[.]

Thursday 11th [May.] The Town was set on fire by a Carcase which burnt several Houses. The Rebels sent out a Flagg soon after, our firing continued without taking Notice of their flag They soon shewed a second Flagg, which was accepted, its contents were begging the Terms that had been offered the last Truce. Sir Henry Clinton Answered them the Firing should cease until he could send and consult Admiral Arbuthnot. the Terms were granted.

Friday 12th [May.] At ten oClock in the Morning the Gates were opened. Genl. Leslie at the Head of the British Grenadiers the Seventh, Sixty third, Sixty fourth Regiments and Hessian Grenadiers marched in and Took posession of Chs. Town. he soon leveled the thirteen Stripes with the Dust & displayed the British [p. 41] Standard on the Ramparts. we still at Lampries Point, this Day Capt. Fredk. DePeyster and I went Sixteen miles up Wando River & took a Quantity of Bark, Salts, Camphor, Opium Jallop, Ipecacuannah, Manna Cantharides &c[.] they had been sent out of Chs. Town & deposited at Doctr. Lococks for safety, I sent in a List of them to Comissary of Captures.

Saturday 13th [May.] Still at Lampries.

Sunday 14th [May.] Went over to Town to view their strong Works. they far exceeded my expectation, saw the Poor deluded Officers much chagrined at not being allowed to wear Side Arms[.]

Monday 15th [May.] A Magazine blew up, it set the Town on fire & burnt several Houses. Capt. Collins & Lieut. Gordon of the Artillery, Lt. McLeod of the forty second Regt. & about thirty Privates besides Inhabitants, perished by the explosion[.] there is no certainty how this accident happened[.] tis conjectured by throwing the Captured Arms into the Store one went off, & set fire to the Powder[.] [p. 42]

Tuesday 16th May 1780[.] The Amn. Volunteers under command of Capt. DePeyster marchd to Sullivan's Island, relieved Capt. Hudson of the Navy and took command of Fort Moultrie[.]

Wednesday 17th [May.] Spent the Day in writing Letters to N. York.

Thursday 18th. Friday 19th Saturday 20 [May.] Nothing extraordinary.

Sunday 21st [May.] Rode to Lamprier Point, from thence to visit Ms.[?] Pinkney[.]

Monday 22d [May.] Orders were recieved to be in readiness for marching, I went to Chs. Town & return'd in the Evening.

Tuesday 23d [May.] Sent the Sick to the Hospital;

Wednesday 24th [May.] Rec'd Orders from Coll. Balfour to lay in Medicine for three Months Campaigne.

Thursday 25th [May.] A Capt. of the Sixty third Regt. relieved our detachment at Fort Moultrie. Capt. DePeyster with the Amn. Vols. moved over the River & took Ground in front of the Lines, the Horses & Baggage was takin to the Ship Yards, two Miles from Town.

Friday 26th [May.] The following Corps got in Motion at three oClock [p. 43] in the Morning, under command of Coll. Balfour of the Twenty third Regt. viz Lt. Infty. Commandd by Major Graham, three Companies of the Seventh by Capt. Peacock, Amn. Vols. Major Ferguson, Prince of Wales's by Lt. Coll. Paterson in Number about six hundred, marched out to the ten Mile House & halted. I remained in Town went on board a Providence Sloop, & got two hundred Limes & half Dozen Pine Apples, at five in the Evening I proceeded as far as Six Mile House with a Wagon & halted, till two in the Morning.

Saturday 27th [May.] Movd at two oClock in the Morning, went six miles up the Dorchester Road, a Dragoon overtook me & told me my Mistake, I passed thro' the woods to the ten Mile House, then passed on till I overtook the Army near twenty three mile House where we took up our Ground.

Sunday 28th [May.] Got in motion at two oClock in the Morning, Marched ten miles to Monks Corner, went & dined at Mr. Giles's with the Ladies [p. 44] whom we protected when we were here the 14th of April.

Monday May 29th 1780[.] Lay encamped in a Wood at Monk's Corner; Mr. Allaire & I were again invited to Dine with Mr Giles.

Tuesday 30th [May.] Moved at five oClock in the Morning & Marched ten Miles to Genl. Moultries Plantation, at Prushee where we halted.

Wednesday 31st [May.] Got in Motion at half past four in the Morning & Marchd Sixteen Miles to Greenland Swamp.

Thursday June 1st 1780[.] Got in Motion at five oClock in the Morning. Marched to Neilson's Ferry Santee River, by express we were informed that Coll. Tarleton on Monday the 29th of May fell in with a Body of Rebels at hanging Rock forty five Miles above Camden, they were commanded by Coll. Bleufort; Coll. Tarleton summoned them to surrender, upon recieving an insolent Answer he immediately charged them; kill'd one Lt. Coll. three Captains, eight Subalterns, one Adjutant, one Quarter Master, & Ninety Nine Sergts. [p. 45] and Rank & file; wounded three Captains, five Subs. and a hundred & forty two Sergts and Rank & file, made Prisoners two Captains one Subaltn. & fifty Sergts. & Rank & file. Total killd Wounded & Prisoners, one Lt. Coll. eight Captains fourteen Subs. one Adjutant, one Quarter Master and two hundred and Ninety one Sergt. & Rank & file taken three Stand of Colours, two Brass six Pounders, two Howitzers, two Waggons with Ammunition, one Artillery forge Waggon, fifty five Barrels of Powder, twenty six Waggons loaded with Cloathing, Camp Equipage, Musket Cartridges Cartridge Boxes Flints &c. killed of the Legion Lieut. McDonald, & Ensign Campbel serving with the Cavalry, two Privates of the Cavalry & one of the Infty. Total killd two Subs. three Rank & file. Wounded Lieut. Patterson of 17th Dragoons & eight Rank & file of the Cavalry, three of the Infantry. Total wounded one Sub. & eleven Rank & file.

Friday 2d [June.] Lay encamped in a Pleasant Field near Neilsons Ferry, ordered to be ready to march at two oClock in the Morning. [p. 46]

Saturday June 3d 1780[.] Moved at two oClock in the Morning, Marched fourteen Miles to Campbles Plantation, halted in the Woods for convenience of Shade, this Plantation is seventy seven Miles from Chs. Town—

Sunday June 4th[.] Lay in the Woods Campbels Plantation, some Prize Wine was shared to the different Corps, in good time to Drink his Majesty's Health.

Monday 5th [June.] Got in Motion at two oClock in the Morning & March'd twelve Miles to Cave Hall, St. Matthews Parish[.] just below our Camp, is a remarkable large Cave, an hundred feet Deep, there is a Room formed by a Rock, Sixty feet long & forty wide, with famous Grand Arches formed by Nature; through the Middle of the Cave runs a beautifull stream of Water, which heads in a Fountain at the farther end of the Cave. This Day twenty Militiamen came in and brought Prisoner the Titular Governor of Georgia. he had taken Protection from Ld. Cornwallis in a [p. 47] Private Character.

Tuesday June 6th 1780[.] Got in motion at three in the Morning and marched thirteen Miles to Coll. Thompson's[.] this Morning on the march two Bucks ran in amongst the men, one of them was so frightened that he could not leap the Fence, was catched. the Militia come from all Quarters, & take Protectn.

Wednesday 7th [June.] Lay encamped at Coll. Thomsons Plantation.

Thursday 8th [June.] Showery afternoon with very heavy Thunder.

Friday 9th [June.] Lay still at Thompsons.

Saturday 10th [June.] Left Thompsons twelve oClock at Night, March'd eighteen Miles to Beaver Creek, & halted[.] Major Graham & two Flank Companies of the Prince of Wales's Amn. Regt. remained at Thomsons[.] a Company of Militia came at four in the afternoon, with their firelocks in order to join us. This day met us Henry Melcolm an old Gentleman eighty one Years old, he had left Home with an intention to go to Chs. Town, & had walked upwards of an hundred Miles when he met us, his errand was to [p. 48] get some kind of assistance, he had been plundered & stript of every thing by the Rebels, what is more remarkable this old Abram. left a Child at Home only two Years old.

Sunday 11th [June.] Got in motion at five oClock in the Morning & March'd five Miles & halted.

Monday 12th [June.] Moved at two oClock in the Morning & march'd fourteen Miles to Congree Stores[.] this Day passed a Plantation where one Man had upwards of four hundred Acres of Indian Corn growing.

Tuesday 13th [June.] Lay at Congree Stores[.] many good friends to Government about here have suffered for their loyalty.

Wednesday 14th [June.] Lay at Congrees, Capt. Peacock with the three Companies of Royal Fusileers, rec'd orders to remain here, Coll. Patterson with the Prince of Wales's Regt to March for Camden.

Thursday 15th [June.] Moved at twelve oClock at Night[.] March'd twelve Miles to Saludy Ferry[.] cross'd the River at five in the Morning & halted.

Friday 16th [June.] Got in Motion at half after four in the Morning[.] Marched seven miles to [p. 49] high hill Creek & halted.

Saturday 17th June 1780[.] Lay still in the Field at high hill Creek.

Sunday 18th [June.] Moved at two oClock in the Morning & Marched fourteen miles to Capt Wrights of Coll. Innes's Corps.

Monday 19th [June.] Got in motion at four oClock in the Morning & Marched fourteen Miles to Cooks Plantation, (Quaker Settlement) he is a Rebel Justice, a Capt. of Militia and a great persecutor of Friends to Government, he is Ordered down to Johns Island, a Place pointed out for the reception of such People.

Tuesday 20th [June.] Marched fourteen Miles to Devenports. (Little River) he was formerly Capt. of Militia under Government, & has the name of a Tory from his Neighbours, tho many of his actions contradict it.

Wednesday 21st [June.] Lay still at Davenports.

Thursday 22d [June.] Got in motion at one oClock in the Morning & march'd ten Miles to the fording Place Saludy River, the Men and Baggage were crossed in a Scow, the Horses forded the River, continued our March six miles to Ninety Six. [p. 50] Ninety Six is a Village or Country Town[.] it contains about twelve dwelling Houses, a Court House & Jail, in which are confined forty odd Rebels brought Prisoners by the friends to Government who have just now got the opportunity to retaliate gladly embrace it, many of them, before this being obliged to hide in Swamps & Caves to keep from Prison themselves. Ninety Six is situate on a Eminence in a Flourishing part of the Country, the Land round about it in General is good, Natural Growth is Oaks, Black Walnut, Hickery, &c which are very large & thrifty, the Land is cleared for a Mile Round the Town, it produces Wheat Indian Corn, Oats, Hemp, Flax, Cotton, & Indigo, the Water is very good, a free open Air & is esteemed, an healthy part of the Country. Seventy Friends to Government were condemned to be hanged at one Court here in April 1779[.] five were hanged the others through Interests of their friends got pardoned.

Friday June 23d[.] lay in the Field at Ninety Six, some friends came in[.] four were wounded, the Militia had embodied at Tuckyseegyford South branch of Catawba River, they [p. 51] were attacked by a Body of Rebels commanded by Genl. Rutherford, the Militia scant of Ammunition were obliged to retreat, they had to swim the River at a Mill Dam, where they were fired on by the Rebels & thirty of them killed. Coll. Ferguson with forty Amn. Vols. pushed with all speed to support the Militia, it is seventy miles from this. the militia are flocking to him from all parts of the Country.

Saturday 24th June[.] The remainder of the Detachment took Quarters in Town[.] Barracks were provided for the Men.

Sunday 25th. Monday 26th. & Tuesday 27th [June]. Were taken up in Clearing the Town & levilling the Parade Ground[.]

Wednesday 28th. Thursday 29th. Friday 30th [June.] Still at Ninety Six nothing extraordinary.

Saturday July 1st[.] Took a ride into the Country for exercise.

Sunday 2d. Monday 3d. Tuesday 4th [July]. No News.

Wednesday 5th [July.] Coll Ferguson returnd without being able to come up with those Gentry.

Thursday 6th Friday 7th, Saturday 8th [July.] Remain'd in Quarters[.]

Sunday 9th [July.] The Amn. Vols. under command of Capt. DePeyster left Ninety Six at seven oClock in the Even. [p. 52] they Marchd. seven Miles to Island ford Saludy River & halted, my friend Allaire & I having Company did not leave our Quarters till Nine oClock, having no Guide we got out of the Road, found our Mistake at a Mill three Miles from the Road we should have taken, we did not lose much by our missing the Road as we supplied ourselves with a feed of Corn for our Horses, we came up with the Detachment at one oClock, in the Morning.

Monday 10th July 1780. Got in Motion at five oClock in the Morning cross'd Saludy in a Flat, march'd Nine Miles to Coll. Williams's Plantation, & halted. Mrs. Williams and The Children were at Home & treated with the utmost civility. Coll. Williams commands a Battn. of Rebels, & is a very violent persecuting Man.

Tuesday 11th [July.] Got in Motion at five oClock in the Morning and Marched eight Miles to Indian Creek and halted during the heat of the Day at one Ryans a Good Friend, and has suffered much for his Loyalty[.] got in motion at six oClock in the Evening & Marched eleven Miles to Dunkins Creek, & halted at a [p. 53] Widow Browns.

Wednesday 12 July 1780[.] Moved at five oClock afternoon, forded Dunkin Creek, & Ennoree River continued our march eight Miles to Capt. Frosts, Paget Creek[.] this Evening met an express with the disagreable News of a Party of ours consisting of seventeen of the Legion, eighteen. N. York. Vols. & twenty Militiamen being defeated at Coll. Bratons Fishing Creek.

Thursday 13th [July.] Lieut. Hunt of the Legion Cavalry came to our Quarters at Capt. Frosts, he was one of the Party defeated, the 12th Inst. he gave us but an imperfect account of the affair, Capt. Huck commanded the Party consisting of one Sub. & Seventeen Privates of the Legion, two Subs. and eighteen N. York Vols. and twenty five Militiamen. they were sent in pursuit of a Rebel party, and arrived at twelve oClock Tuesday Night the 11th Inst. very much fatigued they thought to rest themselves[.] unfortunately a Rebel Party commanded by Coll. Lacy came upon them at four in the Morning [p. 54] of the 12th[.] were in amongst them and had possession of every pass, before they were apprised of it, except a Road leading to North Carolina where Capt. Huck with four Dragoons endeavored to make off. Capt. Huck got shot through the Neck of which he died. Mr. Hunt with one Dragoon took a foot Path leading to a Swamp, the Militia he could give no account off. We left Capt. Frosts about six oClock in the Evening forded Tiger River continued our March twelve Miles to Sugar Creek, where we found two hundred Militia encamped at Waffords old Field Fair Forrest, under command of Major's Plummer & Gibbs, the Rebels we hear are collecting in force at the Catawba Nation & Broad River[.]

Friday 14th [July.] Lay encamped at Waffords old Field, every hour intelligence from different parts of the Country of Rebel Parties doing Mischief.

The Light Infantry of Prince of Wales Amn. Regt. joind us at twelve oClock at Night.

Saturday 15th [July.] Dined with Coll. Fletchall[.] after [p. 55] Dinner went to see his Mill, the Water falls almost perpendicular twenty feet down into a Tub from which runs up a shaft through the Stone & turns it in the same Manner as the Coggs do a double geered Mill. on our return to Camp heared that Capt. Dunlop had retreated from Princes Fort, he had intelligence of a Rebel Party ten miles above him, he attacked them about two oClock in the Morning & drove them off their Ground, took one Prisoner who informed him the Rebels were four hundred Strong[.] upon this information Dunlop thought proper of course to retreat, his Number being only fourteen Amn. Vols. & Sixty Militiamen[.] Dunlop had two Men killed & one made Prisoner a Sergeant & Private wounded. The loss of the Rebels is uncertain, upon this News Capt. DePeyster ordered the Amn. Vols. & Militia to get ready to March to support Dunlop, Capt. F. DePeyster [p. 56] with a hundred Men marched twelve Miles to Mc.Elwains, where we met Dunlop, I went to dress the wounded.

Sunday 16th July 1780[.] Dunlop with the Men under him Marched down five Miles to Whites Plantation Mitchell Creek, where he joined Capt. DePeyster who halted here last Night.

Monday 17th [July.] Lay at Whites, the Militia brought in four Prisoners, one a lad of fifteen Years old badly wounded in the Arm[.] I dressed his Wound[.]

Tuesday 18th [July.] Coll. Ferguson came up from Ninety Six & joind us, by him we were informed that the Light Infty. were on their March to join us.

Wednesday 19th [July.] Still remain'd at Whites Mitchell Creek.

Thursday 20th [July.] Got in motion at five oClock in the Evening & March'd six Miles to Fair Forrest ford, where we halted & lay all Night[.]

Friday 21st [July.] Coll. Balfour with the Light Infty. from Ninety Six joind us, we still remain at the ford.

Saturday 22d [July.] at seven oClock in the Evening the Amn. Vols. Light Infty. & three hundred Militia got in motion, & made a forc'd March of twenty five miles to Lossing's Fork (Pacolet River) to surprize a [p. 57] Party of Rebels that we heared lay here, we arrived at James Woods Plantation at six oClock in the Morning of the 23d greatly disappointed at not finding the Rebels here, we were informed that they were at Green River twenty five Miles farther.

Sunday 23rd July[.] lay all Day in the Tent & Slept.

Monday 24 [July.] Got in motion at one oClock in the Morning & countermarched to our old Ground fair Forrest ford.

Tuesday 25th [July.] Coll. Balfour with the Light Infty. march'd at two oClock in the Morning for Ninety Six.

Wednesday 26th [July.] Lay at our old Ground Fair Forrest.

Thursday 27th [July.] Moved at Nine oClock in the Morning forded Fair Forrest River marched three miles & halted in the Woods[.]

Friday 28th [July.] Got in motion at seven in the Morning[.] Marched eight Miles to Coll. Henderson's Plantation, he has near two hundred Acres of Indian Corn growing in one Field, he is Prisoner at Chs. Town.

Saturday 29th [July.] Moved at eight in the Morning[.] Marched five Miles to Thickety River, & halted[.] one of the Men killed a Rattle Snake with thirteen Rattles on. [p. 58]

Sunday 30th July 1780[.] Moved at three in the morning, countermarched twelve Miles to Armstrong Creek Fair Forrest,[.] this Day came into Camp express from Anderson's Fort; Capt. Cook aged Sixty Years, he has buried four Wives & now has his fifth on her last Legs.

A timber rattlesnake such as Johnson probably saw on July 29, 1780, when its thirteen rattles prompted his friend Anthony Allaire to sardonically dub it a "Continental rattle-snake." Mark Catesby, *The Natural History of Carolina, Florida, and the Bahama Islands . . .* (London, 1731–1743). Courtesy of Rare Books and Special Collections, University of South Carolina Libraries

Monday 31st [July.] Got in Motion at six oClock in the Morning & Marched ten Miles to Mitchell Creek fair forrest, a very wet disagreable Day[.] we got thoroughly soaked.

Tuesday August 1st. Lay at Mitchell Creek[.] had intelligence that Coll. Turnbull had been attacked at Rocky Mount but were not able to learn how the affair ended[.]

Wednesday 2d [August]. Got in Motion at four oClock in the Morning Marched four Miles to Tiger River forded it & continued our March to Capt. Boboes & halted, here we reciev'd Intelligence that Coll. Turnbull beat of the Rebels, Capt. Hulett got wounded in the Head. Genl. Sumpter commanded the Rebel party, he sent in a Flagg & demanded [p. 59] the Post, Coll. Turnbull sent out Word he must come & take it if he wanted it. Sumpter then made his attack, but was soon obliged to retreat with considerable loss. Coll. Turnbull took two Prisoners that had been in his Camp some Days before drew Ammunition & then joind the Rebels, & were heard to say when firing, take back your Ammunition again, they were both hang'd as a reward for their Treachery.

Thursday Augt. 3d[.] Lay at Bobos[.] nothing Extra[.]

Friday 4th [August.] At six in the Evening[.] moved three quarters of a Mile for convenience of Ground.

Saturday 5th [August.] Lay on the heights in the Woods near Bobos, had intelligence that Fort Anderson, (on Thickety) was taken in which were Sergt. Blacksley of ours and eighty Militiamen commanded by Capt. More. the Rebels summoned it on Sunday 30th of July, & More gave it up in a Dastardly Manner without exchanging a Single Shot.

Sunday 6th [August.] at seven oClock in the Evening we left the heighths near Boboes, upon hearing the Rebels [p. 60] were collecting in force at Fords Mill. we made a forced march of sixteen Miles, marched all Night in order to surprize them, we took up our Ground at six oClock in the Morning of the 7th at Jemmy's Creek, here we were informed the Rebels had moved seven Miles to Philip Fords.

Monday Augt. 7th 1780[.] Built Bowers & slept all Day, moved at seven in the Evening & made another forc'd March for them; forded Jemmy's Creek, the South, & North Branches of Tiger River[.] got to the Ground the Rebels had been encamped on about four oClock in the Morning of the 8th. They got intelligence of our move, & were likewise alarmed by the firing of a Gun in our Ranks they sneaked from their Ground about half an Hour before we got to it.

Tuesday 8th [August]. Intelligence came in that the Rebels Waggon's were only three Miles in our Front at Cedar Springs[.] Capt. Dunlop, with fourteen Mounted Amn. Vols. and a hundred & thirty Militia were dispatched to take the Waggons, he met three Rebels coming [p. 61] to reconnoitre our Camp, he gave chase, took two of them, the other got to the Rebels and gave the Alarm, in pursuing this Man Dunlop and his party rush'd into the Centre of the Rebels where they lay in Ambush, before he knew where they lay, a Skirmish ensued in which Dunlop got slightly wounded, between twenty & thirty killed, & Wounded (including Rebels), Ensign McFarlin & one Private taken Prisoners, Major Smith & Capt. Potts of the Rebels are among the killd[.] as soon as the Firing began the remainder of the Amn. Vols. & Militia marched in pursuit of them, we follow'd them five Miles to the Iron Works, but were not able to come up with them they being Mounted[.] we then countermarched to Cedar Springs, and halted to refresh, we remain'd here during the heat of the Day, at six in the Evening Marchd and took aheighth near the Ground the Rebels left.

Wednesday 9th [August.] Lay on the heighth[.] nothing extraordinary.

Thursday 10th [August]. Sent the Wounded [p. 62] to Musgroves Mill Ennoree River to be attended by Doctr. Ross, we Marched seven Miles to Culversons Plantation Fair Forrest. in the Evening express arrived from Coll. Turnbull Rocky Mount, with Orders for us to join him without loss of time, by the express we were informed that Genl. Sumpter had attacked our Troops at hanging Rock, the 6th Inst. The North Carolinians were first attacked and gave way[.] Browns Corps came up but were obliged to fall back, the Legion Cavalry came in the Rear of the Rebels, & soon gain'd the Day, with the assistance of Browns Corps which suffered much three Officers killed & three wounded, and one hundred made Prisoners.

Friday 11th Augt. 1780[.] Moved at six oClock in the Morning, & March'd ten Miles to Major Gibbs Plantation, & halted[.]

Saturday 12th [August.] Moved at seven in the Morning[.] Marched seven Miles to a Rebel Capt. Stripplings Plantation, he has taken protection, Major Rutherford came in with a Flagg, in consequence [p. 63] of his coming in our rear without giving signal by Drum or Trumpet, was detained all night.

Sunday 13th Augt. 1780[.] Got in Motion at five oClock in the Morning & Marched Nine Miles to Tinker Creek, halted during the heat of the Day, at six in the Evening Marched five Miles to Smiths Mills, on Swift Creek, and halted all Night.

Monday 14th [August]. Moved at four in the Morning. Marched Nine Miles to Quaker ford Tiger River, forded the River continued our March four Miles to Coll. James Lisles. Plantation, Lisle is in the Rebel Service, his family were home.

Tuesday 15th [August]. Moved at Seven in the Morning. Marched two Miles to Lisles ford, forded Broad River, proceed on seven Miles to Mr Colemans, Morberley Settlement[.] halted during the heat of the Day, moved at seven in the Evening, Marched two Miles to the Camp of the Y. Vols. where we got intelligence that, Genl. Gates lay within three Miles of Camden [p. 64] with seven thousand Men, Coll. Turnbull rec'd Orders the 12th to retreat from Rocky Mount and act as he saw proper, to get to Camden if possible. G. Sumpter appeared with Canon at Rocky Mount about twelve Hours after Coll. Turnbull left it, in order to make a second trial for the post, he found not so harsh a reception as his first Visit.

Wednesday Augt. 16th 1780. Moved at seven in the Morning. Marched two Miles for convenience of Ground, halted at Morberley Meeting House.

Thursday 17th [August.] got in Motion at Nine oClock in the Morning & Marched six Miles to Coll. Winn's Plantation, Winn is Prisoner at Chs. Town.

Friday 18th [August.] Lay at Winns waiting News from Camden having Spyes out upon every Quarter.

Saturday 19th [August.] Still at Winns[.] an Express arrived from Camden with the agreable News, of Lord Cornwalls attacking and totally defeating Gl. Gates on the Morning of the 16th. Twelve hundred were killd & wounded [p. 65] Wounded left in the Field, one Thousand taken Prisoners, Eight brass Field pieces being all they had in the Field were taken several stand of Colours, all their Ammunition Waggons, a hundred & fifty Waggons of Baggage, Provisions, & stores of different kinds. Genl. DeKalb is among the killd, among the Wounded & Prisoners are Genls. Rutherford and Gregory, all this with the Trifling loss on our side of not more than ten Officers killed and wounded, and not more than two hundred and fifty Non commissd. Officers & Privates. after this we rec'd Orders to pursue Genl. Sumpter he being the only remains of what the Rebels can call a Corps in these parts at present. at six in the Evening we Ordered our Waggons forward, that we might pursue Sumpter with Vigour, at seven we got in motion, that very moment Express arrived from Coll. Innes (who was on his way to join us from Ninety Six) informing us that [p. 66] he had been attacked that Morning by a Body of Rebels at Musgroves Mill, Ennoree River, that himself and Major Fraser of his Corps were wounded, likewise Capt. Peter Campbel Lieut. Chew & Camp of Coll. Allens; he must immediately have assistance as many of the Militia had left him; this to our great Mortification altered the course of our March, and at Eleven at Night we got in motion march'd all Night forded Broad River at Sunrising on the Morning of the 20th continued our March four Miles farther to Peters Creek, took up our Ground and lay Sunday all Day at Peters Creek very much fatigued with our Nights March, being eighteen Miles. A Mr Smith was executed (at Winn's, Saturday the 19th Inst.) for joining the Rebels after he had taken protection & embodied himself with our Militia.

Monday 21st Augt. 1780[.] Moved at one oClock in the Morning, & Marched six Miles to a Rebel Capt. Liphams, (Paget Creek) took up our ground at five [p. 67] oClock in the Morning, it was so cold we were all glad to hover round a large fire as soon as we halted. About one oClock a Mr Duncan came to our Camp, with the agreable News that Coll. Tarleton with the Legion Cavalry, and 3 Compys of Light Infty fell in with Genl. Sumpter about twelve oClock on Saturday the 19th. They were all asleep after the fatigue of two Nights rapid retreat, their Horses were all at pasture, their first alarm was the light Infty. firing on them. Coll. Tarleton with his usual success, compleatly defeated Genl. Sumpter, took two brass field pieces Six hundred Horses, thirty Waggons, made two hundred Prisoners, relieved a hundred of Browns Men that were taken at hanging Rock[.] Capt. Duncan was Prisoner to the Rebels, & made his escape during the action. We got in Motion at Eleven oClock at Night & Marched ten Miles to Tiger River, forded it at Break of Day[.]

Tuesday Morng. the 22d [August.] continued our March four Miles to Harrison's Plantation Fair Forrest where we halted. __O__ [*sic*] [p. 68]

Wednesday Augt. 23d 1780[.] Moved at six oClock in the Morning & Marched six Miles to John Blasingham's Plantation, Sugar Creek, where we took up our Ground. Coll. Ferguson set out for Camden at seven this Evening. I rode in Company with him Eleven Miles to see Capt. Gists Wife. Capt. DePeyster took command in the absence of Col. Ferguson.

Thursday 24th [August.] Lay at Blasingham's.

Friday 25th [August.] Still at Blasinghams Plantation[.]

Saturday 26th [August.] Movd at five in the Morning, Marchd six Miles to John Waffords Plantation, Cluers Creek[.] in the Evening I rode six Miles to see a Militiaman that got wounded through the Body at Cedar Springs.

Sunday 27th [August.] Rode back & joind the Detachmt. at Cluers Creek.

Monday 28th [August.] Moved at five oClock in the Morning & marched six Miles to Culversons Plantation Fair Forrest River Orders came for the York. Vols. to March for Camden. Capt. DePeyster expecting hourly to recieve News from Coll. Ferguson, who had promised to do his best to get us all relieved from the disagreable service in the back Woods [p. 69] detained the Y. Vols. till the 29th in hopes to recieve Orders to March with them to Camden—

Tuesday Augt. 29th 1780[.] Orders came to Capt. DePeyster to send the Y. Vs. & Light Compy of Browns Corps to Camden, this of course greatly mortified us, for now we began to see our destiny was fixd to do duty in the back Woods seperate from the Main Army, with the Militia. The Y. Vs. & Lt. Compy of Browns left us at six oClock in the Evening.

Wednesday 30th. Thursday 31st [August]. Lay still at Culversons[.]

Friday Septemr. 1 1780[.] Coll. Ferguson return'd from Camden & joind us at Culversons, with the certain tho disagreable News that we were to be seperated from the Army, & act on the Frontiers with the Militia.

Saturday 2d [September]. got in motion at Eleven oClock in the Morning, & marched ten Miles to the Iron Works. Lossings Fork. Pacolet River[.] I went to see a Militiaman that was in the Skirmish at Cedar Springs the 8th of Augt. he got wounded in the Arm[.] it was taken off by one Frost a Black Smith, with a Shoemakers knife & Carpenters Saw, he stopd the Blood with Fungus of W[?] Oak without taking up a blood vessel[?][.] [p. 70]

Sunday Septemr. 3d 1780[.] Bathed in the River at the Iron Works in Company with my friend Allaire[.]

Monday 4th [September.] Moved at six oClock in the Morning and Marched ten Miles to Cases Creek. I was very unwell took a Vomit which throw'd me into convulsions and almost killd me in the operation.

Tuesday 5th [September.] Moved at five in the Evening, & Marchd. a mile & half to Pacolet River, the fresh so high that we could not ford it. I took quarters at Mr Colemans a quarter of a Mile from Camp. Mrs Coleman is a very warm Tory, she has two Sons in Coll. Inness's Corps[.] She has a family of small Children & has been Mother of five in two Years, they have been greatly distressd by the Rebels for their Loyalty, the House strip'd of all the Beds & other furniture, & the Children of all their Cloaths.

Wednesday 6th [September.] Got in Motion at eight oClock in the Morning, forded Pacolet River, marchd six Miles to Buck Creek, I took Quarters at one Neilsons[.] here was a remarkable hearty old Man, named Willm. Case, he is a hundred & Nine Years old, is a Native of New England, of which he gives some faint description [p. 71] his Memory began to fail at a hundred Years old and his Eye Sight left him eighteen Months ago, he is otherwise remarkably hail, talks very strong & walks amazingly Spry, & to shew his activity danced a jigg for us.

Thursday 7th Septr. 1780[.] Moved at seven in the Morning crossd Buck Creek & the division line between South & North Carolina, marched six

Miles & halted. Col Ferguson with fifty Amn. Vs. & three hundred Militia marched at six oClock in the Evening for Gilbert Town, to surprize a Rebel party that we heard lay there. Capt. DePeyster, Lt. Allaire & I remaind on the Ground we took in the Morning[.]

Friday 8th [September.] We got in motion at eight in the morning & marched six Miles to Broad River took a heighth & waited for Orders from Coll. Ferguson.

Saturday 9th [September.] Recievd intelligence from Coll. Ferguson to keep our post he was returning, to keep a good look out as the Georgians [*new page—not numbered*] were come towards us.

Sunday Sept 10th 1780[.] Coll. Ferguson joined us at Eleven oClock at Night[.]

Monday 11th [September]. Moved at four oClock in the afternoon, forded Broad River, continued our March ten Miles to James Adaires Plantation.

Tuesday 12th [September.] Coll. Ferguson with forty Amn. Vols. & a hundred Militia Marchd. at two oClock in the Morning, they marched fourteen Miles thro the Mountains to the Head of Cane Creek to surprize a Party of Rebels. Capt Ryerse Mr Flecher and I remained at Adaires till Sunrise, we then Marched four Miles to Coll. Walkers, where I took Quarters not able to March any farther, the Rebels that Coll. Ferguson was in pursuit of got intelligence of his coming, in consequence of which, they thought proper to withdraw; however he was lucky enough to take a different route from what they expected, & met them on their way to Burk Court House, the Rebels drew up on an eminence seemingly with a desire to have a Battle[.] upon the approach of our Men they fired & gave way [*new page—not numbered*] they were totally routed, one Private killed & a Capt. White wounded, seventeen of them were taken, twelve Horses, & all their Ammunition which was only twenty weight of Powder; our loss was one killed & two wounded.——

Wednesday Sept. 13th 1780[.] Capt. Dunlop who was one of the Wounded in the Skirmish Yesterday was brought to Coll. Walkers. I dressed his Wounds, one ball went through the left Ilium the other through the right Thigh both, flesh Wounds.

Thursday 14th [September.] Coll. Ferguson with thirty Amn. Vs. & three hundred Militia, Marched at six oClock in the Evening to the Head of Cane Creek[.] the deluded People came in very fast, they say they never heared of any Terms being offered but have always been kept in ignorance, & told of the Cruelty of the English, one Poor Woman expressed great surprize at seeing our Men so mild, she asked if there was not Heathens in our Army that eat Children, she had been told there was, they have never seen a Proclamation. [p. 72]

Friday Sept. 15th 1780[.] Capt. DePeyster with the remainder of the Amn. Vs. & Militia Marchd after Coll. Ferguson; Capt. Chitwood & twenty Militia were left as a Guard for Capt. Dunlop & I, at Coll. Walkers House, they put Abbitees, & built a Worm Fence around the House & put in proper order to fight out off in case of an attack upon us.

Saturday 16th. Sunday 17th. Monday 18th. Tuesday 19th. Wednesday 20th. Thursday 21st [September.] I Lay at Walkers very Sick.

Friday 22d [September]. Coll. Ferguson & the Detachment came to us at Walkers in the Evening[.] he Marched four Miles to Capt. Turners Plantation for forage, Coll. Ferguson gave Dunlop & I orders to get ready to move.

Saturday 23d [September.] Lay at Walkers.

Sunday 24th [September.] Waggons were sent to move Dunlop & I to Gilbert Town, Dunlop was carri'd on a Litter, & I in a covered Waggon fixed on a Bed, we took quarters at Gilberts House, here we found Coll. Ferguson & the Detachment.

Monday 25th [September.] Express from Ninety Six informed that a Body of Rebels under Coll. Clerk had attacked Coll. Brown at Augusta, they had taken the Town & many Indian Stores, & drove Coll Brown [p. 73] into the Fort. This so enraged the Indians that a Body of five hundred of them came down to Coll Browns assistance, upon which Brown sallied out, & drove them from the Town, took some Prisoners, drove two hundred into Savannah River, they swam across & took to a Fort calld fort Independence, here Coll. Cruger came upon them & routed them, retook some of the Cannon & Stores they had got from Augusta, took fifty odd Prisoners with protections in their Pockets[.] twenty seven of them were hanged at Augusta, & twenty seven brought to Ninety Six to share the same fate. Coll. Brown & his Men were three Days in the Fort without, Bread or Water, he got wounded himself through both Thighs, & lost eighty Men during the Siege.

Tuesday 26th [September.] Lay at Gilbert Town, Lt. Stevenson joind us With two hundred Militia;

Wednesday 27th [September.] Coll. Ferguson with the Detachment moved at four in the afternoon to Capt. Turners for convenience of Forage, he left Dunlop & I at Gilbert Town, with Orders [p. 74] A description of Hillsborough to be read after Page Ninety Six . . . [*The description is written on pages 74 and 75 in the original journal, but the editors have placed it on pages 36–38 of this transcription in accordance with Johnson's intention.*] [p. 76] to proceed to Adaires in the Morning.

Thursday 28th Sept. 1780[.] This Morning almost White frost on the Ground, the first this fall. at ten oClock Dunlop & I got fixed in our Carriages & proceeded to Adairs where we met Coll. Ferguson Lt. Tayler &

Fletcher with some Mounted Men. Capt. DePeyster with the Amn. Vs. & Militia had gone forward towards White Oak, Coll. Ferguson and the other Gentlemen followed at three in the afternoon, having intelligence that Coll. Clerk was coming this Way from Georgia. A Guard with the Baggage, Prisoners &c. were left with Dunlop & I at Adairs, in the Evening Express from Coll. Ferguson to keep a good look out, that Mr Allaire's Servt. had been taken prisoner by remaining a little behind the detachment to cook Dinner. Coll. Husband with a hundred & fifty Men joined us about ten oclock at Night, about Eleven our Pickets were fired on by some Skulking Rascals, that were creeping about endeavouring to Steal Horses. [p. 77]

Friday Sept 29th 1780. Constant information that the Rebels were collecting in force at Burk Court House, under Colls Shelby, McDoul, & Cleveland[.]

Saturday 30th [September]. Mr. Boyle came to us from Coll. Ferguson to take command of the Baggage Guard with Orders for us to move to Broad River, we got in motion at eight oClock in the Morning, & Marchd to Denards ford, forded the River, took a heighth & halted, I took quarters at Mr Powers's House.

Sunday Octr. 1st. Coll. Ferguson joind us from White Oak, no certain Intelligence of Clerk.

Monday 2d [October]. Coll. Ferguson with the American Vols. & Militia Marched at five in the Evening in pursuit of Col. Greyms & a Party. Mr. Boyle commanded the Baggage Guard, & Prisoners, consisting of a hundred Militiamen, his Orders were to march for Thickety. Capt. Dunlop & I remained all Night at Mr Powers's Broad River.

Tuesday 3d [October.] We left our Quarters at five in the Morning, proceeded ten Miles to Buck Creek, where we overtook the Baggage [p. 78] Dunlop & I went on two Miles to Cases Creek and halted to refresh ourselves, the Baggage was sent over Pacolet River, at five oClock in the Evening Mr Boyle & I left Dunlop at Cases House, we forded Pacolet River, we followed the Baggage ten Miles overtook it at Willm. Abbots Plantation[.] here we halted all Night.

Wednesday Octr. 4th 1780[.] We moved at six oClock in the Morning, & Marched twelve Miles to Sharps, stopped to Dine then went on three Miles to Tates Plantation[.] Tate was out with the Rebels his family Home. he has a very pretty plantation, pleasantly situated on Broad River, we rec'd Orders from Coll Ferguson to proceed to Kemps over Broad River, our Waggon Horses being tired down we were obliged to remain all Night at Tates.

Thursday 5th [October.] Express from Coll. Ferguson at four in the Afternoon, informd us there was a strong Party near the fording Place watching for us, Orders by the same Express to be as expeditious as possible in getting the Baggage [p. 79] over (at the Ferry & not venture down to the ford) which we affected about ten oClock in the Evening[.] then we proceeded a Mile & half to Buffalow Creek where we joind Coll. Ferguson & the Detachment.

Friday 6th Octr. 1780[.] Moved at six oClock in the morning & marched sixteen Miles to Kings Hill and took up our Ground.

Saturday 7th [October]. Lay on Kings Hill; about three oClock in the Afternoon we were alarmed, & got under Arms ready for action, the Enemy were directly upon us & made the attack, they were commanded by Genl. Williams who got killed in the action. Coll. Campble then took command, under him were Colls. Shelby, Lacy, Brannon, Hampton, Greyms, Severe, Cleveland, Thomas, Robinson, & Chandler, ————————— There Number was about two thousand five hundred, they advanced up the Hill pretty rapidly, as soon as they got to the Brow of the Hill the Amn. Vols. charged them with success [p. 80] and drove them down the Hill, but were not able to pursue, our Number being so small, we then retreated in order to gain the heighth & prevent their[?] getting possession of it; The North Carolina Militia had twice repulsed a Body that attacked their Line, unfortunately their Ammunition being now exhausted they were obliged to give way. Capt. DePeyster with the first Division of Amn. Vols. charged the Enemy again at the Point of the Hill and drove them a second time; the North Carolinians having quit their line it hove the others into confusion, and the Enemy (whos Numbers enabled them to compleatly surround us,) encouraged by the confusion of our Militia rushed on; Coll. Ferguson gave the Word to charge again, he then rushd in amongst the Rebels with about half a Dozen Men, he was soon shot from his Horse; Capt. DePeyster then gave the Word to form & charge, the cry throughout the Militia line was, we are out of [p. 81] Ammunition, this being our unhappy condition, and the Militia (tho they stood & fought bravely while their Ammunition lasted) were now getting into the utmost disorder, it was thought most expedient to send out a Flagg to save a few brave Men that had survived the heat of action. The engagement lasted an Hour and five Minutes, we were then reduced to the Necessity of Yielding to far Superior Numbers, we had only Seventy Amn. Vols. (fifty of whom got killed & wounded, among the killd was Coll. Ferguson, and Ensign Mc.Ginnis of Coll. Allen's Corps, among the wounded was Capt. Ryerse) and eight hundred Militiamen engaged, two hundred & twenty five Militiamen were killed, & seventy two Wounded. How many of the Enemy got kill'd is uncertain, not far inferior to ours if [p. 82] we judge from the Number of their wounded which was equal to ours, I being employed to dress them in preference to their own Surgeon enabled me to get the Number.

Sunday Octr. 8th 1780[.] Eleven oClock in the Morning, our Men were Marched from this Ground. I remained till Evening dressing the Wounded; Coll. Lacy with about two hundred Men remained behind, he gave Paroles to the Wounded Militiamen that were not able to March, at eight oClock in the Evening we left Kings Hill & Marched about eight Miles, overtook the Waggons & halted all Night.

Monday 9th [October.] Moved at Daylight[.] marched about four Miles, to a Tory's Plantation, here I found our Men & Coll. Campbel with his Men &c. After I dressed their Wounded here, they Moved at two oClock in the Afternoon, we went about two Miles, forded Broad River & halted at a Torys Plantation.

Tuesday 10th [October]. Moved at six in the Morning marchd twenty Miles & halted in the Woods, where we lay contented with our lot on [p. 83] the cold Ground.

Wednesday 11th Octr. 1780[.] Moved at eight oClock in the Morning and marched twelve Miles to Coll Walkers, Tryon County[.]

Thursday 12th [October.] Lay at Walkers Plantation, had the Mortification to see our Baggage, divided to the difft. Corps.

Friday 13th [October.] Moved at ten oClock in the Morning, Marched six Miles to Bickerstaff Settlement, a Flagg came to us this Day from Ninety Six, the Gentlemen of the Flagg were detained, *pro certis Causis bene Nemine Notis.* left Capt Ryerse, at Walkers, he obtaind a Parole. in the Evening their liberality extended so far as to send five Shirts to Nine of us as a Change of Linnen, other cloathing in like proportion, one old Shirt was sent me all torn to pieces, by way of fulfilling their promise, as every Field Officer had given his Honour I should have all my Baggage for attendg their Wounded. Where honour binds I find Promise can be broke. query? would not hemp do the business better[?]? [p. 84]

Saturday October 14th 1780[.] Ten oClock in the Morning their Guard Paraded & formed a circle, Capt. DePeyster & the rest of us Officers were ordered within the ring, they then proceeded to trying the Militiamen for treason, thirty of them were condemned and bound under the Gallows, we were kept throughout the Day in the Rain Spectators of this disagreable Days Work, at seven oClock in the Evening they began to execute them. Coll. Mills, Capt. Wilson, Capt. Chitwood, and six others were hanged for their Loyalty to their Sovereign[.] they died like Romans saying they died for their King & his Laws. What increased this Melancholy scene, was the seeing Mrs. Mills take leave of her Husband, & two of Capt. Chitwoods Daughters take leave of their Father, the latter were comforted with being told their Father was pardoned, they then went to our Fire where we had made a Shed to keep out the Rain, they had scarce sat down when News was brought that their Father was dead [p. 85] here words can scarce describe the Melancholy Scene, the two Young Ladies swoon'd away, and continued in fits all Night.—Mrs. Mills with a Young Child in her Arms set out all Night in the Rain with her Husbands Corps, & not even a Blanket to cover her from the inclemency of the Weather, one of the condemned named Baldwin at the foot of the Gallows, broke through their Guards & made his escape; The crime of one Walter Gilky that was executed, was his wounding the lad that was brought in to us at Whites the 17th of July. the Boy appeared to evidence against Gilky; a poor retaliation for the Lenity shewn him in our Camp, & his being set at liberty upon promising to go home to his Parents.

Sunday 15th [October.] Moved at five oClock in the Morning, & Marched thirty two Miles, a very disagreable wet Day, very bad Road, we cross'd Cane Creek Nineteen times in going three Miles, forded [p. 86] Catawba River at Island ford, Burk County ten oClock at Night, thirty odd of the Prisoners made their escape on the March, tho very much fatigued & allmost famished with hunger, having no Meat for three Days; Capt. DePeyster obtained permission for himself & Officers to go to Coll. Mc.Douls House to dry ourselves & lodge, we were well entertained & got a good Supper which we stood in great need of having eat nothing all Day but a Raw Turnip which I beg'd from the Guard.

Monday 16th [October.] Moved at two in the afternoon[.] forded the North Branch of Catawba and Johns River, marched five Miles & halted at a Tory Plantation.

Tuesday 17th [October.] Movd at eight in the Morning[.] Marched fifteen Miles to Capt Holts Plantation[.] three Prisoners endeavouring to make their escape, one got shot through the Body, the other two got off.

Wednesday 18th [October.] The Poor Man hanged that got wounded last Night attempting to get off, we moved at [p. 87] eight oClock in the Morning, & Marched eighteen Miles to Moravian Creek in Wilkes County & halted.

Thursday Octr. 19th 1780[.] Moved at eight in the Morning forded Moravian Creek, passed Wilkes Court House, marched Sixteen Miles to Hogwoods Plantation & halted.

~~Saturday~~ Friday 20th [October.] At Eleven oClock in the Morning Marchd. six Miles to Sales Plantation[.]

Saturday 21st [October.] Some Tory Women brought us in Milk, Butter, Honey & other comforts[.] we Marchd at ten oClock in the Morning, fourteen Miles to HeadPiths Plantation, he is with Lord Cornwallis, we lodged at Edwd. Clantons[.] he is likewise with our Army.

Sunday 22d [October.] Moved at ten in the Morning, we got permission to go forward with Coll. Shelby to Salem[.] we Marched ten Miles, forded Yadkin River at Shallow ford, continued on eighteen Miles farther to Salem [p. 88] in the Evening we went to the Moravian Meeting were highly entertained with their Musick & the civility of the People, the most of them are Friends to Gt. or hard Money. Salem contains about twenty Houses & a Church, they are all Mechanicks that live in this Town, there are two Moravian Towns above this where the Farmers dwell.

Monday Octr. 23d 1780[.] Lay at Salem, in the Evening two Continental Officers called at our Quarters on their way to join the Army.

Tuesday 24th [October.] Marched at ten in the Morning & joind the Camp at the old Moravian Town called Bethabara, this Town is about as large as Salem tho not so regularly laid out; soon after Mr Allaire & I got to bed were disturbed by a Capt. Campbel who came into our Room and demanded our Bed, Mr Allaire was obliged to go to Coll. Campbel, before we could get the Ruffian turned out of the Room, he strutted about in a truly [p. 89] coward like manner with his Sword drawn and threatening to Murder us, he is an exact Picture & has all the actions of Jos. Ridgeway[.]

Wednesday 25th Octr. 1780[.] Kept my Bed all Day being very unwell.

Thursday 26th[.] Friday 27th[.] Saturday 28th. Sunday 29th [October.] Still unwell & kept my Room.

Monday 30th [October]. Walked out.

Tuesday 31st [October.] Rode to Salem in Compy. with Capt. DePeyster Mr Allaire & Supple. this Night was very cold, froze Ice half an Inch thick, the first Ice this fall.

Wednesday Novemr. 1st[.] Cold blustering Day, I went to see the Prisoners, got permission from Coll. Cleveland to go within the Ring & dress the wounded Prisoners, when dressing one McCatchum Coll. Cleveland came to me and said he was a Damnd Villain & deserved the Gallows[.] I asked him what he was guilty of, he repeated that he was as Damnd Villain as I was and deserved [p. 90] hanging, he then very passionately said he had found out my Villainies, & had a great mind to cut me up, no sooner said than done, he struck me over the Head with his Sword, and levil'd me, he repeated his stroke & cut my Hand[.] I then desired to know my Crime, he said I was a Damn'd Traitor to my Country, & that he would confine me in the Guard with the other Villains[.] Coll. Armstrong took command in the Evening & relieved Cleveland a happy exchange to the Prisoners[.]

Thursday Novemr. 2d 1780[.] Walked three Miles to Bethania in Compy. with Capt. DePeyster Mr Allaire & Tayler, this Town contains about thirty

Houses & a Place of Worship is very regularly laid out, the Inhabitants are Farmers.

Saturday [*sic*] Friday 3d [November.] Nothing extraordinary.

Saturday 4th [November.] Major Reed returnd from Genl. Gates with a Letter directed to C. Cleveland. C. Armstrong proceeded to meet Cleveland to know what were the Orders respecting us, we could not learn our Destiny. [p. 91]

Sunday Novr. 5th 1780[.] Rode to Salem[.] Coll. Armstrong returned, without seeing Cleveland, he opened the Letter; we could not yet learn our fate, in the Evening Lieut. Taylor, Stevenson & Allaire, went off, their departure was discovered about Eleven oClock.

Monday 6th [November.] Rode to Salem met a Man from Virginia who gave certain account that ~~Sir H. Clinton~~ the English had landed at Plymouth in Virginia.

Tuesday 7th [November.] No News.

Wednesday 8th [November.] Rode to Salem in Compy. with Capt. DePeyster, when we returnd, recieved orders to be ready to March the Militia, had most of them enlisted in the Continental Service rather than suffer Death by inches Starving with cold & hunger.

Thursday 9th [November.] Capt. DePeyster had Orders to Parade the Officers & Men, at one oClock afternoon[.] this Morning near twenty of the Soldiers made [p. 92] their escape, being apprehensive of a disagreable March over the Mountains, the remainder of our Men with the Militia that had not yet enlisted were Marched at four in the afternoon about one Mile up the Mountain Road to a Plantation called the Branch. Coll. Armstrong gave permission for the Officers to stay all Night at their old Quarters.

Friday Novr. 10th 1780[.] Coll. Armstrong ordered us to March for Salem at four in the Afternoon, we arrived there in the Evening where we are to take Quarters till Genl. Gates gives Orders where we are to be stationed.

Saturday 11th [November.] Coll. Armstrong sent Express to Genl. Gates with our Letters, he & the other Continental Officers then left us at Salem.

Sunday 12th [November.] Major Winston sent aHorse to Capt. DePeyster.

Monday 13th[.] Tuesday 14th[.] Wednesday 15th [November.] Lay in Quarters[.] nothing extraordinary.

Thursday 16th [November.] Rode to Bethabara & took Dinner in Compy. [p. 93] with Capt. DePeyster & Mr Supple, when we returned to our Quarters found one Smith, an Irishman[.] he gave avery good description of our Works at Camden, Ninety Six, Augusta & even Chs. Town, he said that he had been at each place as aSpy, he was taken up at Ninety Six and confined in Irons, & was releasd by Coll. Kirkland while Coll. Cruger was gone to Augusta.

Friday 17th Novr. 1780[.] No News, still at Salem[.]

Saturday 18th [November.] Express arrived from Genl. Gates with a Letter for Capt DePeyster Ordering us to March with Capt. Wood to Hillsborough.

Sunday 19th [November.] Prepared for our Move.

Monday 20th [November.] Left Salem at Nine oClock in the Morning, Capt DePeyster Mr Supple & I Rode forward with Mr Ashbourne a Lieut. of Militia, we rode fifteen [p. 94] Miles & stopped at Mr Bullocks and fed our Horses, could get nothing for ourselves, notwithstanding there was plenty of Beef in the House; we proceeded eight Miles to Friend Anthanks a Quakers where we got some cold meat, after eating mounted and rode on Seven Miles to Guilford Court House[.] passed a House where the Cherry trees were in Blossom; we stopped at Guilford Ct. House expecting to put up for the Night, on finding the Landlord like most of his Neighbours, perfectly disposed to disoblige as much as he could we again Ordered our Horses Saddled & rode one Mile to another Tavern, where we met much the same treatment, we rode on two Miles farther to a Mr Logan's, his Doors were fast & he, nonse ipse, swore vengeance to any that attempted to enter, after a long [p. 95] altercation between Mr Logan & Ashbourn our conductor, we got admittance, had our Horses put out & we, laid ourselves on a Bed upon the Floor, Mr Logan kept most of the Night, marching about the Floor & examining his Muskets pretending, fear of the Tories. we were not without our apprehensions he had some design upon us, & were accordingly on our Guard.

Tuesday 21 Novr. 1780[.] Mounted our Horses at seven in the Morning and Rode eight Miles to Coll. Pacely's, fed our Horses with Public Forage, here again the People refused to get us any thing to eat, they all seemed determined to make us fast for the good of our Souls. We mounted our Horses again at twelve oClock & rode twelve Miles through [p. 96] the Rain to Major ONiels, here we put up for the Night, found Mrs Oniel perfectly disposed to make us comfortable, we got some thing to eat & were for once thank God, very decently entertained.

Wednesday 22d Novr. —80[.] Took Breakfast with Mrs ONiel, left her Home at eight in the Morning Rode four Miles forded Haw River. Rode on eighteen Miles farther, ~~took Quarters in Hillsborough~~ to Hillsborough, we put up & took Dinner at Mr Courtneys. [*A note in the entry for this day refers the reader back to the misplaced description of Hillsborough found on pages 74 and 75 of the original journal. The editors have accordingly inserted the*

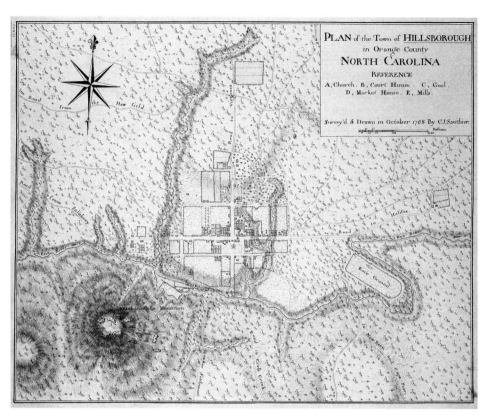

This map of Hillsborough was the first of ten plans depicting the chief towns of North Carolina drawn between 1768 and 1771 by C. J. Sauthier, a skilled French surveyor and draftsman who accompanied Governor William Tryon to North Carolina. © The British Library Board. All Rights Reserved. Maps. K. Top. 122.59

description here.] A description of Hillsborough to be read after Page Ninety Six. It is an inland Town in Orange County North Carolina about a hundred & Seventy Miles distant from Wilmington & nearly the same distance from Newbern; it is laid out in Square lots four acres in alot, these are again divided into building lots, of one Acre each. There is a Ridge of Hills on the Southwest Side, whence it gets its Name, between this & the Town there runs a large stream of Water called Eno River on which Stands aGrist Mill & Saw Mill[.] it contains about thirty dwelling Houses an English Church, a Court House, Jail and Market. A Mr Korben was the first proprietor of the Land, he laid down the [p. 75] Plan of the Town, binding every one that purchased a Lott to build a frame House twenty by sixteen, with floors above & below, having Stone or Brick Chimneys. two years was the time limited to build in[.] the Land was forfeited in case of failure. It has been aflourishing little Town, before this War & will be again, as the Country around it is good Land. Produces Wheat, Indian Corn, Cotton, Tobacco, &c. and the Country People formerly kept large Stocks of Cattle & Hoggs; it is a very good Situation for Mercantile Business, or Mechanicks. Capt. DePeyster waited on Genl. Stevenson for directions, he ordered Coll. Thomas D.Q.G. to provide us with Quarters, he directed us to Mr Leonards Tavern, at Leonards likewise quartered Coll. Thackston a Continental Colonel.

Thursday 23d [November.] The Soldiers arrived, under the Militia Guard [p. 97] The Soldiers were put into Hillsborough jail.

Friday Novemr. 24th —80[.] Genl. Stevenson ordered us to Quarters in the Country & restricted us to two Miles Circumference: we chose rather to be confined to aHouse than to such Narrow limits in a Country where the Houses were two or three Miles distance from each other; Genl. Stevenson left Town[.] Coll. Gunby took Command.

Saturday 25th [November.] I Inoculated Mr Newman's & Mr Chapmans Families for the SmallPox.

Sunday 26th [November]. I remained in Town while Capt. DePeyster rode into the Country with Coll Thomas to look Quarters for us; in the Evening Genl Green arrived at Hillsborough on his way to take the Comd. of the Southern Continental Army. Coll. Morris and Major Burnet, AideCamps to G Green called to see us, by them we heard of our friends to the Northward. [p. 98]

Monday 27th Novemr. 1780[.] Coll. Thomas sent out & procured us Quarters, we sent our Servants to get the Room in Order.

Tuesday 28th [November.] Capt. DePeyster & I rode five Miles into the Country and took Quarters at Saml. Allens House, we signd Parol's of honour to confine ourselves to this House & the Neighbourhood of Hillsborough[.]

Wednesday 29th [November.] I rode to Town on Business.

Thursday 30th [November]. Friday 1st Decemr. Remaind in Quarters nothing extraordinary.

Saturday 2d [December]. I went to Town & Inoculated Mr Sharps Family for the Small Pox.

Sunday 3d [December]. Coll. Gunby sent for me to Town in the Evening, upon my arrival he acquainted me that he had been informed I was Inoculating for the Small Pox without permission; It was hinted to me that this Complaint [p. 99] had been lodged by some Narrow Minded Gentlemen of the Faculty who were jealous that if I was permitted to Inoculate, my Practice would exceed theirs. Coll. Gunby after an extraordinary reprimand, for attempting (as he said) an undertaking so prejudicial in its consequences acquainted me I must keep my Room till further Orders; In justification of my Conduct I acquainted Coll. Gunby that I had consulted and got permission of the Magistrates of the Town in whom I judged the Liberties of the People were vested, & that I likewise thought they had proper Authority to give direction in Matters where the Inhabitants were more concerned, than the Army, that I had not brought the Disorder into [p. 100] the Place it was done by his Surgeon before I attempted any thing of the kind. My not paying due respect to Col. Gunby as Comman Officer and obtaining his permission seemed the occasion of my being restrict within the Narrow Limits of a Room.

Monday 4th Decr. Kept my Room at Mr Leonards agreable to Orders, in the Evening a Letter was handed me from Coll. Gunby with Orders to take my old Quarters, and consider myself confined to Mr Samuel Allens House with an hundred Yards Square, I was not to administer any Medicine to the Inhabitants of the Country, nor exceed my limits on any pretence whatever till further permission, and that I must deliver up all my Medicines to Doctr. Elbert.

Tuesday 5th [December.] Wrote to Coll. Gunby assuring him I had no [p. 101] Ill design in Inoculating those Families, and I made no doubt he was before this convinced I had not. Neither would the Infection Spread farther from those that I had Inoculated, than from those to whom the Surgeons of the Hospital had communicated the Infection. Agreable to his Order I should shortly take myself out of Town. With regard to the Medicine what few Articles I had, I would deliver to Doctr. Elbert whenever he would call for them, or I would send them to any Place in Town that Coll. Gunby would please to direct. I sent to Doctr. Brickell[.] Borrowed his Horse & Rode to my Quarters. Doctr. Brickell called & dined with me.

Wednesday Decr. 6th 1780[.] Coll. Thackston and Mr Johnston called to see us and Dined with us. [p. 102]

Thursday Decemr. 7th 1780[.] I was invited to Dine with Mr Monro, could not do myself that Pleasure on account of my narrow limits. Capt. DePeyster Dined with him, in the Evening Capt. DePeyster & Mr Allen went to hunting Turkeys[.] catched one.

Friday 8th. Saturday 9th [December.] Rainy Weather[.] uncommonly Warm for the Season.

Sunday 10th [December.] Doctr. Brickell called to see us & took Dinner with us.

Monday 11th [December]. Unsettled Weather remarkably Warm, Capt. Brown of the Militia, called to see us, in Company with Mr Turner & Supple.

Tuesday 12th [December.] Nothing Extraordinary.

Wednesday 13th. Thursday 14th[.] Friday 15th[.] Saturday 16th [December.] Kept my Quarters[.] not allowed to go out.

Sunday 17th [December.] Doctr. Brickell called to bid me good by, he left Hillsborough [p. 103] and set out for Halifax to Inoculate the Inhabitants of that Place.

Monday 18th Decemr. 1780, Tuesday 19th[.] Wednesday 20th[.] Thursday 21st[.] No News. Dull Weather, but remarkably Warm.

Friday 22d [December]. Unwell, took Physick.

Saturday 23d [December]. Bled myself.

Sunday 24th [December.] Very pleasant Warm Weather[.]

Monday Decemr. 25th[.] High Winds & Cool[.] Wrote a Letter to Coll. Thackston, desiring him to intercede with Coll. Gunby, & get me the Privilidges limited in my Parol of Honour[.] aCold Night Very high Winds.

Tuesday 26th [December.] Cold Day & high Wind.

Wednesday 27th [December.] Still Cold & Dry.

Thursday 28th[.] Friday 29th [December.] Cool & pleasant. Coll. Gunby wrote me a note informing me I was released from confinement [p. 104] in consequence of a Letter that I had wrote Coll. Thackston. Recieved an Invitation to Dine with Mr Monro on Sunday.

Saturday 30th. 1780 [December.] Sent for by Mr Monro to see a little Boy that lay Ill at his House[.]

Sunday 31st [December]. Dined at Mr Monro's[.] return'd to my Quarters in the Evening.

Monday January 1st 1781[.] Pleasant Weather. Sent Letter to Major Burnet, (Genl. Green's Aid-de Camp) asking Parol to go within our lines in case the Exchange did not take place.

Tuesday 2d [January.] Went to see Mr Frazer's Child, and Mr Monro's little Boy, lodged at Monroe's.

Wednesday 3d [January.] Returned to my Quarters, very Warm Weather for the Season.

Thursday 4th [January]. Warm Rainy Day.

Friday 5th [January.] Rode to Mr Supples Quarters [p. 105] and Dined; returned to my Quarters in the Evening. Pleasant Weather.

Saturday 6th January 1781[.] Some Thunder in the Morning[.] Warm & Showery through the Day. Took a Ride for Exercise.

Sunday 7th [January.] Rainy and Warm with Southerly Winds.

Monday 8th [January.] Took a Ride & Dined with Mr Monro. Pleasant Weather. Express went through Hillsborough from Virginia, to Genl. Green informing that the British Troops had landed at Sandy Point in Virginia.

Tuesday 9th [January]. Rode to my Quarters. Rainy Evening.

Wednesday 10th [January]. Dull Weather. Warm Southerly Winds. In the Evening Mr Allen return'd from Genl Greene's Camp with Answers to our Letters. Major Burnet sent Forty Continental Bills of Sixty Dollars each, Capt. DePeyster & I divided [p. 106] them between us. Heavy Squall this Eveng attended with Thunder and Lightening.

Thursday Jany. 11th 1781[.] Capt. DePeyster and I Dined at Mr Supples, went home with Mr Monro and lodged at his House. Pleasant Weather.

Friday 12th [January.] Mr Monro rode to Mr Whitted's to procure us quarters with him[.] we dined with Mr Monro, after Dinner rode to our old Quarters.

Saturday 13th [January.] Cap. DePeyster & I rode to Hillsborough where we met Mr Monro & rode out with him to Mr Whitteds to see his Room, left aServant to keep possession[.] we rode back to our old Quarters again.

Sunday 14th [January]. Capt. DePeyster & I rode five Miles up the Country to see a Mr Lynch a good friend. Cold Evening.

Monday 15th [January.] Remaind at Mr Allen's. ACold Day.

Tuesday 16th [January]. Dry and Cold. Capt. DePeyster & I left [p. 107] Mr Samuel Allens and took Quarters at Mr William Whitteds.

Wednesday 17th Jany 1781[.] Remaind in Quarters[.] Pleasant Weather.

Thursday 18th [January]. Rainy but not Cold.

Friday 19th [January.] Dull Weather, warm for the Season[.]

Saturday 20th [January]. Mr Burd called on me to Inoculate his Family for the Small Pox. I sent him to Coll. Gunby to obtain his permission, as I had given my Word, that I would not Inoculate without the approbation of the Commanding Officer of Hillsborough. In the Evening I was sent for to Town by Coll. Gunby. I chearfully gave my attendance not the least doubting that Coll. Gunby was going to extend his generosity so far as to permit me to Inoculate afew Families at aDistance [p. 108] from the Town, here I was greatly disappointed, upon meeting Coll. Gunby he began to interrogate me in avery serious Manner whether I had Inoculated any body since his Orders forbidding it. I Answered by Asking whether I did not give my Word that I would not Inoculate any without the approbation of the Comdg. Officer; he then told me there had been a Woman who said I had Inoculated her Child[.] I desired to see the Woman, she was called for but could not be found. I offered to take Oath that I had not broke my Word, & the Woman must be mistaken or disposed to do Mischief I then Asked if Mr Burd had not spoke to him respecting his Family; Coll. Gunby said [p. 109] he had, but it could not be allowed[.]

Sunday 21st Jany. 1781. Capt. DePeyster & I walked to Town & Dined with Mr Hog we lodged in town at Mr Farmers.

~~Tuesday~~ Monday 22d [January.] Walked out to our Quarters, Rainy afternoon with Thunder & Lightening; Clear and Cold Night Smart Frost.

Tuesday 23d [January.] I Rode out about three Miles to see Mr Kelly a Sharp cold Morning.

Wednesday 24th [January.] I was called out of Bed about three oClock in the Morning to see Mr Brantons Child. Pleasant Weather.

Thursday 25th [January.] Rode to Mr Munroe's[.] returnd and drank Tea at Mr Hogs.

Friday 26th [January.] Dull Rainy Weather.

Saturday 27th [January.] Still rainy[.] No News[.]

Sunday 28th [January.] Very fine Weather.

Monday 29 [January.] Cold & Dry.

Tuesday 30th [January.] Report prevails of [p. 110] a severe action between Genl. Leslie & Genl. Morgan, that Genl. Morgan totaly defeated Genl. Leslie & Made five hundred Prisoners. Coll. Gunby sent a Note to Capt. DePeyster informing him that he had agreable News if he would come to Town.

Wednesday 31st Jany 1781[.] Capt. DePeyster & I rode to Town to see Coll. Gunby, he informed Capt. DePeyster that a Comissary of Prisoners was on his way to Hillsborough & that Capt. DePeyster would be Paroll'd to Charles Town.

Thursday Feby. 1st[.] Dull Weather.

Friday 2d [February]. Pleasant Weather & Warm for the Season. Capt DePeyster & I dined with Coll. Gunby. [p. 111]

Saturday Feby. 3d 1781[.] Capt. DePeyster & I rode out to see our old Landlady Mrs Allen.

Sunday 4th [February.] Showery & high Wind[.] had the Pleasure of two Ladies Company to Dine with us. Mrs Williams & Mrs Lynch.

Monday 5th [February]. Dined with Mr Monro[.] Express arriv'd in Town with News that Ld. Cornwallis was advancing[.]

Tuesday 6th [February.] Coll Gunby sent for Cap. DePeyster & I to come to Town with our Baggage, upon our arrival we were Ordered to get ready to March to Virginia[.] Capt. DePeyster & I Rode out to Mr Monroe's, in the Evening we returnd to our old Quarters again[.]

Wednesday 7th [February.] I signed aParol to Proceed to Virginia by way of Dixs Ferry on Dan River, I left Hillsborough at three oClock in the afternoon & rode five Miles to Mr Rileys where I put up[.]

Thursday 8th [February.] Left Rileys at eight in the Morning & Rode twenty five Miles to [p. 112] Coll. Moores Plantation upon Country line Creek where I put up all Night. This Day I met a Cursed Villain[.] after he found I was unacquainted with the Road, endeavoured to lead me astray. I enquired the Way to Coll. Moores, he told me I was ten Miles too high up the County. I was suspicious he was a Rogue, & did not choose to follow his directions. I kept on my old course about Seven Miles when coming to aCabbin I enquired which way the Road led, the Good Lady of the House told me to Coll. Moores[.] This[?] convinced me that the Scoundrel I met had some Mischief in View.

Friday 9th Feby. 1781[.] At eight in the Morning I mounted my Horse to proceed, Mr Arnold who kept the House where I lodged advised me to go no farther, as the Country was alarmed & there were many would not stick at Murdering me if they found out [p. 113] I belonged to the British, I took his advice and went back to Peter Harts where I lodged all Night, I got Very Wet, it being a Rainy disagreable Day, I was very Sick all Night through fatigue & being Wet.

Saturday 10th Feby. 1781[.] Returnd to Hillsborough expecting to be put under Guard for returning, was agreably disappointed upon Meeting Coll. Gunby with the agreable News that I was Permitted to go to Charls Town.

Sunday 11th [February]. Went to Mr Monro to get a Horse.

Monday 12th [February]. Capt DePeyster & I Dined with Mr. Monroe. He came to Hillsborough to let me see a Horse if it would suit me, I did not like the Price.

Tuesday 13th [February]. I went up to Mr Rileys & bought aHorse.

Wednesday 14th [February.] I Rode to Mr Monros to see Mr Decon[?] & fix the Time for setting out towards Chas. Town. Mr Monro Satisfied Riley for his Horse. [p. 114]

Thursday 15th Feby. 1781[.] Capt. DePeyster & I Set out for Chs. Town[.] we left Mr Whitted at twelve oClock & Rode to Mr Monroe's & Lodged.

Friday 16th [February.] Left Mr Monroe's at Seven oClock in the Morning[.] we Rode twelve Miles to Mr Tenings, & stopp'd to feed our Horses, at twelve oClock we left Tenings, we rode three Miles to Woody's Ferry (Haw River)[.] we crossed the River in aFlatt, & Rode three Miles to William Lindleys, an honest Quaker where we put up.

Saturday 17th [February]. Left Mr Lindleys at Seven in the Morning & Rode twelve Miles to the Widow Mc.Carrols, where we took Breakfast[.] at twelve we left Mrs McCarrols & Rode twenty Miles to Deep River, forded the River at Searcey's Ferry, my Horse fell over a Rock by which I got very wet. we rode two Miles beyond the [p. 115] River to the Dutch Butchers, where we put up, lay before the fire upon some Straw[.] This Day we Started a Drove of Deers not less than a Dozen in Number.

Sunday 18th Feby. 1781[.] Left the Dutch Butchers at Seven in the Morning & Rode twenty Seven Miles to Samuel Parsons & put up.

Monday 19th [February.] Left Parsons at eight in the Morning. Parsons Rode with us ten Miles to Capt. Kimboroughs, where we stopp'd to feed[.] he has suffered much for his Loyalty, we left Kimboroughs at twelve oClock & Rode three Miles to Cornelius Robinson's an honest Countryman[.] he had no Forage, we Rode on Mr Robinson went with us five Miles to his Brother Charles Robinsons where we put up, they have suffer'd for their Loyalty. [p. 116]

Tuesday 20th Feby 1781[.] Left Robinsons at Seven in the Morning & Rode twelve Miles to Mr Bluets & Stoppd to feed, left Bluets at ten & Rode twenty Miles to Mr Pegues a Wealthy Man Plenty of every thing around him & Wishes for Peace.

Wednesday 21st. Thursday 22d [February]. Remained at Mr Pegues[.]

Friday 23d [February]. Left Pegues at Nine in the Morning crossed the Pedee in his Flatt, passed through a Village called Cheraw, passed by Anson Court House at the long Bluff[.] Rode twenty five Miles to Mr Williamsons, where we put up. he and his Family have suffered very much for his Loyalty.

Saturday 24th [February.] left Mr Williamsons at Six in the Morng. [p. 117] after Riding Seven Miles met a Party of Militia commanded by a Major James[.] They had twenty four Prisoners belonging to the Kings Amn. Regt. we Rode on ten Miles farther to Mr Jouets & Stoppd to Breakfast[.] we left Jouets at twelve crossed black Creek in a Flatt[.] Rode twelve Miles to Mr Finkleys at Jeffs'n Creek fed our Horses, we left Finkleys at four in the Evening & Rode ten Miles to Mr Burch's an Italian Gentleman, where here we put up.

Sunday 25th [February]. Left Mr Burches at Six in the Morning & Rode Sixteen Miles to Lynches Creek, crossed the Ferry in a Flatt and Rode three Miles to Mr Joness where we fed our Horses, left Jones's at 12 oClock & Rode twelve [p. 118] Miles to Black Mingo Ferry, here we met about forty of Genl. Marrians Party Mounted on Horses. They examined our Parols & let us pass[.] we crossed the Ferry in a Flatt & Rode two Miles to Capt. Tweeds[.] here we put up all Night[.]

Monday 26th Feby. 1781[.] left Capt Tweeds at eight in the Morning[.] Rode Nine Miles to Potatoe Ferry[.] crossed our baggage in a Canoe & Swam our Horses, after leaving the Ferry two Miles we were directed to take a path thro the Woods as a short cut to the Main Road to George Town, we pursued the path till we got lost in the Woods, we Wandered about in the Woods Near four Hours, at last luckily came upon a Road that led us to a Planta-tion [p. 119] belonging to Mr Ford[.] we got a Pilot to put us in to the Road, we then Rode fifteen Miles & arrived at George Town about Six oClock in the Evening. Remarkable Warm Weather[.] the Trees all in Bloom thro the Country.

Tuesday 27th. Wednesday 28 Feby. 1781[.] Spent the Time in Viewing George Town[.] it Contains about fifty Dwelling Houses some very Good ones, an English Church & Court House, some valuable Rice Plantations adjacent to the Town, the River is Navigable up to the Town, it is laid out for an hundred Acres as the Town Platt, & has been a Flourishing Town. [p. 120]

Thursday March 1st 1781[.] Left George Town at ten o Clock in the Morning crossed Samppitt River in a Flatt, we Rode twelve Miles to North Santee & crossed the Ferry in a Flatt. Rode over a very bad Causway three Quarters of a Mile, & crossed South Santee[.] we then Rode four Miles to Mr Fords & Stoppd to feed our Horses, after bating the Mares we Mounted & Rode twenty Six Miles to Whites Tavern[.] here we put up all Night.

Friday 2d [March.] Left Whites at eight in the Morning & Rode Seventeen Miles to Hibbens Ferry, where to our great joy we were informed of our exchange, we crossed the Ferry over to Charles Town, where I found Mr Hidden & Allaire.

Saturday 3d. Sunday 4. & Monday 5th [March.] Remained in Town[.] [p. 121]

Tuesday March 6th 1781[.] Capt. DePeyster was Ordered to take command at Neilsons Ferry, & I to attend as Surgeon at that Post[.] we left Chs. Town at twelve oClock & Rode to Monks Corner where we put up all Night[.]

Wednesday 7th [March]. Left Monks Corner at eight in the Morning & Rode to Neilsons Ferry.

Notes to the Journal

3.5.80 Gen. James Paterson, as a colonel of the Sixty-third British Regiment, served as adjutant general to the army in America from the summer of 1776 until the summer of 1778, when he returned to England for a year's leave. Back in America, he was in command of four units during the American capture of Stony Point, New York (1779). By 1780, when he was in charge of the reinforcements that Sir Henry Clinton summoned from Georgia to aid in the attack on Charles Town, South Carolina, Paterson was brigadier general "in America." Harold E. Selesky, ed., *Encyclopedia of the American Revolution,* 2nd ed. (Detroit, Mich.: Charles Scribner's Sons, 2006), 2:875 [a revised and expanded version of Mark M. Boatner's *Encyclopedia of the American Revolution,* published in 1966.]; John Peebles, *John Peebles' American War: The Diary of a Scottish Grenadier, 1776–1782,* ed. Ira D. Gruber (Mechanicsburg, Pa.: Stackpole Books, 1998), 521.

Maj. Charles Graham, as a captain, commanded the grenadier company of the Forty-second Regiment of Foot, or Royal Highland Regiment (also known as the Black Watch), beginning in August 1776. In 1778 he became a major and in 1782 lieutenant colonel of the regiment. Peebles, *John Peebles' American War,* 517; Philip R. N. Katcher, *Encyclopedia of British, Provincial, and German Army Units, 1775–1783* (Harrisburg, Pa.: Stackpole Books, 1973), 52–53.

Composed of the tallest and strongest men in the regiment, the grenadier company was originally designed to heave heavy grenades at the enemy; however, by the late eighteenth century, use of grenades was discontinued, and the grenadier company had become an elite unit positioned on the right flank when the regiment was drawn up in formation. The other flank company, also an elite unit, was the light infantry, theoretically composed of men in the best physical condition, who generally served as scouts and rangers. Both companies frequently operated separately from the other companies in their regiments. Katcher, *Encyclopedia of British, Provincial, and German Army Units,* 14; Edward E. Curtis, *The Organization of the British Army in the American Revolution* (1926; repr., Yorkshire, U.K.: E. P. Publishing, 1972), 3–4.

Maj. Archibald McArthur had been promoted to captain in the Fifty-fourth Regiment of Foot in 1771 and to major of the Seventy-first Regiment on November 16, 1777. He would be captured by the Americans at the battle of Cowpens, South Carolina, on January 17, 1781. Three months later, after being exchanged, he became lieutenant colonel of the Third Battalion of the Royal Americans (Sixtieth) Regiment. Selesky, *Encyclopedia of the American Revolution,* 2:703.

Lt. Col. George Turnbull was an officer of the New York Volunteers, a Tory regiment that had been raised by Oliver DeLancey (the elder). Two battalions served in the Southern Campaign. Turnbull would successfully defend the British outpost at Rocky Mount, South Carolina, on August 1, 1780. Selesky, *Encyclopedia of the American Revolution,* 2:1175; Lorenzo Sabine, *Biographical Sketches of Loyalists of the American Revolution with an Historical Essay* (1864; repr., Baltimore: Genealogical Publishing Co., 1979), 2:367.

For the American Volunteers and Patrick Ferguson, see the introduction to this volume.

Lt. Col. John Hamilton (d. 1816), a partner in a Glasgow trading firm, immigrated to America in 1760. Operating branches of the firm in Virginia and North Carolina, he and his brothers prospered until the Revolution intervened. He then raised a unit of Loyalists, later designated the Royal North Carolina Regiment, which would embody more than seven hundred men. This regiment served in numerous battles, including the siege of Charles Town and the unsuccessful defense of Yorktown. Hamilton was thrice wounded and twice captured. Although Charles, Earl Cornwallis termed him "an obstante blockhead" and blamed him for a premature uprising of Loyalists in Tryon County, North Carolina, during June 1780, Hamilton later served as a surprisingly popular British consul at Norfolk. William S. Powell, ed., *Dictionary of North Carolina Biography* (Chapel Hill: University of North Carolina Press, 1979–1996), 3:16–17; Gregory Palmer, *Biographical Sketches of Loyalists of the American Revolution* (Westport, Conn.: Meckler, 1984), 352–53; Robert Scott Davis Jr., "Colonel John Hamilton of the Royal North Carolina Regiment," *Southern Campaigns of the American Revolution* 3 (May 2006): 32–34, available at http://www.southerncampaign.org/newsletter/v3n5.pdf (accessed August 3, 2010); Cornwallis quoted in Robert S. Lambert, *South Carolina Loyalists in the American Revolution* (Columbia: University of South Carolina Press, 1987), 126–27.

Lt. Col. Alexander Innes, a Scotsman, arrived in Charles Town in April 1775 as secretary to the royal governor of South Carolina, Lord William Campbell. As such, he filed several secret reports to keep the secretary of state posted on local affairs. In September 1776 he was commissioned an ensign in the Forty-second Regiment of Foot and a lieutenant in August 1778. Meanwhile, he assumed the duties of inspector general of provincial forces. In January 1780 he became colonel of the South Carolina Royalists, a provincial unit composed of Carolina refugees in Florida. He would be severely wounded at the battle of Musgrove's Mill, South Carolina, on August 18, 1780. Bradley Bargar, "Charles Town Loyalism in 1775: The Secret Reports of Alexander Innes," *South Carolina Historical Magazine* 63 (July 1962): 125–36; Worthington C. Ford, comp., *British Officers Serving in the American Revolution, 1774–1783* (Brooklyn, N.Y.: Historical Printing Club, 1897), 100; Paul H. Smith, *Loyalists and Redcoats: A Study in British Revolutionary Policy*

(Chapel Hill: University of North Carolina Press, 1964), 49; K. G. Davies, ed., *Documents of the American Revolution, 1770–1783,* vol. 16, *Calendar 1779–1780, July–December* (Shannon: Irish University Press, 1977), 44; Lambert, *South Carolina Loyalists,* 71–72, 133.

Maj. Charles Cochrane was a lieutenant in the Seventh British Regiment of Foot in 1768 and a captain in the Fourth Regiment in 1774. He became a major under Lt. Col. Banastre Tarleton and commanded the infantry of the British Legion. He would be killed at Yorktown after delivering information from the British head-quarters in New York about General Clinton's last-ditch plans to save Cornwallis's army before it surrendered. Ford, *British Officers in the American Revolution,* 49; Banastre Tarleton, *A History of the Campaigns of 1780 and 1781, in the Southern Provinces of North America* (1787; repr., Spartanburg, S.C.: Reprint Co., 1967), 7, 390; Henry Clinton, *The American Rebellion: Sir Henry Clinton's Narrative of His Campaigns, 1775–1782, with an Appendix of Original Documents* (New Haven, Conn.: Yale University Press, 1954), 580; Franklin Wickwire and Mary Wickwire, *Cornwallis: The American Adventure* (Boston: Houghton Mifflin, 1970), 377–78.

Dragoons were mounted soldiers who moved about like cavalry but fought on foot as well as on horseback. Terry M. Mays, *Dictionary of the American Revolution* (Lanham, Md.: Scarecrow Press, 1999), 88.

The identity of the Captain Campbell who commanded the Georgia dragoons may be lost forever in the thicket of Campbells that peopled the British army. No fewer than eleven Archibald Campbells who were junior officers at the time appear in the army lists, and six of them were in the Seventy-first Regiment. Who-ever commanded the second troop of Georgia Light Dragoons had been trans-ferred from the Seventy-first Regiment and commissioned as captain in December 1778 or January 1779. Lt. Col. Archibald Campbell had no issue, so it is not clear if he was related to Captain Archibald. Murtie June Clark, ed., *Loyalists in the Southern Campaign of the Revolutionary War* (Baltimore: Genealogical Publishing Co., 1981), 1:453–55; Archibald Campbell, *Journal of an Expedition against the Rebels of Georgia in North America under the Orders of Archibald Campbell Esquire, Lieut. Colol. of His Majesty's 71st Regimt., 1778,* ed. Colin Campbell (Darien, Ga.: Ashan-tilly Press, 1981), 83, x.

Geridous Plantation was probably Giradeau's Bluff (also known as Brewton Hill) on the Savannah River about twelve miles above present-day Tybee Island and about a mile from Savannah. The plantation was occupied by John Giradeau when British troops landed there on December 20, 1778. Campbell, *Journal of an Expe-dition,* 21, 23, 108n49; Works Progress Administration of Georgia, Federal Writers' Project, Savannah Unit, "Causton's Bluff, Deptford, Brewton Hill: Three Allied Plantations," part 2, *Georgia Historical Quarterly* 23 (June 1939): 139–40.

Cherokee Hill was located by Lt. Col. Archibald Campbell as being eight miles, presumably from Savannah, north along a sandy road abounding with swamps and creeks. Cherokee Hill Cemetery, Chatham County, appears on the 7.5 minute Port Wentworth, Georgia, quadrangle map of the United States Geological Survey approximately two miles west of the Savannah River. Campbell, *Journal of an Expedition*, 32.

Abercorn was a small settlement fifteen to sixteen miles upriver from Savannah. Founded about 1734, it was abandoned by 1751. Kenneth Coleman, *Colonial Georgia: A History* (Millwood, N.Y.: KTO Press, 1989), 39–40. Abercorn Creek also appears on the Port Wentworth quadrangle map.

3.6.80 Ebenezer had been settled originally in 1734 by Lutheran refugees from Salzburg at a site laid out by James Ogelthorpe. Two years later the inhabitants moved to the juncture of Ebenezer Creek and the Savannah River, approximately twenty-two miles north of Savannah, where Johnson found the village. The Lutheran church, built in 1767, still stands and is on the National Register of Historic Places. Coleman, *Colonial Georgia*, 43–45, 234–35.

High Dutch refers to Germans from the higher elevations of south Germany and to their language. *Oxford English Dictionary*, 2nd ed., s.v. "Dutch."

Redoubts were traditionally small, enclosed, detached outworks clustered around a larger fortification to cover approach routes, although they could be stand-alone structures. Selesky, *Encyclopedia of the American Revolution*, 2:972.

Allaire's journal says four redoubts. "Diary of Lieut. Anthony Allaire," in Lyman C. Draper, *King's Mountain and Its Heroes: History of the Battle of King's Mountain, October 7th, 1780, and the Events Which Led to It* (1881; repr., Spartanburg, S.C.: Reprint Co., 1967), 484.

3.7.80 John and James may have been among the few Indians that Lt. Col. Alexander Innes was to bring with him "so that they would be awed by the size of the king's army." Most of the Cherokee and Creek Indians who had planned to join the expedition were left behind on Clinton's orders because he feared adverse political effects from their possible depredations—this despite a report that they behaved exceptionally well during Gen. Augustine Prevost's incursion into South Carolina the year before. Edward J. Cashin, *The King's Ranger: Thomas Brown and the American Revolution on the Southern Frontier* (Athens: University of Georgia Press, 1989), 104; Clinton to Alexander Innes, Feb. 19, 1780, in Royal Commission on Historical Manuscripts, *Report on American Manuscripts*, 2:92–93; David Taitt to Clinton, [c. June 11, 1779], in Campbell, *Journal of an Expedition*, 88.

Allaire omitted the fact that Ferguson joined them. "Diary of Allaire," in Draper, *King's Mountain*, 484.

3.8.80 Almost certainly Johnson referred to poison oak and poison ivy here. That both Allaire and Johnson were apparently unfamiliar with these weeds, which were then, as now, widespread in New York and New Jersey, is a bit puzzling. See Peter Kalm, *Peter Kalm's Travels in North America: The English Version of 1770*, ed. Adolph B. Benson (New York: Wilson-Erickson, 1937), 1:38, 43–45, 93–94.

3.9.80 Two Sisters Bluff was the site referred to in a statute of 1769 vesting a ferry there in William Williamson for fourteen years. Thomas Cooper and David J. McCord, eds., *Statutes at Large of South Carolina* (Columbia: printed by A. S. Johnston, 1836–1841), 9:226–27; Archibald Campbell, "Colonel Archibald Campbell's March from Savannah to Augusta, 1779," ed. Doyce B. Nunis Jr., *Georgia Historical Quarterly* 45 (September 1961): 280.

3.10.80 Tuckassa King was a plantation on relatively high ground, approximately three miles north of the Two Sisters, according to Archibald Campbell's Journal, 1779. Campbell, "March from Savannah to Augusta," 280.

The editors have been unable to identify Lieutenant Johnson with certainty. He may have been Samuel Johnson of North Carolina, who was severely wounded at the battle of Kings Mountain. But we have been unable to place this Johnson on the south side of the Savannah River in March 1780; accordingly we suspect that Richard Johnson, who eventually served as a captain in the South Carolina militia regiment of refugees from Georgia commanded by Col. Samuel Hammond, was the most likely individual. Uzal Johnson, *Uzal Johnson, Loyalist Surgeon: A Revolutionary War Diary*, ed. Bobby G. Moss (Blacksburg, S.C.: Scotia Hibernia Press, 2000), 6n21; Draper, *King's Mountain*, 460–61; Lucian Knight, comp., *Georgia's Roster of the Revolution* (1920; repr., Baltimore: Genealogical Publishing Co., 1967), 100; Accounts Audited of Claims Growing Out of the Revolution in South Carolina, 1775–1876, 4050 A, South Carolina Department of Archives and History.

Allaire's version of the last sentences reads "ground we left in the morning, where I and part of the detachment lay all night. One division crossed the river—the others to follow us expeditiously as possible." "Diary of Allaire," in Draper, *King's Mountain*, 485.

Capt. Abraham DePeyster, born in 1753, was a Loyalist from New York. A captain in the King's American (New York Provincial) Regiment since 1776, he was present at the siege of Charles Town and the battle of Musgrove's Mill. As the ranking officer after Ferguson's death at Kings Mountain, he would assume command and order the British surrender. He later settled in New Brunswick, where he served as treasurer of the province and colonel of militia. Bobby G. Moss, *Roster of the Loyalists in the Battle of Kings Mountain* (Blacksburg, S.C.: Scotia-Hibernia Press, 1998), 22–23.

3.12.80 Gen. William Moultrie (1730–1805) was a longtime member of the colonial Commons House of Assembly and successor revolutionary bodies. As commander of the Second South Carolina Regiment of Foot, on June 28, 1776, he directed the successful defense of the American fort on Sullivans Island against a British naval attack. As a result the fort was renamed in his honor. When the regiment was taken into the Continental service in September 1776, he was promoted to brigadier general. Captured at the fall of Charles Town, he remained a prisoner of war until 1782, when he was exchanged for the British general John Burgoyne, who was then a prisoner of the Americans on parole in England. On October 15, 1782, Moultrie was promoted to major general. During 1785–87 and 1792–94 he served as governor of South Carolina. Walter B. Edgar and N. Louise Bailey, *Biographical Directory of the South Carolina House of Representatives*, vol. 2, *The Commons House of Assembly, 1692–1775* (Columbia: University of South Carolina Press, 1977), 485–88.

In 1779 Moultrie had encamped at Black Swamp (where Uzal Johnson currently was positioned) as the British moved toward Charles Town. William Moultrie, *Memoirs of the American Revolution, So Far as It Related to the States of North and South Carolina, and Georgia.* 2 vols. (1802; repr., 2 vols. in 1, New York: New York Times and Arno Press, 1968), 1:376–77.

Given the plethora of Campbells in the British units, positive identification of this individual is difficult. One of the two most likely candidates is Colin Campbell, who served in the First Battalion of the New York Volunteers, which was on this march. The other, more likely, possibility (because Allaire identified him as "Mr. Campbell of the Georgia Dragoons") is Lt. Smollet Campbell, who was transferred from the Seventy-first British Regiment to the Second Troop of Georgia Light Dragoons. His commission dated from December 24, 1779. Johnson, *Loyalist Surgeon: War Diary,* 3, 7; "Diary of Allaire," in Draper, *King's Mountain,* 485; M. J. Clark, *Loyalists in the Southern Campaign,* 1:453.

3.13.80 For Bee Creek, and Coosawhatchie and Tulifinny rivers, see the Beaufort District map in Robert Mills, *Mills' Atlas: Atlas of the State of South Carolina, 1825* (1825; repr., Easley, S.C.: Southern Historical Press, 1980). The British were following the roads over which General Moultrie retreated as Prevost pushed north in 1779. See Moultrie, *Memoirs,* 1:364–410.

William Middleton (1710–1775 or 1785) was a member of the South Carolina Royal Council from 1740 to 1755. Thereafter he resided in Suffolk, England. His son Thomas lived at Crowfield Plantation in St. James Goose Creek Parish. At his death in 1779, Thomas owned Turkey Hill Plantation, which he had attempted to sell in 1772. His advertisement stated that it was within three miles of "the Sisters" and included eighteen hundred acres—four hundred of which were under good fence—and "Negro Houses" for one hundred workers. The surveyor Joseph Purcell made a plat of the property in 1786. George W. Lane, "The Middletons of Eighteenth-Century South Carolina: A Colonial Dynasty, 1678–1787" (Ph.D. diss., Emory University, 1990); Henry Laurens, *The Papers of Henry Laurens,* vol. 9, *April 19, 1773–Dec. 12, 1774,* ed. George C. Rogers Jr. and David R. Chesnutt (Columbia: University of South Carolina Press, 1981), 372n9; N. Louise Bailey and Elizabeth I. Cooper, *Biographical Directory of the South Carolina House of Representatives,* vol. 3, *1775–1790* (Columbia: University of South Carolina Press, 1981), 494–95; *Gazette of the State of South Carolina,* February 24, 1772; Plat of Turkey Hill

Plantation by Joseph Purcell, St. Peter's, Beaufort, June 15, 1786 (32–30–8), South Carolina Historical Society, Charleston.

For the subsequent history of the plantation, see Jessica Stevens Loring, *Auldbrass: The Plantation Complex Designed by Frank Lloyd Wright: A Documented History of Its South Carolina Lands* (Greenville, S.C.: Southern Historical Press, 1992).

Battle at Coosawhatchie Bridge. Whig forces composing the rear guard of General Moultrie's regiments engaged British troops under General Prevost on May 3, 1779, on the western bank of the Coosawhatchie River near this bridge. The Whigs, commanded by Lt. Col. John Laurens, suffered eleven casualties and were forced to retreat. Terry W. Lipscomb, "South Carolina Revolutionary Battles: Part 2," *Names in South Carolina* 21 (Winter 1974): 23; Howard H. Peckham, ed., *The Toll of Independence: Engagements and Battle Casualties of the American Revolution* (Chicago: University of Chicago Press, 1974), 60; Gregory De Van Massey, *John Laurens and the American Revolution* (Columbia: University of South Carolina Press, 2000), 132–36.

3.14.80 John Stafford supplied provisions to "sundry Troops and Waggoners" in 1778 and 1779. Records of the South Carolina Auditor and Accountant General, 1778–1788, pp. 19, 93, South Carolina Department of Archives and History.

Isaac McPherson (1739–1787), a planter whose holdings included more than five thousand acres and 151 slaves at the time of his death, served in the revolutionary First and Second Provincial Congresses and the state General Assembly from 1776 to 1780. Edgar and Bailey, *Biographical Directory of the South Carolina House of Representatives,* 2:450–51.

John McPherson (d. 1806), Isaac McPherson's nephew, was also a planter and a member of the South Carolina Assembly (1782–1784, 1787–1791) whose military experience included service in Francis Marion's brigade (2.25.81 below) and the Third South Carolina Regiment of Rangers. He eventually became a brigadier general in the state militia. Will of Isaac McPherson, proved Sept. 22, 1787, Charleston County Will Transcripts, vol. 22 (1786–1793), p. 180, South Carolina Department of Archives and History; Suzanne C. Linder, *Historical Atlas of the Rice Plantations of the ACE River Basin—1860* (Columbia: South Carolina Department of Archives and History, 1995), 379–80.

The mistaken engagement Johnson described occurred near the present town of McPhersonville. Lipscomb, "South Carolina Battles," 21:24–25.

Lt. Donald McPherson of the British Legion was born in Scotland and would serve in the provincial corps for a total of seven years. On-Line Institute for Advanced Loyalist Studies, "Biographical Sketches on Infantry Officers of the British Legion, 1778–1782," copyright Donald J. Gara, New Jersey, available at http://www .royalprovincial.com/military/rhist/britlegn/blinf1.htm (accessed August 3, 2010); M. J. Clark, *Loyalists in the Southern Campaign,* 2:218–21; 3:343, 354, 402–8.

For variations in the time of day, distances, and substantive wording, see Allaire's diary in Draper, *King's Mountain,* 485–86.

3.16.80 For the sighting of some rebels, see Allaire's entry for this date in Draper, *King's Mountain,* 486.

3.18.80 Saltketcher Bridge was referred to on the Beaufort District map in Robert Mills, *Mills' Atlas,* but modern maps label the river the Combahee at this point. Lipscomb, "South Carolina Battles," 21:25–26.

Major Ladson was evidently Thomas Ladson of South Carolina. He served as a captain and major in the South Carolina militia between 1779 and 1781. Francis B. Heitman, *Historical Register of Officers of the Continental Army during the War of the Revolution, April 1775 to December 1783* (1914; repr., Baltimore: Genealogical Publishing Co., 1982), 337.

Captain Mills was probably William Mills of the St. Bartholomew Parish volunteer militia. Alexander S. Salley Jr., comp., *South Carolina Provincial Troops, Named in the Papers of the First Council of Safety of the Revolutionary Party in South Carolina, June–November 1775* (Baltimore: Genealogical Publishing Co., 1977), 223–24. See also Henry Laurens, *The Papers of Henry Laurens,* vol. 10, *Dec. 12, 1774–Jan. 4, 1776,* ed. David R. Chesnutt (Columbia: University of South Carolina Press, 1985), 411n3.

Maj. Charles Graham. See 3.5.80 above.

Maj. James Wright Jr. (c. 1747–1816), the son of the last royal governor of Georgia, Sir James Wright, was the owner of two plantations on the Ogeechee River in Georgia. Commissioned major on May 1, 1779, he commanded one of the companies of Georgia Loyalists. When the British evacuated Savannah in the summer of 178?, he went to Nova Scotia and subsequently to Jamaica. M. J. Clark, *Loyalists in the Southern Campaign,* 1:435–36; Laurens, *Papers,* 9:103n6.

Charles Ogilvie, a prominent Charles Town merchant, traded as a partner in various firms, including Ogilvie, Forbes and Michie. In 1761 he moved to Great Britain, where he continued in business. In June 1780, however, he returned to Charles Town, then occupied by the British, and was appointed deputy commissioner of sequestered [seized] property. When British forces evacuated the city in December 1782, he again moved to England, and he died there in the late 1780s. The plantation to which Johnson referred was really three separate but adjoining tracts owned by Ogilvie and his two minor sons. Located on the Combahee River near the intersection of the roads to Saltketcher Ferry and Augusta, Georgia, these properties provided "great Assistance and Supplies" to Gen. James Paterson's troops. W. Robert Higgins, "Charles Town Merchants and Factors Dealing in the External Negro Trade, 1735–1775," *South Carolina Historical Magazine* 65 (October 1964): 213; Loring, *Auldbrass,* 53–68, quotation 59.

Indian Land was the area between the Savannah and Combahee rivers that the legislature had set aside for the Yemasee Indians in 1707 and subsequently confiscated from them after the Yemasee War. The primary village in the area was Pocataligo, which was itself often termed Indian Land. In 1778 a traveler noted that it was "not properly a village but a number of houses at a distance from, and yet within site of each other." Robert M. Weir, *Colonial South Carolina: A History* (1983; repr., Columbia: University of South Carolina Press, 1997), 83; Ebenezer Hazard, "A View of Coastal South Carolina in 1778: The Journal of Ebenezer Hazard," ed. H. Roy Merrens, *South Carolina Historical Magazine* 73 (October 1972): 187.

3.19.80 The bridge had been rebuilt by the time Francis Asbury, the great Methodist itinerant preacher, passed this way more than a decade later, but the house at which he stopped to pay the toll reeked with "the scent of rum, and men filled with it!" Francis Asbury, *The Journal and Letters of Francis Asbury,* ed. Elmer T. Clark (Nashville, Tenn.: Abingdon Press, 1958), 1:747.

Perhaps Gipson was William Gibson, who was on the jury lists for St. Bartholomew Parish for 1778–1779. Evelyn M. F. Bryan, *Colleton County, South Carolina: A History of the First 160 Years, 1670–1830* (Jacksonville, Fla.: Florentine Press, 1993), 193, 195.

3.20.80 Godfrey's Savannah seems to have been the swampy area near Walterboro crossed today by S.C. Route 41 and labeled Bluehouse Swamp and Calfpen on modern maps. Lipscomb, "South Carolina Revolutionary Battles: Part 7," *Names in South Carolina* 26 (Winter 1979): 33.

3.21.80 Fish Pond was on the Ashepoo River where the road to Jacksonborough crossed. The bridge there appears on the Colleton District map in *Mills' Atlas.*

Lt. Col. Banastre Tarleton (1754–1833) in 1778 became the lieutenant colonel commandant of the British Legion, which he led to victories that made him legendary. But in January 1781 Gen. Daniel Morgan defeated him at the battle of Cowpens, South Carolina, and in October he was captured at Yorktown, Virginia. Paroled to England, he later served as a member of Parliament from Liverpool, 1790–1812. His *History of the Campaigns of 1780 and 1781, in the Southern Provinces of North America,* in which he indicated that all the cavalry horses drowned when a vessel foundered on the voyage southward (p. 4), remains a valuable primary account. H. C. G. Matthew and Brian Harrison, eds., *Oxford Dictionary of National Biography in Association with the British Academy: From the Earliest Times to the Year 2000* (Oxford: Oxford University Press, 2004), 53:784–86; Anthony J. Scotti Jr., *Brutal Virtue: The Myth and Reality of Banastre Tarleton* (1995; repr., Bowie, Md.: Heritage Books, 2002).

3.22.80 Horseshoe Creek is now crossed by S.C. Route 64 about ten miles southeast of Walterboro. The horseshoe-shaped marsh on the west side of the creek was called Horseshoe Savannah. Lipscomb, "South Carolina Battles," 26:31.

Jacksonborough, settled in 1706, became the temporary capital of South Carolina when the legislature met there from January 8 to February 26, 1782, while the British occupied Charles Town. J. F. D. Smyth, a captain of the Loyalist Queens Rangers who toured the United States after the war, noted that the Jacksonborough area was "remarkable for rich widows, frolic, and feasting." Bryan, *Colleton County*, 124–26, 158; J. F. D. Smyth, *A Tour in the United States of America; Containing an Account of the Present Situation of That Country* (Dublin: Price, Moncrieffe [etc.], 1784), 2:34, 271; P. H. Smith, *Loyalists and Redcoats*, 48–49. For another brief description of Jacksonborough, see Hazard, "View of Coastal South Carolina in 1778," 187.

The Tory physician was probably Dr. John De la Howe (c. 1717–1797), who was a justice of the peace in the area before the British reached it in 1780 and a private in the Jacksonborough company of the Loyalist Colleton County militia under the occupation. De la Howe's estate was amerced and subjected to a confiscatory tax of 12 percent in 1782 as punishment for his Loyalist activities, but he was permitted to remain in South Carolina. About 1785 he moved to Abbeville District in the South Carolina upcountry, where he continued to practice medicine successfully enough to make his house the "the most elaborate" in the area. Dying without children, he left his property to establish a public school for poor children; girls as well as boys were to learn mathematics and chemistry as well as reading and writing. This school is reported to have been the first manual training school in the country. *Gazette of the State of South Carolina*, February 9, 1780; M. J. Clark, *Loyalists in the Southern Campaign*, 1:170; Joseph Ioor Waring, *A History of Medicine in South Carolina, 1670–1825* (Charleston: South Carolina Medical Association, 1964), 345; Mary K. Davis, "The Feather Bed Aristocracy: Abbeville District in the 1790s," *South Carolina Historical Magazine* 80 (April 1979): 149–50; Mabel L. Webber, comp., "Marriage and Death Notices from *The City Gazette*," *South Carolina Historical and Genealogical Magazine* 23 (October 1922): 210–11; David D. Wallace, *The History of South Carolina* (New York: American Historical Society, 1934), 3:25.

Another, less likely, possibility is that the physician was Dr. Peter Spence, who joined British forces in Christ Church Parish in April 1780. A Scot who settled in Jacksonborough about 1767, he built an extensive medical practice that he maintained during the Revolution. Spence was a surgeon to Whig militia in Charles Town between 1777 and 1778 before he joined the British. He barely escaped capture in 1781 and left the country until 1782. On his return he was jailed and later discovered that his property had been confiscated; after a stay at St. Augustine, he was allowed to sail for England. His claim of lost possessions amounted to £12,974. Witnesses in support of his claim believed that he was "a friend to the British Constitution," but he had married "an American Lady, and her Friends took part with the Americans." Waring, *History of Medicine in South Carolina*, 316, 345, 386; Lambert, *South Carolina Loyalists*, 27; American Loyalist Claims, March 12, 1784, AO 12/50/124, National Archives, Kew, Richmond, Surrey, United Kingdom; Palmer, *Biographical Sketches of Loyalists*, 814.

3.23.80 Gov. Thomas Bee (1739–1812) was a planter and lawyer who owned land on the east side of the Edisto (Pon Pon) River across from Jacksonborough. He was active during the Stamp Act crisis and served in the Royal Assembly (1762–1768, 1772–1775) and the First and Second Provincial Congresses (1775–1776), as well as the General Assemblies of 1776–1778 (during which he was Speaker) and 1783–1788. In 1780–1782 he was a delegate to the Continental Congress. In 1779 he was lieutenant governor of South Carolina. As a member of the state ratifying convention in 1788, he would vote to approve the U.S. Constitution. Edgar and Bailey, *Biographical Directory of the South Carolina House of Representatives,* 2:69–72; Lipscomb, "South Carolina Battles," 21:26.

Whether the engagement at Bee's plantation involved troops under Lt. Col. William Washington (4.13.80 below) or American militia is unclear; historians differ on the question. See Tarleton, *History of the Campaigns of 1780 and 1781,* 8–9; Lipscomb, "South Carolina Battles," 21:26; Edward McCrady, *The History of South Carolina in the Revolution, 1775–1780* (1901; repr., New York: Russell & Russell, 1969), 450–51; Mark M. Boatner, III, *Landmarks of the American Revolution,* 2nd ed. (Detroit, Mich.: Charles Scribner's Sons, 2006), 328; Stephen E. Haller, *William Washington: Cavalryman of the Revolution* (Bowie, Md.: Heritage Books, 2001), 53; and Scotti, *Brutal Virtue.*

3.24.80 Thomas Ferguson (d. c. 1786) was a prominent public official. One of his six wives was a daughter of Christopher Gadsden, whose revolutionary zeal he shared. Ferguson served in the Commons House of Assembly (1762–1775), First and Second Provincial Congresses (1775–1776), and General Assembly (1776–1780, 1782–1786), usually representing St. Paul Parish. This plantation (Spoon's Savannah)—one of several that he owned—contained 7,830 acres. Henry Laurens, *The Papers of Henry Laurens,* vol. 5, *Sept. 1, 1765–July 31, 1768,* ed. George C. Rogers Jr. and David R. Chesnutt (Columbia: University of South Carolina Press, 1976), 493; Edgar and Bailey, *Biographical Directory of the South Carolina House of Representatives,* 2:248–50; Will of Thomas Ferguson, proved May 20, 1786, South Carolina Will Transcripts, vol. 22 (1786–1793), p. 11, South Carolina Department of Archives and History.

Captain Saunders was probably John Sanders of South Carolina; he was a lieutenant with the Horse Shoe Company of the Colleton County Regiment of Foot in 1775. A captain by 1779, he was later promoted to lieutenant colonel. He lived at Round O in St. Bartholomew Parish and represented that district in the General Assembly during 1789–1790. Bailey and Cooper, *Biographical Directory of the South Carolina House of Representatives,* 3:632–33.

Captain Wilkinson was doubtless Ens. Morton Wilkinson (1745?–1790), who had served under John Sanders in the Colleton County Regiment of Foot in 1775. He would be captured at the fall of Charles Town and later exiled to St. Augustine. He served in the South Carolina General Assembly in 1782 and in the Privy Council in 1782–83, as well as the state senate from 1783 to 1784. Bailey and Cooper, *Biographical Directory of the South Carolina House of Representatives,* 3:724–25.

The procedural problem here arose because commanders took great pains to prevent spying under cover of a flag of truce. For George Washington's orders on the subject, see General Orders, Headquarters, Cambridge, July 12, 1775, in George Washington, *Writings of George Washington from the Original Manuscript Sources, 1745–1799*, vol. 3, *Jan. 1770–Sept. 1775*, ed. John C. Fitzpatrick (Washington, D.C.: Government Printing Office, 1931), 335. General Paterson's denunciation of the "unmilitary and irregular manner in which your flag of truce, has presumed to approach His Majesty's Army" appears in Brig. Gen. James Paterson to Brig. Gen. [Isaac] Huger, March 24, 1780, *Yearbook, City of Charleston, South Carolina, 1897*, pp. 346–47. Robert Donkin, *Military Collections and Remarks* (New York: H. Gaine, 1777), 120, contains specific suggestions for using a flag of truce for espionage.

3.25.80 Stono or Wallace's Bridge crossed Wallace Creek, a tributary of the Stono River. In *Mills' Atlas,* the bridge is located near the boundary between Charleston and Colleton districts.

3.26.80 Rantowles Creek flows into Wallace Creek approximately one mile before Wallace Creek empties into the Stono River. The route Paterson's force took here corresponds roughly to U.S. Highway 17, which crosses the neck of land between Wallace and Rantowles creeks. Rantowle's Bridge is identified on the Charleston District map of *Mills' Atlas.* Lipscomb, "South Carolina Battles," 21:26.

The commander in chief was Sir Henry Clinton (1730–1795), who was raised in New York and became a lieutenant in the Coldstream Guards in 1751. By 1758 he was lieutenant colonel of the Grenadier Guards. During the Seven Years' War he served credibly in Europe and was wounded. Rising through the officers' ranks, he reached lieutenant general in 1777; in 1778 he became commander in chief in America. The capture of Charles Town in 1780 marked the apex of his career; Sir Guy Carleton would succeed him in 1782. In 1793 Clinton was promoted to full general, and the next year he was made governor of Gibraltar. His history of the American Revolution was published in 1954 as *The American Rebellion: Sir Henry Clinton's Narrative of His Campaigns, 1775–1782,* edited by William B. Willcox. Intelligent and knowledgeable, he was nevertheless temperamentally unqualified for the role of commander in chief. Matthew and Harrison, *Oxford Dictionary of National Biography,* 12:140–43; William B. Willcox, *Portrait of a General: Sir Henry Clinton in the War of Independence* (New York: Knopf, 1964).

American forces had information about Clinton's visit and planned to capture him at Gov. John Rutledge's plantation. They sprang the trap a day late, however, for Clinton returned to Charles Town before the Whigs reached Rutledge's on the twenty-seventh. Lipscomb, "South Carolina Battles," 21:26; Franklin B. Hough, ed., *The Siege of Charleston by the British Fleet and Army Under the Command of Admiral Arbuthnot and Sir Henry Clinton* (1867; repr., Spartanburg, S.C.: Reprint Co., 1975), 161.

Allaire omitted Clinton's narrow escape. "Diary of Allaire," in Draper, *King's Mountain,* 488.

3.27.80 Lt. Col. John Hamilton was previously identified at 3.5.80.

Mr. Smith was probably Robert Smith, a Virginian who served as surgeon to the British General Hospital staff; on June 1, 1782, he was identified as a "prisoner." M. J. Clark, *Loyalists in the Southern Campaign,* 1:543.

A more remote possibility is Dr. Nathan Smith, a physician from Long Island who served in the First Battalion of DeLancey's Corps of New York Volunteers, a unit that was in Paterson's march from Savannah to Charles Town. K. G. Davies, ed., *Documents of the American Revolution, 1770–1783,* vol. 21, *Transcripts 1782–1783* (Shannon: Irish University Press, 1981), 227, 237.

Gov. John Rutledge (1739–1800) served in the colonial Commons House from 1761 to 1775, the First and Second Provincial Congresses in 1775 and 1776, and the General Assembly from 1776 through most of the 1780s, as well as participated in the U.S. Constitutional Convention in 1787. He was the governor of South Carolina between 1779 and 1782 and was later an associate justice of the U.S. Supreme Court and the chief justice of South Carolina. Among his approximately thirty thousand acres in lowcountry South Carolina, the tract to which Johnson refers was Rutledge's Stono Plantation, which was about a mile east of Rantowle's Bridge. His main residence was in Christ Church Parish. Edgar and Bailey, *Biographical Directory of the South Carolina House of Representatives,* 2:577–80; Lipscomb, "South Carolina Battles," 21:26.

This brief battle involved the advance guard of Banastre Tarleton's dragoons and a rear guard of patriot cavalry under Lt. Col. William Washington (4.13.80 below). There is no record of any patriot casualties. Lipscomb, "South Carolina Battles," 21:26; Peckham, *Toll of Independence,* 68–69; Tarleton, *History of the Campaigns of 1780 and 1781,* 8–9.

Allaire is more specific about the British wounded. "Diary of Allaire," in Draper, *King's Mountain,* 488.

3.28.80 Ashley Ferry was approximately six miles northeast of Rantowle's Bridge. Charleston District map, *Mills' Atlas.*

Lining's Plantation was six miles below Ashley Ferry on the south side of the Ashley River across from Charles Town. It belonged to Dr. John Lining (1708–1760), a scientifically inclined physician who reported on yellow fever, experimented with electricity, and made significant meteorological studies. *American National Biography,* ed. John A. Garraty and Mark C. Carnes (New York: Oxford University Press, 1999–2005), 13:706–7; Waring, *History of Medicine in South Carolina,* 254–60.

Allaire omitted the entire description of lowcountry South Carolina and Georgia. "Diary of Allaire, in Draper, *King's Mountain,* 489.

3.29.80 The Hessians were troops from Hesse-Cassel hired to the British by their ruler. This state supplied nearly seventeen thousand soldiers—more than half the troops from Germany that fought in the Revolution; Americans therefore tended to call all Germans Hessians, whatever their origin. The jaegers (German for "hunters") were riflemen from various German corps. Johann Ewald, *The Diary of the American War: A Hessian Journal; Captain Johann Ewald, Field Jager Corps,* trans. and ed. Joseph P. Tustin (New Haven, Conn.: Yale University Press, 1979), provides an excellent account of some of the jaegers' service, as well as information about the Hessians.

3.30.80 Lord Caithness, John Barriedale, the Eleventh Earl of Caithness, was a volunteer aide-de-camp to Sir Henry Clinton. Barriedale began military service in 1772 and was a major with the Seventy-sixth Foot during the Revolution; he eventually rose to the rank of lieutenant colonel. He survived this wound but committed suicide in 1789 at the age of thirty-three. Clinton, *American Rebellion,* 163n8; George Edward Cockayne, *The Complete Peerage of England, Scotland, Ireland and the United Kingdom,* vol. 2, rev. ed., ed. Vicary Gibbs (London: St. Catherine Press, 1912), 482.

3.31.80 Maj. James Moncrieff (1744–1793) was a Scotsman trained as an engineer at Woolwich who served in America and the West Indies during and after the Seven Years' War. Having been responsible for the defensive works at Savannah that withstood the American attack in 1779, he directed siege operations against Charles Town, which included use of prefabricated apparatus brought from New York. Clinton justifiably considered him an engineer *"who understood his business."* L. Edward Purcell, *Who Was Who in the American Revolution* (New York: Facts on File, 1993), 329–30; Clinton, *American Rebellion,* 150, 164, 432.

For variant information about the redoubts, see Allaire's diary in Draper, *King's Mountain,* 489.

For a clear map of this area, see Carl P. Borick, *A Gallant Defense: The Siege of Charleston, 1780* (Columbia: University of South Carolina Press, 2003), 51.

4.3.80 Henry Middleton's Plantation, known as Middleton Place, now Middleton Gardens, was the country seat of Henry Middleton (1717–1784), who was first elected to the South Carolina Commons House of Assembly in 1742. From 1747 to 1755 he was Speaker of the House before becoming a member of the Royal Council. Beginning in 1774, he served in various revolutionary bodies, including the First Continental Congress, of which he was president. After the fall of Charles Town, he took protection from the British. Edgar and Bailey, *Biographical Directory of the South Carolina House of Representatives,* 2:458–59. See also the dissertation by George Lane, "The Middletons of Eighteenth-Century South Carolina: A Colonial Dynasty, 1678–1787" (Emory University, 1990).

Drayton Hall, owned since 1974 by the National Trust for Historic Preservation, is located approximately twelve miles above Charles Town on the Ashley River. Built beginning in 1738 by John Drayton, a wealthy planter, it was situated amid sumptuous gardens and contained more than seventy-six hundred square feet. John, who died in 1779, disinherited his son William Henry Drayton, so Johnson (and others) erred in believing that he had owned Drayton Hall; it actually descended to his brother Charles. William Henry Drayton (1742–1779), a complex, prominent, and influential revolutionary leader, served in the Commons House of Assembly and the Royal Council before becoming a member of the Continental Congress. Keith Krawczynski, *William Henry Drayton: South Carolina Revolutionary Patriot* (Baton Rouge: Louisiana State University Press, 2001), 1, 2, 309–10, 320–21. See also Robert M. Weir, ed., *The Letters of Freeman, Etc.: Essays on the Nonimportation Movement in South Carolina* (Columbia: University of South Carolina Press, 1977).

By March 28, 1780, General Clinton had established his headquarters at Drayton Hall. Peter Russell, "The Siege of Charleston: Journal of Captain Peter Russell, December 25, 1779 to May 2, 1780," ed. James Bain Jr., *American Historical Review* 4 (April 1899): 493.

4.4.80 Capt. John Peebles of the Forty-second Regiment indicated that the Americans came up the Cooper River with a brig and two galleys. Peebles, *John Peebles' American War,* 356.

4.8.80 A "feu de joie," or fire of joy, was the term for martial celebrations of significant events. This American celebration was so noisy that many British soldiers mistakenly thought they were under attack. Contrary to Johnson's report, however, the reinforcements evidently numbered only 750 Virginia Continentals commanded by Gen. William Woodford, not Gen. Charles Scott. General Scott of Virginia had actually arrived at Charles Town on March 30, but without troops. Bonnie S. Stadelman, "The Amusements of the American Soldiers during the Revolution" (Ph.D. diss., Tulane University, 1969), 59–70; Walter J. Fraser Jr., *Patriots, Pistols, and Petticoats: "Poor Sinful Charles Town" during the American Revolution,* 2nd ed. (Columbia: University of South Carolina Press, 1993), 123–24; Henry M. Ward, *Charles Scott and the "Spirit of '76"* (Charlottesville: University of Virginia Press, 1988), 74–75.

To pass Fort Moultrie, the commander of the British fleet, Adm. Marriot Arbuthnot (4.9.80 below), took advantage of wind and tide during an afternoon thunderstorm to send nine ships past the fort. Having neutralized the defensive value of the fort, the British ships anchored off James Island, within cannon range of Charles Town. The HMS *Richmond* carried thirty-two guns and was commanded by Capt. Charles Hudson (5.7.80 below). The transport *Aeolus* sustained rudder damage and ran aground near Haddrell's Point (4.26.80 below). Fraser, *Patriots,*

Pistols, and Petticoats, 124; Peebles, *John Peebles' American War,* 357–58; Hough, *Siege of Charleston,* 21, 72–73.

4.9.80 Adm. Marriot Arbuthnot (1711–1794) became a lieutenant in 1739 and a captain in 1747. Promoted to admiral in 1777, he became commander in chief of the British navy in American waters in February 1779. He cooperated well enough with Clinton for them to succeed in the attack on Charles Town, but it was not an easy relationship. As Clinton's biographer maintained, Arbuthnot, although generally unpredictable, "could be relied upon not to follow through any course of action according to plan." Selesky, *Encyclopedia of the American Revolution,* 1:23–24; John A. Tilley, *The British Navy and the American Revolution* (Columbia: University of South Carolina Press, 1987), 163–65; Willcox, *Portrait of a General,* 514.

4.11.80 The correspondence between Clinton and Arbuthnot, on the one hand, and the American commander of Charles Town, Benjamin Lincoln, on the other, is printed in Hough, *Siege of Charleston,* 87–115.

4.12.80 North Carolinians were put under Ferguson's command because their colonel, John Hamilton, had been captured. See 3.5.80 above for Hamilton.

Bacon's Bridge crossed the Ashley River near Dorchester; the bridge on S.C. 165 in present-day Dorchester County corresponds to its colonial predecessor. Colleton District map, *Mills' Atlas.*

4.13.80 Dorchester, at the time of the Revolution, was the third-largest village in South Carolina. Located southwest of present-day Summerville along the Ashley River, it was the site of St. George's Church, the ruins of which may be seen today in Dorchester State Park. A detailed account of Dorchester is found in Henry A. M. Smith, "The Town of Dorchester, in South Carolina—A Sketch of Its History," *South Carolina Historical and Genealogical Magazine* 6 (April 1905): 62–95.

Middleton's Plantation at Goose Creek was owned by Henry Middleton. Known as The Oaks, this plantation in St. James Goose Creek Parish contained 1,630 acres. Although Henry made Middleton Place (4.3.80 above) along the Ashley his chief residence, The Oaks was the original plantation of the Middleton family; Henry's grandfather, Edward Middleton, had established it around 1680. Henry returned to The Oaks in 1780 after the fall of Charles Town, and upon his death the plantation descended to his second son, Thomas Middleton. Edgar and Bailey, *Biographical Directory of the South Carolina House of Representatives,* 2:458–60; Lane, "The Middletons."

Moncks Corner was strategically located at the intersection of important trade routes. The Charles Town Road divided here; the northern fork connected with roads from the Pee Dee and Georgetown areas; the western fork led to the Cherokee Nation. J. Russell Cross, *Historic Ramblin's through Berkeley* (Columbia, S.C.:

R. L. Bryan, 1985), 190–93; Elias B. Bull, "Community and Neighborhood Names in Berkeley County," part 2, *Names in South Carolina* 12 (Winter 1965): 36–37.

Patriot cavalry and militia were stationed at Moncks Corner in order to guard the last route of escape from Charles Town. In what William Moultrie (3.12.80 above) remembered as a "shameful surprise," dragoons under Banastre Tarleton (3.21.80 above) attacked and scattered the patriot force under Gen. Isaac Huger and Lt. Col. William Washington. Moultrie, *Memoirs*, 2:72.

Lt. Col. William Washington (1752–1810) was born in Virginia. In 1776 he became captain of the Third Virginia Regiment of Continental troops; in 1777 he was promoted to major of the Fourth Continental Dragoons and in November 1778 to lieutenant colonel of the Third Continental Dragoons. He saw action in numerous battles from Long Island in August 1776 to Eutaw Springs in September 1781. Wounded and captured in the latter, he remained in Charles Town as a prisoner for the rest of the war. During the 1780s and 1790s he served in both houses of the South Carolina legislature and was a delegate to the state convention that ratified the U.S. Constitution. Bailey and Cooper, *Biographical Directory of the South Carolina House of Representatives*, 3:749–52. See also Haller, *William Washington*.

Although Theodorick Bland and Casimir Pulaski's corps were involved in this battle, the leaders of these units were not present. Bland, a colonel of Continental dragoons from Virginia, withdrew from military service in December 1779, and Pulaski, a Polish nobleman serving as a brigadier general, was mortally wounded in October of the same year. Selesky, *Encyclopedia of the American Revolution*, 1:77; 2:945–46.

Owree was Colonel Daniel Horry Jr. (d. 1785). A member of the Commons House of Assembly from 1760 to 1771, the First and Second Provincial Congresses, 1775–1776, and the General Assembly, 1776–1778, he became a colonel of light dragoons by 1778. During the British march northward from Savannah, Horry's horsemen kept a watchful eye on their movements before withdrawing to Bacon's Bridge and the area north of Charles Town. Edgar and Bailey, *Biographical Directory of the South Carolina House of Representatives*, 2:329–30; Borick, *Gallant Defense*, 32, 50, 54.

Peter Horry (1747–1815), who later became famous for his service with Francis Marion (2.25.81 below), was evidently not involved in the action at Moncks Corner. When the Fifth South Carolina Regiment was consolidated with another, he lost his command and went home briefly before joining American forces in North Carolina after the fall of Charles Town. Bailey and Cooper, *Biographical Directory of the South Carolina House of Representatives*, 3:346–48.

Gen. Isaac Huger (1743–1797) was a South Carolinian who served in the Royal Assembly in 1772, the First Provincial Congress in 1775, and the General Assembly in 1779–1780 and 1782–1784. Appointed lieutenant colonel in the South Carolina militia in 1775, he became a brigadier general in the Continental line by 1777. After his escape at Moncks Corner, he would command Virginians in the battle of Guilford Court House and the second battle of Camden, 1781. Edgar and Bailey, *Biographical Directory of the South Carolina House of Representatives,* 2:341–43.

Maj. Peter J. F. Vernie, commissioned on February 23, 1779, and Louis I de Beaulieu, a Frenchman serving as a lieutenant under Pulaski, were the two casualties noted by Johnson. Commissioned in March 1779, Beaulieu was wounded at Moncks Corner and placed on leave until the end of the war. Heitman, *Historical Register,* 560 (Vernie), 95 (Beaulieu).

Casualties for the Americans probably totaled fourteen killed, nineteen wounded, and sixty-four captured, versus three wounded for the British. Peckham, *Toll of Independence,* 69.

4.14.80 The explosion of the storehouse occurred at 7 P.M. according to Allaire (who does not mention DePeyster's exploit). This incident should not be confused with a much larger explosion in Charles Town on May 15, 1780. "Diary of Allaire," in Draper, *King's Mountain,* 491.

Ann Fayssoux was the wife of Dr. Peter Fayssoux (d. 1795), the senior physician to the Southern Department of the Continental establishment. To escape the siege of Charles Town, she went to Fairlawn Plantation, the home of Lady Jane Colleton, who was the widow of Sir John Colleton (d. 1777), the fourth baronet and a descendant of one of the original lords proprietors. Chalmers G. Davidson, *Friend of the People: The Life of Dr. Peter Fayssoux of Charleston, South Carolina* (Columbia: Medical Association of South Carolina, 1950), 26–27, 35–36; Edgar and Bailey, *Biographical Directory of the South Carolina House of Representatives,* 2:161–62.

Betsy Giles was Elisabeth Giles, the daughter of John Giles, who with his brother Thomas Giles and John Lesley operated a store at Moncks Corner. She would marry Capt. George Warley in 1786. *South Carolina and American General Gazette,* November 18, 1771; Mabel L. Webber, comp., "Extracts from the Journal of Mrs. Ann Manigault, 1754–1781," *South Carolina Historical and Genealogical Magazine* 20 (April 1919): 141.

Jane Russell was the daughter of Alexander Russell (d. 1771), a ship's carpenter of Charles Town, who appointed John Giles as one of the executors of his will and a guardian of his children. Identified as a "spinster" in 1783, Jane married Henry Lanchester in 1789. Caroline T. Moore and Agatha A. Simmons, eds., *Abstracts of the Wills of the State of South Carolina, 1760–1784* (Columbia, S.C.: R. L. Bryan, 1969), 150; Brent Holcomb, *Probate Records of South Carolina* (Easley, S.C.: Southern Historical Press, 1978), 2:215; Barbara R. Langdon, *South Carolina Marriages,* vol. 2, *1735–1885, Implied in South Carolina Law Reports* (Aiken, S.C.: Langdon & Langdon Genealogical Research, 1993), 148.

The treatment given Ann Fayssoux was typical for the period. Dr. George Harral, a Savannah physician of the early nineteenth century, described bleeding as "the first and most essential remedy in all accidents from external violence." The anodyne was dispensed to relieve pain. Harral is quoted in Robert C. Wilson,

Drugs and Pharmacy in the Life of Georgia, 1733–1959 (Atlanta, Ga.: Foote and Davies, 1959), 83.

As detailed in Lady Colleton's deposition, Henry McDonough and several others unknown were the culprits in this incident. When they were apprehended, Patrick Ferguson was for putting them to "instant death," but the ranking British officer on the scene sent the offenders to headquarters, where they were apparently tried and whipped. Deposition against Henry McDonough, April 15, 1780, Clinton Papers, William L. Clements Library, University of Michigan, Ann Arbor; Charles Stedman, *The History of the Origin, Progress, and Termination of the American War* (Dublin: printed for Messr. P. Wogan . . . , 1794), 2:183n.

4.15.80 Thomas Broughton, governor of South Carolina from 1735 to 1737, acquired 4,423 acres of Fairlawn Barony in 1708 and built Mulberry Mansion in 1714. The house, now called Mulberry Castle, still stands south of Moncks Corner but is not open to the public. At the time of the Revolution, one of Governor Broughton's descendants, an ardent patriot also named Thomas Broughton, owned Mulberry Plantation. Cross, *Historic Ramblin's,* 69–73; Daniel W. Barefoot, *Touring South Carolina's Revolutionary War Sites* (Winston-Salem, N.C.: John F. Blair, 1999), 46–47.

Allaire evidenced more interest in the ladies. "Diary of Allaire," in Draper, *King's Mountain,* 491.

The British would keep a detachment at Twenty Three Mile House during 1781 to guard the main road to Charles Town from the Santee River and Moncks Corner. Nathanael Greene, *The Papers of General Nathanael Greene,* vol. 8, *30 March–10 July 1781,* ed. Dennis M. Conrad (Chapel Hill: University of North Carolina Press, 1995), 483 and n5.

4.16.80 Strawberry Ferry was on the western branch of the Cooper River at Childsbury ten to twelve miles east of Twenty Three Mile House. Bonneau Ferry, which crossed the eastern branch of the Cooper River approximately three miles before the two branches merged, was established as early as 1712 to provide a crossing for the roads in St. Thomas Parish. Henry Laurens, *The Papers of Henry Laurens,* vol. 3, *Jan. 1, 1759–Aug. 31, 1763,* ed. Philip M. Hamer and George C. Rogers Jr. (Columbia: University of South Carolina Press, 1972), 41n4; Henry Laurens, *The Papers of Henry Laurens,* vol. 4, *Sept. 1, 1763–Aug. 31, 1765,* ed. George C. Rogers Jr. (Columbia: University of South Carolina Press, 1974), 588n8, 590n3; Charleston District map, *Mills' Atlas.*

Maj. Pierce Butler (1744–1822) was a brigadier general in the South Carolina militia but preferred to be known as major, the rank he had held in the British army before retiring in 1773. A native of county Carlow, Ireland, he married a South Carolina heiress, Mary Middleton, and became a wealthy planter and statesman. From 1776 through the 1790s Butler served at various times in the South Carolina General Assembly, in the U.S. Senate, and as a delegate to the U.S. Constitutional

Convention of 1787. Bailey and Cooper, *Biographical Directory of the South Carolina House of Representatives,* 3:108–14. See also Malcolm Bell Jr., *Major Butler's Legacy: Five Generations of a Slaveholding Family* (Athens: University of Georgia Press, 1987).

The British capture of Butler's household goods prompted a local resident to observe, "In some places the Ennemy have behaved very well . . . in others very Ill, some houses they plundered because there was nobody at home, others have been plundered alto they were at home. . . . Mrs. Butler, Wife to the Major, had every thing taken from her." Major Butler apparently "hid in the Swamp & got off." John Louis Gervais to Henry Laurens, April 28, 1780, in Henry Laurens, *The Papers of Henry Laurens,* vol. 15, *Dec. 11, 1778–Aug. 31, 1782,* ed. David R. Chesnutt and C. James Taylor (Columbia: University of South Carolina Press, 2000), 288. (Terry Lipscomb kindly called the editors' attention to this passage.)

4.17.80 "Miller" appears on Henry Mouzon's "Accurate Map of North and South Carolina" (1775) about ten miles as the crow flies southeast of Bonneau Ferry.

Wando River. See Charleston District map, *Mills' Atlas.*

Two structures served as the parish church for St. Thomas and St. Denis Parish. The first church, a brick building constructed in 1708, burned in 1815. The successor and a vestry house dating from the eighteenth century are now just west of state Secondary Road 98 in Berkeley County. Suzanne C. Linder, *Anglican Churches in Colonial South Carolina: Their History and Architecture* (Charleston, S.C.: Wyrick and Co., 2000), 33–38.

4.19.80 Lempriere's Point, Lempriere's Creek (now known as Shem Creek), and ferry were named for Captain Clement Lempriere (d. 1778), who owned a nearby plantation and shipyard that constructed large vessels for the transatlantic trade as well as smaller boats. He served in the South Carolina Commons House (1765–1768) and the revolutionary Provincial Congresses (1775–1776) and the first state General Assembly in 1776. He also commanded colonial privateers and at least two state vessels during the Revolution. Petrona McIver, "Some Towns and Settlements of Christ Church Parish," *Names in South Carolina* 13 (November 1966): 47; Henry Laurens, *The Papers of Henry Laurens,* vol. 6, *Aug. 1, 1768–July 31, 1769,* ed. George C. Rogers Jr. and David R. Chesnutt (Columbia: University of South Carolina Press, 1978), 591n8, 181n8; Edgar and Bailey, *Biographical Directory of the South Carolina House of Representatives,* 2:401.

The patriot fortification is labeled "Lempries" on some maps of the siege of Charles Town. This post was evidently meant to serve as an evacuation point if Charles Town had to be abandoned. Borick, *Gallant Defense,* 146; Fraser, *Patriots, Pistols, and Petticoats,* 123; Hough, *Siege of Charleston,* 165.

4.20.80 Allaire stipulated twenty cannon. "Diary of Allaire," in Draper, *King's Mountain,* 492.

4.21.80 Capt. Samuel Ryerse [or Ryerson] (1752–1812) was raised in Bergen County, New Jersey. Ryerse (his preferred spelling) joined the New Jersey Volunteers and became a captain on March 25, 1777. He would be wounded at the battle of Kings Mountain, captured, and paroled in February 1781. At the end of the war he went to Canada, where he ultimately settled in Norfolk County in the province of Upper Canada. There his gristmills and sawmills would provide the nucleus of Port Ryerse. Ryerse later became colonel of the local militia and in 1800 district judge. His daughter, Amelie Harris, published a memoir of their family life at Port Ryerse. Francess G. Halpenny, ed., *Dictionary of Canadian Biography Online,* vol. 5, *1801–1820* (Toronto: University of Toronto Press, 1983), 732–35; Amelie Harris, "Memoir," in *Loyalist Narratives from Upper Canada,* ed. James J. Talman (1946; repr., New York: Greenwood Press, 1969), 109–48; Samuel Ryerse to George Ryerse, May 19, 1781, in Larry R. Gerlach, ed., *New Jersey in the American Revolution, 1763–1783: A Documentary History* (Trenton: New Jersey Historical Commission, 1975), 261–62.

4.24.80 Charles, Earl Cornwallis (1738–1805), who was promoted to lieutenant general in January 1778, was second in command to General Clinton, the commander in chief in North America. He served in Europe during the Seven Years' War (1756–1763) and became a member of the House of Lords in 1762 upon his father's death. His job after the capture of Charles Town was to hold the South for the British. In this he failed, and his surrender at Yorktown, Virginia, on October 19, 1781, brought the war to a virtual close, but he went on to a distinguished career as governor general in both India and Ireland. Matthew and Harrison, *Oxford Dictionary of National Biography,* 13:474–82; Wickwire and Wickwire, *Cornwallis.*

4.25.80 Wapeta [Wappetaw] Bridge and Meeting House. Wappetaw Bridge over Wappetaw Creek was moved to where Johnson crossed it by act of the Commons House of Assembly in 1767. The Wappetaw community dated from about 1696, when settlers from New England established the Wappetaw Independent Congregational Church or meetinghouse. After quartering troops in the church, the British would burn the building when they evacuated in 1782. McIver, "Towns and Settlements in Christ Church Parish," 46–47; Mabel L. Webber, "Inscriptions from the Church Yard of the Independent or Congregational Church at Wappetaw, Christ Church Parish," *South Carolina Historical and Genealogical Magazine* 25 (July 1924): 136–37.

Allaire noted that the volunteers of Ireland joined them. "Diary of Allaire," in Draper, *King's Mountain,* 493.

4.26.80 Hibben's Ferry, the first ferry to run directly between Charles Town and Mount Pleasant, was operated by Andrew Hibben beginning around 1770. The ferry was located just north of Shutes Folly Island on the Cooper River. Andrew Hibben, a Christ Church planter, was among those who had their property

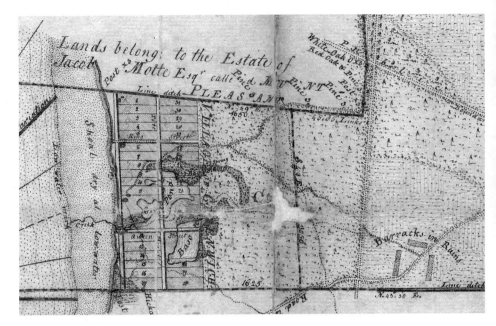

A rare depiction of the unfinished barracks at Mount Pleasant that Johnson termed "very good" if completed. From a plat of the "Estate of Jacob Motte Esqr. called Mount Pleasant" surveyed and drawn by Joseph Purcell, September 27, 1784, contained in Charleston County, Court of Common Pleas, Petitions for Dower, 1791, No. 11a. Courtesy of the South Carolina Department of Archives and History

confiscated after the war for being Loyalists. Hibben, however, maintained that he was forced to cooperate with the British and that, among other activities, he had helped American prisoners of war escape from captivity. In 1785 the legislature exempted him from the confiscation act, but he died before obtaining relief. McIver, "Towns and Settlements in Christ Church Parish," 48; Charleston District, *Mills' Atlas*; Kathy R. Coker, "The Punishment of Revolutionary War Loyalists in South Carolina" (Ph.D. diss., University of South Carolina, 1987), 211–13.

Construction of these barracks evidently began in 1777 inasmuch as the Treasury Journal entries for May 1778 recorded sums due for surveying the site, laying out roads, and wagon hire from December 1, 1777, to April 30, 1778, but the facilities were still unfinished a decade later when the South Carolina legislature directed the governor to expedite their completion. Although not large enough to satisfactorily accommodate all of the 274 officers who were quartered at Haddrell's Point as prisoners of war after the British capture of Charles Town, these barracks housed some of them. Records of the South Carolina Treasury, 1775–1780, pp. [35?] and [38?], South Carolina Department of Archives and History; McIver, "Towns and Settlements in Christ Church Parish, 49; William E. Hemphill, Wylma A.

Wates, and R. Nicholas Olsberg, eds., *State Records of South Carolina: Journals of the General Assembly and House of Representatives, 1776–1780* (Columbia: University of South Carolina Press, 1970), 197, 201; Moultrie, *Memoirs*, 2:116–17. These barracks are depicted on a plat of the "Estate of Jacob Motte Esqr. called Mount Pleasant" made by surveyor Joseph Purcell, September 27, 1784, now located in Charleston County, Court of Common Pleas, Petitions for Dower, 1791, No. 11a, South Carolina Department of Archives and History.

The editors have been unable to identify the doctor captured at the hospital. A document endorsed "List of Officers late at Haddrell's Point, 4th: August, 1781" (*Yearbook, City of Charleston*, 1897, pp. 417–25) provides an extensive roster of names, including those of men who had already been exchanged. It includes surgeons attached to the general hospital and fourteen regimental surgeons, with dates of capture. None of these individuals was captured on April 26, 1780.

Haddrell's Point is now part of Mount Pleasant, South Carolina.

Christopher Gadsden's bridge stretched across the water between Sullivans Island and the mainland in approximately the same location as its predecessor, which had been built to provide an escape route for troops on Sullivans Island in 1776. A floating plank bridge, this temporary structure sank as two hundred men tried to cross it. Gen. Christopher Gadsden (1724–1805), a leading Whig and longtime member of the colonial Commons House of Assembly and successor revolutionary bodies, then oversaw construction of its replacement, which began in September 1776 and lasted about nine months. The finished structure was 3,517 feet long and wide enough for a dozen men to walk abreast; a northern observer termed it "an amazing work," declaring that there was "nothing like it on the continent." Christopher Ward, *The War of the Revolution*, ed. John R. Alden (New York: Macmillan, 1952), 2:675, 677; quote from E. Stanley Godbold, *Christopher Gadsden and the American Revolution* (Knoxville: University of Tennessee Press, 1982), 164–66; Edgar and Bailey, *Biographical Directory of the South Carolina House of Representatives*, 2:259–63. Ewald, *Hessian Journal*, 223, provides a map of the area showing the location of the bridge.

Christ Church was the second Anglican church on this site. Fire destroyed the first building in 1725; and a second, dedicated in 1728, would be burned by the British in 1782. A third structure incorporated the walls of the second in 1794. The site is just south of U.S. 17 in Mount Pleasant. Linder, *Anglican Churches*, 26–31.

"Sing content with our hard fate on the cold ground" is a variant of two lines from the first verse of "A Soldier's Song," which was popular with Loyalists. *Songs, Naval and Military* (New York: printed by James Rivington, 1779), 45–46, Early American Imprints, Series 1: Evans, 1639–1800, Readex Digital Collections No. 16530.

4.28.80 Fort Lempriere. See 4.19.80 above.

4.30.80 Lempriere Ferry was to operate every day of the year, day and night, as authorized by the colonial legislature in 1765. Clement Lempriere was also required to compensate passengers for unreasonable delays. Cooper and McCord, *Statutes at Large of South Carolina,* 9:208–9.

5.2.80 Captain Doyle was probably Sir John Doyle (1750–1834), who began his army career as an ensign in 1771; two years later he was promoted to lieutenant. After distinguishing himself at the battle of Brooklyn (1776), he helped Lord Rawdon raise the Volunteers of Ireland (a Loyalist regiment recruited in America). Becoming a captain of this unit in 1778, Doyle participated in the battle of Monmouth Courthouse. A distinguished military career ensued, and he would eventually become a full general, member of Parliament, a baronet, and Knight of the Bath. Matthew and Harrison, *Oxford Dictionary of National Biography,* 16:836–38; Katcher, *Encyclopedia of British, Provincial, and German Army Units,* 77, 101.

Lt. John Taylor (1742–1822), a member of the New Jersey Volunteers, became a lieutenant on July 2, 1776, and a captain on August 26, 1780. Captured at the battle of Kings Mountain, he escaped on November 5, 1780, with Lt. Anthony Allaire and others. At the end of war, he moved to Nova Scotia. Jonas Howe, "Major Ferguson's Riflemen—The American Volunteers," *Acadiensis* 6 (October 1906): 240; Moss, *Roster of the Loyalists in the Battle of Kings Mountain,* 80.

A Lt. John Wilson is probably the man to whom Johnson referred, but which John remains in doubt. Both the Queens Rangers and the Volunteers of Ireland had Lts. John Wilson, and both units were operating in the vicinity after Clinton strengthened the forces on the north side of the Cooper River with newly arrived troops from New York. Because the other officers referred to were in provincial, not militia, units, and the date is very early for the South Carolina Loyalist militia to be serving in this area, it is unlikely that this Lieutenant Wilson was a militia officer. W. O. Raymond, "Roll of Officers of the British American or Loyalist Corps, 1775–1783," *Collections of the New Brunswick Historical Society* 5 (1904): 259; Clinton, *American Rebellion,* 166–67.

Haddrell's Point. See 4.26.80 above.

A fort on a causeway is located on Johann Ewald's contemporary "Plan of the Siege of Charlestown in South Carolina" in Ewald, *A Hessian Journal: Captain Johann Ewald,* 223.

5.3.80 The capture of the hospital ship was described in more detail by another British officer: "Last night two boats with sailors boarded an unrigg'd ship lying at anchor in Cooper River a little above the Town & towed her up to the Ship yard, they tho't she was a prison ship, but she proves to be an hospital for the small pox, above 30 people in her." Peebles, *John Peebles' American War,* 369.

5.4.80 Allaire's proud entry differs considerably. "Diary of Allaire," in Draper, *King's Mountain,* 494.

5.6.80 Lieutenant Nash is identified by another British officer as Lt. Lovett Ashe. Ashe served with the Thirty-eighth Regiment and was commissioned ensign in 1772 and lieutenant in 1776. Peebles, *John Peebles' American War,* 370; Ford, *British Officers in the American Revolution,* 19.

This engagement, known as the battle of Lenud's Ferry, was another major victory for Tarleton and his dragoons. The patriot cavalry force, commanded by Col. Anthony White, suffered high casualties: eleven men were killed, thirty wounded, and sixty-seven captured. The British Legion lost two men. Peckham, *Toll of Independence,* 70; Tarleton, *History of the Campaigns of 1780 and 1781,* 19–20.

Col. William Washington and Daniel Horry Jr. See 4.13.80 above.

5.7.80 Capt. Charles Hudson of the Royal Navy commanded the HMS *Richmond* (32 guns). He had previously been captain of the *Orpheus,* which was burned at Rhode Island in 1778. On September 5, 1781, he participated in the crucial battle of the Chesapeake Capes, which led to French control of the waters around Yorktown and Cornwallis's surrender on October 19; meanwhile, Hudson and his vessel were captured by the French on September 11. Hudson, however, was eventually promoted to rear admiral. William L. Clowes, *The Royal Navy: A History from the Earliest Times to the Present* (London: Sampson Low, Marston & Co., 1897–1903), 4:48, 75, 109, 111; Clinton, *American Rebellion,* 631.

Col. William Scott of South Carolina was left in command of Fort Moultrie when Col. C. C. Pinckney and the majority of the First South Carolina Regiment were withdrawn into Charles Town. Following the capitulation of the fort, Scott remained a prisoner until his exchange in June 1781. Heitman, *Historical Register,* 486; McCrady, *South Carolina in the Revolution, 1775–1780,* 483; Borick, *Gallant Defense,* 205–6.

Lunt was the matchcord with which guns were fired. *Oxford English Dictionary,* 2nd ed., s.v. "lunt."

Interestingly enough, both Johnson and Allaire counted only regulars, not militia, in their tallies of the number of men under Scott's command. "Diary of Allaire," in Draper, *King's Mountain,* 494–95.

Black cattle was a loose term referring variously to Spanish stock from the West Indies, horned cattle in general, and, as were most of the above, any cattle raised for beef instead of milk. Lewis C. Gray, *History of Agriculture in the Southern United States to 1860* (1933; repr., Gloucester, Mass.: Peter Smith, 1958), 1:203–4; Mart Stewart, "'Whether Wast, Deodand, or Stray': Cattle, Culture, and the Environment in Early Georgia," *Agricultural History* 65 (Summer 1991): 5; Terry G. Jordan, *Trails to Texas: Southern Roots of Western Cattle Ranching* (Lincoln: University of Nebraska Press, 1981), 39.

5.8.80 Gen. Benjamin Lincoln (1733–1810), born in Massachusetts, was a farmer, a member of the colonial legislature, the provincial congress, and a lieutenant colonel of the local militia before the war. On February 19, 1777, he was commissioned major general in the Continental line. In September 1778 Congress named him to command the Southern Department, and he reached Charles Town in December. Captured at the fall of Charles Town, he was exchanged and would command troops under Washington at the siege of Yorktown. From 1781 to 1783 he was secretary of war. He also enjoyed a respectable scholarly career, becoming a member of the American Academy of Arts and Sciences and the Massachusetts Historical Society. Selesky, *Encyclopedia of the American Revolution,* 1:637–39. See also David B. Mattern, *Benjamin Lincoln and the American Revolution* (Columbia: University of South Carolina Press, 1995).

The "insolent request" probably referred to Articles VII and X of Benjamin Lincoln's proposed Articles of Capitulation. The first would have allowed the garrison to "march out with shouldered arms, drums beating, and colours flying"; the second would have given a year to inhabitants who did not "choose to continue under the British government, to dispose of their effects, real and personal, in the State, without any molestation whatever, or to remove such part thereof as they choose, as well as themselves and families. . . ." Clinton and Marriot Arbuthnot rejected both provisions. Borick, *Gallant Defense,* 247–50, includes the quotations.

A carcase is an artillery projectile filled with flammables designed to set fire to wooden defenses and buildings. *Oxford English Dictionary,* 2nd ed., s.v. "carcass, carcase."

5.12.80 Gen. Alexander Leslie (c. 1740–1794) served as lieutenant colonel of the Sixty-fourth Regiment in Massachusetts in 1775 and the northern campaigns thereafter. A major general by 1780, he would operate briefly in Virginia during the fall of 1780 and with Cornwallis in North Carolina in 1781. In October he succeeded Cornwallis as the commander of the southern theater and presided over the British evacuation of Charles Town in December 1782. Selesky, *Encyclopedia of the American Revolution,* 1:620–21.

Capt. Frederick DePeyster (1758–1834), known as "Feady," was a brother of Abraham DePeyster (3.10.80 above). His first command was a company of the Loyalist Nassau Blues, a unit that was absorbed into the New York Volunteers by late 1779; his commission as captain was awarded October 18, 1781. After service with the volunteers in South Carolina, he went to St. John, New Brunswick, but later returned to New York. Sabine, *Biographical Sketches of Loyalists,* 1:374; Philip Klingle, "Soldiers of Kings," *Journal of Long Island History* 12 (Spring 1976): 29, 34.

The drugs which Johnson secured were fairly common, but three merit explanation. "Jallop": *Phytolacca americana,* commonly known as pokeberry or jalap, was used as a purgative or for treating rheumatism. It also served as "an ointment for sore eyes," as well as a poultice for insect bites. Quotation from Nelson Coon, *Using Plants for Healing* (Emmaus, Pa.: Rodale Press, 1979), 156. See also Harold B. Gill Jr., *The Apothecary in Colonial Virginia* (Charlottesville: University Press of Virginia, 1972), 47.

Ipecacuannah: *Euphorbia ipecacuanhae,* commonly known as ipecac, was used as an emetic and purgative during the Revolution. Coon, *Using Plants for Healing,* 216; Gill, *Apothecary in Colonial Virginia,* 47.

Cantharides were derived from the dried insect *Cantharsis vesicatoria,* or Spanish fly, which contains the anhydride of cantharidic acid. Cantharides provided the chief active ingredient in blistering plasters during the Revolution. Gill, *Apothecary in Colonial Virginia,* 47; Walter H. Lewis and Memory P. F. Elvin-Lewis, *Medical Botany: Plants Affecting Man's Health* (New York: John Wiley & Sons, 1977), 326.

Dr. William Locock, commissioned a surgeon during the Cherokee War (1759–1761), subsequently maintained a smallpox hospital for African Americans at his home in Charles Town. Waring, *History of Medicine in South Carolina,* 263.

Allaire omitted the time of the British entry into Charles Town as well as Johnson's and DePeyster's acquisition of drugs. "Diary of Allaire," in Draper, *King's Mountain,* 495.

5.14.80 Allaire called Johnson's "Poor deluded Officers" "Rebel dogs"; other changes in the wording were less substantive. "Diary of Allaire," in Draper, *King's Mountain,* 495.

5.15.80 The location of the magazine was "the south side of Magazine-street, to which it gave the name, about midway between Archdale and Mazyck-streets." The explosion set the town on fire, which "was got out by the activity of the Militia inhabitants & Negroes before evening, having burnt a Barrack, the gaol, & house of Correction. . . . Very Strange Management to Store up loaded Arms in a Magazine, of Powder." Peebles, *John Peebles' American War,* 374. For Whig accounts of this explosion, see Joseph Johnson, *Traditions and Reminiscences Chiefly of the American Revolution in the South* (1851; repr., Spartanburg, S.C.: Reprint Co., 1972), 274–75, and General William Moultrie, who noted that a British officer told him that had the ten thousand pounds of powder stored in the nearby magazine all gone off, it would have blown "your town to hell!" Moultrie, *Memoirs,* 2:109–11.

Capt. Robert Collins was commissioned first lieutenant in the Royal Artillery in 1771. Lt. Alexander McLeod of the Forty-second Regiment was commissioned ensign in 1775 and promoted to lieutenant in 1777. Ford, *British Officers in the American Revolution,* 50, 121.

Another British officer identified Lieutenant Gordon as Lt. John William Gordon of the artillery. Peebles, *John Peebles' American War,* 374.

5.18.80–5.20.80 Allaire compressed the dates. "Diary of Allaire," in Draper, *King's Mountain,* 496.

5.21.80 Mr. or Mrs. Pinckney. This entry is illegible and it is impossible to tell whether Johnson wrote Mr. or Mrs. Pinckney. Mrs. Charles (Frances Brewton)

Pinckney was the wife of Charles Pinckney Sr. (1732–1782), whose Snee Farm was located in Christ Church Parish only a short ride from Lempriere's Point. Charles Pinckney Sr. was a member of the governor's council and as such on April 13 escaped from Charles Town with Gov. John Rutledge and two other councilors. Rutledge ultimately reached North Carolina, but Pinckney and fellow councilor Daniel Huger returned to Charles Town sometime after May 24 and took British protection. The Pinckneys' son, Charles Jr., a militia officer, was captured by the British when the city fell and paroled to his home in town. Given the absence of the two men when Johnson was there, Mrs. Pinckney was then probably the one in charge of the plantation. Edgar and Bailey, *Biographical Directory of the South Carolina House of Representatives,* 2:522–24; James Haw, *John and Edward Rutledge of South Carolina* (Athens: University of Georgia Press, 1997), 134–39; Marty Mathews, *Forgotten Founder: The Life and Times of Charles Pinckney* (Columbia: University of South Carolina Press, 2004), 18.

5.23.80 Allaire mentioned that he saw sixty or seventy ships entering the harbor that afternoon. "Diary of Allaire," in Draper, *King's Mountain,* 496.

5.24.80 Lt. Col. Nisbet Balfour (1743–1823) had been an ensign in the Fourth Regiment in 1761; promoted to captain in 1770, he was wounded in the battle of Bunker Hill five years later. In 1778 he became lieutenant colonel of the Twenty-third Regiment, or Royal Welsh Fusiliers. After the fall of Charles Town, he led the expedition into the backcountry that Johnson chronicles and for some time commanded the British post at Ninety Six (6.22.80 below). In August 1780 he succeeded Gen. James Paterson as commandant of Charles Town, a post which he retained during most of the British occupation of the city. Ironically, despite his sophisticated understanding of the relationship between military measures and "the fluctuating State of Politicks," he further alienated Whigs by sanctioning the execution of a prominent South Carolinian, Col. Isaac Hayne, who had violated his parole. Following the war, Balfour served in Parliament, participated in the campaigns on the Continent in the 1790s, and became a full general in 1803. George S. McCowen, *The British Occupation of Charleston, 1780–82* (Columbia: University of South Carolina Press, 1972), 13; Selesky, *Encyclopedia of the American Revolution,* 1:50–51; Matthew and Harrison, *Oxford Dictionary of National Biography,* 3:541–42.

Allaire omitted Balfour's orders. "Diary of Allaire," in Draper, *King's Mountain,* 496.

5.25.80 The shipyard on Charles Town neck outside of town was established about 1763 by Captain Robert Cochran (c. 1735–1824), who originally came from Massachusetts. After leasing the facility to Paul Pritchard for awhile, he offered it and five workmen to the state in March 1777 for £1,200 per year, which the commissioners of the navy accepted. David Hamilton was hired to manage it. But proximity to town tempted the workers and sailors from ships under repair to go to town, "get Drunk," and quit their posts. So the commissioners turned to Pritchard, who in 1778 sold the state a three-quarters interest in his larger shipyard across the Cooper River at Hobcaw Point. Laurens, *Papers*, 10:385n; Alexander S. Salley Jr., ed., *Journal of the Commissioners of the Navy, October 9, 1776–March 1, 1779* (Columbia, S.C.: The State Co., 1912–13), 51, 55, 59, 177, 197.

Allaire, who went to the shipyard, provides additional detail. "Diary of Allaire," in Draper, *King's Mountain*, 496.

5.26.80 Maj. Charles Graham. See 3.5.80 above.

Capt. George Peacock of the Seventh Regiment of Foot (Royal Fusiliers) had been commissioned lieutenant March 2, 1763; on January 18, 1777, he was promoted to captain. Katcher, *Encyclopedia of British, Provincial, and German Army Units*, 31; Ford, *British Officers in the American Revolution*, 142.

Although referred to as Lt. Col. Paterson by both Johnson and Allaire, he was probably Lt. Col. Thomas Pattinson, who, according to Sabine, died at Charles Town before December 1782. Nevertheless, on April 21, 1783, someone at Flushing, New York, identified as "Thomas Pattinson, Lt. Col." signed a document describing the current distribution of the Prince of Wales Volunteers. However, no Pattinson appeared with the Prince of Wales Regiment on the extensive "List of Officers . . ." under the command of Sir Guy Carleton, dated November 25, 1783, in Davies, *Documents of the American Revolution*, 21:227–50. Sabine, *Biographical Sketches of Loyalists*, 2:153; K. G. Davies, ed., *Documents of the American Revolution, 1770–1783*, vol. 19, *Calendar 1781–1783 and Addenda 1770–1780* (Shannon: Irish University Press, 1978), 397; "Diary of Allaire," in Draper, *King's Mountain*, 496.

Ten Mile House was located ten miles from Charles Town on the main road going west out of the city. It and similar taverns or their successors were long-lived institutions; as early as 1740, for example, Ten Mile House had become a known reference point; thirty-five years later sailors absent without leave frequented it; and in 1781 the British posted troops there. Henry A. M. Smith, "Goose Creek," *South Carolina Historical and Genealogical Magazine* 29 (January 1928): 2; Greene, *Papers*, 8:483.

The fresh fruit was used to prevent and treat scurvy. Dr. James Lind of the HMS *Salisbury* demonstrated the benefits of citrus fruits and published the results of his experiments as early as 1753, but the navy did not officially adopt his findings until 1795. In the interim, however, individual commanders could act on his recommendations. Oscar Reiss, *Medicine and the American Revolution: How Diseases and Their Treatments Affected the Colonial Army* (Jefferson, N.C.: McFarland, 1998), 130–32.

Six Mile House is identified on the Charleston District map, *Mills' Atlas*, at the convergence of the Goose Creek and Dorchester roads.

Allaire noted that temporary bough houses were used as shelter from the sun by the troops near Ten Mile House. "Diary of Allaire," in Draper, *King's Mountain*, 496.

5.27.80 Twenty Three Mile House. See 4.15.80 above.

Allaire, who was not with Johnson at this point, has an entirely different entry. "Diary of Allaire," in Draper, *King's Mountain,* 496.

5.28.80 Moncks Corner. See 4.13.80 above.

John Giles. See 4.14.80 above.

Allaire named the ladies. "Diary of Allaire," in Draper, *King's Mountain,* 496.

5.29.80 Allaire indicated they spent the afternoon at Lady Colleton's. "Diary of Allaire," in Draper, *King's Mountain,* 496.

5.30.80 Gen. William Moultrie owned the 800-acre North Hampton Plantation in Upper St. John Parish. Pooshee Plantation, consisting of 1,290 acres, lay just east of North Hampton and was first owned by Pierre De St. Julien before being acquired by the Ravenel Family. Pooshee is thought to have been named for the nearby Pooshee Swamp. Both plantations are now covered by Lake Moultrie. George D. Terry, "Eighteenth Century Plantation Names in Upper St. John's, Berkeley," *Names in South Carolina* 26 (Winter 1979): 16–17.

5.31.80 Greenland Swamp, which was named for John Greenland, one of the initial landholders in the area, branched off from the Santee River and is identified on the Charleston District map of *Mills' Atlas.* Henry Mouzon's original plan for the Santee Canal connected the natural water courses of Greenland Swamp with various parts of the Cooper River. George D. Terry, "'Champaign Country': A Social History of an Eighteenth Century Lowcountry Parish in South Carolina, St. John's Berkeley County" (Ph.D. diss., University of South Carolina, 1981), 51; Cross, *Historic Ramblin's,* 208.

6.1.80 Nelson's Ferry crossed the Santee River north of Eutawville between Charleston and Sumter districts (*Mills' Atlas*). Although James Beard initiated the ferry, Jared Nelson operated it by 1762. It had been most recently vested in him in 1779. Anne King Gregorie, *History of Sumter County, South Carolina* (Sumter, S.C.: Library Board of Sumter County, 1954), 121; Terry W. Lipscomb, "South Carolina Revolutionary Battles: Part 3," *Names in South Carolina* 22 (Winter 1975): 38; Cooper and McCord, *Statutes at Large of South Carolina,* 9:268.

This engagement, known as Buford's Massacre or the battle of the Waxhaws, should not be confused with the battle of Hanging Rock, which occurred on August 6, 1780. Although the details of the battle of the Waxhaws remain controversial, the Continental commander, Col. Abraham Buford of Virginia, who realized his position was indefensible against cavalry, surrendered shortly after the battle began. But some of Tarleton's dragoons probably continued to kill Continental soldiers. The resulting "massacre" and its mythological exaggeration outraged backcountry Carolinians whose memories of "Tarleton's Quarter" converted many previously neutral individuals to the patriot cause. Tarleton, *History of the Campaigns of 1780 and 1781,* 27–32; J. Tracy Power, "'The Virtue of Humanity Was Totally Forgot': Buford's Massacre, May 29, 1780," *South Carolina Historical Magazine* 93 (January 1992): 5–14; Scotti, *Brutal Virtue,* 173–78. Also see the introduction, p. xxx.

Lt. Lachlan McDonald of the British Legion had served in Fraser's Highlanders during the Seven Years' War as a sergeant and later became captain of a volunteer company. After the war, he settled in New York. In the 1776 expedition against Charles Town, he was taken prisoner but escaped two years later and joined the British at Philadelphia. Appointed lieutenant, he served in the Caledonian Volunteers until the unit was merged into the British Legion in July 1778. He then continued with the British Legion. Memorial of Lachlan McDonald of New York by Lt. Col. Banastre Tarleton, from Henry Clinton Papers, vol. 101, item 45, William L. Clements Library, University of Michigan, available from the On-Line Institute for Advanced Loyalist Studies, "Infantry Officers of the British Legion"; Katcher, *Encyclopedia of British, Provincial, and German Army Units,* 84.

Ensign Campbel was probably Peter Campbell, an infantry officer serving with the cavalry of the British Legion in Capt. James Edwards's company. On-Line Institute for Advanced Loyalist Studies, "Infantry Officers of the British Legion"; Tarleton, *History of the Campaigns of 1780 and 1781,* 84.

Lieutenant Patterson was probably Thomas Patterson, who on December 31, 1777, was made cornet of the Seventeenth Light Dragoons, one troop of which served with the British Legion in the South. Ford, *British Officers in the American Revolution,* 141; Katcher, *Encyclopedia of British, Provincial, and German Army Units,* 24. Tarleton's *History of the Campaigns of 1780 and 1781,* however, identifies the wounded dragoon as Lieutenant Pateschall (p. 84).

6.3.80 "Camble" appears on Mouzon's map (Mouzon, "Accurate Map of North and South Carolina," 1775) near a fork in the Congaree Road just west of the Santee River. An Alexd. Camble and sixty-four other inhabitants of St. Marks Parish signed a petition advocating leniency toward a local Loyalist in 1783. Theodora J. Thompson and Rosa S. Lumpkin, eds., *Journals of the House of Representatives, 1783–1784,* State Records of South Carolina (Columbia: University of South Carolina Press, 1977), 21.

6.4.80 The fourth of June was the birthday of King George III.

6.5.80 Cave Hall, previously known as Wright's Bluff, was the plantation of William Russell Thomson, who had served as a lieutenant in the Third South Carolina Regiment of Continental Troops. His grandfather, Col. Moses Thomson, purchased the land from the estate of Chief Justice Robert Wright in 1755. The cave described by Johnson is one of several in the limestone formations of the area. Alexander S. Salley Jr., "Colonel Moses Thomson and Some of His Descendants,"

South Carolina Historical and Genealogical Magazine 3 (April 1902): 108–10; Sarah Brice, "Cave Hall," ms., 1997, Calhoun County Museum and Cultural Center, as well as information kindly supplied by Deborah Rowland, director of this facility.

The titular governor of Georgia was John Adam Treutlen, for on the fifth and sixth of June the commander of the expedition, Lt. Col. Nisbet Balfour, reported that "Mr. Treutle, the late Governor of Georgia" who had been paroled by Cornwallis before his identity was known, had been captured by local inhabitants and was being sent to headquarters. Balfour to Gen. James Paterson, June 5, 1780, New York Public Library, *Calendar of the Emmet Collection of Manuscripts etc. Relating to American History* (New York: presented to the New York Public Library by John S. Kennedy, 1900), 348; Balfour to Cornwallis, June 6, 1780, Cornwallis Papers, PRO 30/11/2 f. 96–98, South Carolina Department of Archives and History.

A native of Württemberg or Austria, Treutlen became a merchant, schoolteacher, planter, and the first elected governor of Georgia. He served in that office from May 1777 until January 1778. Sometime after the incident related here, he was released and returned to a plantation near Orangeburg, South Carolina, where in the spring of 1782 he was killed for personal or political reasons. That a Loyalist, James Swinney, claimed credit for the murder suggests that politics figured in his death. Kenneth Coleman and Charles S. Gurr, eds., *Dictionary of Georgia Biography* (Athens: University of Georgia Press, 1983), 2:999–1000; Lambert, *South Carolina Loyalists,* 226n18. For a philosophical summary of Treutlen's rise and fall by a man who knew him, see Henry Melchior Muhlenberg, *The Journals of Henry Melchior Muhlenberg,* ed. Theodore G. Tappert and John W. Doberstein (Philadelphia: Evangelical Lutheran Ministerium of Pennsylvania and Adjacent States, 1942–1958), 3:216–17. Edna Q. Morgan, *John Adam Treutlen, Georgia's First Constitutional Governor: His Life, Real and Rumored* (Springfield, Ga.: Historic Effingham Society, 1998) provides a recent biography.

"Titular" governor became "new fangled" governor in Allaire's version. "Diary of Allaire," in Draper, *King's Mountain,* 497.

6.6.80 Although two Colonel Thomsons, a father and son, were prominent in this area of St. Matthew Parish, this figure was the father, Col. William Thomson (1727–1796). He served with the Continental forces until 1778, when he resigned to lead the Orangeburg militia. His plantation, Belleville, was confiscated and garrisoned by the British after the fall of Charles Town. Belleville was located along the Congaree River in modern-day Calhoun County, "within sight" of the British post at Fort Motte. Alexander S. Salley Jr., *The History of Orangeburg County, South Carolina* (1898; repr., Baltimore: Regional Publishing Co., 1969), 377–79. For a biographical sketch emphasizing Thomson's public offices, see Edgar and Bailey, *Biographical Directory of the South Carolina House of Representatives,* 2:669–71.

"To take protection" was to attest to one's loyalty to the British Crown. Protection and allegiance were considered the reciprocal duties of a sovereign and his or her subjects.

6.10.80 Beaver Creek. Big Beaver Creek flows into the Congaree River approximately nineteen miles southeast of Congaree Stores (6.12.80 below). Orangeburg District map, *Mills' Atlas.*

Maj. Charles Graham. See 3.5.80 above.

A firelock is a "gun-lock in which sparks produced . . . ignite the priming." Thus a weapon so equipped. *Oxford English Dictionary,* 2nd ed., s.v. "firelock."

Henry Melcolm could not be identified.

6.12.80 Congaree Stores was "a few hundred yards below Granby," a small settlement at Friday's Ferry on the western side of the Congaree River. Known first as "The Congarees," it was called Granby by the time of the Revolution, presumably in honor of Charles Manners, the Marquis of Granby, who was a supporter of colonial rights. John Hammond Moore, *Columbia and Richland County: A South Carolina Community, 1740–1990* (Columbia: University of South Carolina Press, 1993), 29.

In 1774 John Chestnut advertised the sale of several properties; these included his firm's "commodious and well situated stores" at Granby on the Congaree River. *South Carolina and American General Gazette,* September 2, 1774.

Lt. Col. Alexander Innes amplified Johnson's observation about the productivity of the area by noting, "Thank God the Rebels have good stores and with proper care much may be drawn for the supply of Charles Town the Army and the poor Country people if care is only taken." Innes to Cornwallis, June 8, 1780, Cornwallis Papers, PRO 30/11/2, f. 114ff., South Carolina Department of Archives and History.

6.14.80 Capt. George Peacock and Col. Thomas Patterson [or Pattinson]. See 5.26.80 above for their identifications.

6.15.80 Saludy Ferry was operated by Moses Kirkland, who owned sawmills and flour mills in the lower portion of the fork between the Broad and Saluda rivers. In 1765 he was granted the right to operate a ferry between his lands on both sides of the Saluda River. Henry Laurens, *The Papers of Henry Laurens,* vol. 7, *Aug. 1, 1769–Oct. 9, 1771,* ed. George C. Rogers Jr. and David R. Chesnutt (Columbia: University of South Carolina Press, 1979), 297n8.

6.16.80 High Hill Creek flows into the Saluda River. Lexington District map, *Mills' Atlas.*

6.18.80 Lt. Col. Alexander Innes. See 3.5.80 above.

Capt. James Wright, of the South Carolina Royalists, was the owner of two hundred acres of land in the Ninety Six District (6.22.80 below). He was imprisoned and tried for treason in 1775. Released upon taking an oath, he later made his way to Florida and joined the British at St. Augustine in 1778. After the war, he settled in Shelburne, Nova Scotia. Palmer, *Biographical Sketches of Loyalists,* 948–49.

6.19.80 Several Cooks lived in the area, but this plantation probably belonged to Isaac Cook, whose holdings were along Beaver Dam Creek, a tributary of the Saluda River about four miles northwest of Bush River. Newberry County was an important center of early Quakerism in South Carolina, and until 1822 a large number of Friends worshiped at Bush River Monthly Meeting. However, many of them moved to Ohio to escape the expansion of slavery in upcountry South Carolina, and their loss dealt "a severe blow" to Newberry County. Because the Quakers usually disowned members who bore arms, Captain Cook may not have been a member of this meeting. Arthur Barnett, Unrecorded Plat for Land Not Granted on the Saluda River and Beaver Dam Creek, Series S213197, Box 1, Item 53, South Carolina Department of Archives and History; Thomas H. Pope, *The History of Newberry County, South Carolina* (Columbia: University of South Carolina Press, 1973), 1:83–84.

Cornwallis ordered that "the field-officers of the Rebel Militia, members of their council, assembly men, and acting magistrates" were "to go on their paroles to the islands on the coast between Charlestown and Beaufort . . ." until their backgrounds and principles could be investigated. Isolating them there, Cornwallis hoped, would also neutralize their influence with others on the mainland. Cornwallis to Sir Henry Clinton, June 30, 1780, *Correspondence of Charles, First Marquis Cornwallis,* ed. Charles Ross (London, John Murray, 1859), 1:499.

6.20.80 Several Davenports, including Francis, James, and Joseph, lived on or near Little River in the Revolutionary era, and at least James and Joseph provided supplies for American troops. Joseph, who served as a local road commissioner, appears to have been the most prominent during the pre-Revolutionary period and may therefore have been a captain in the colonial militia. A bridge crossed Little River at his place in 1789. Accounts Audited of Claims, Files 1754 and 1755, South Carolina Department of Archives and History; *South Carolina Gazette,* December 17, 1772; Brent Holcomb, comp., *Newberry County, South Carolina: Minutes of the County Court, 1785–1798* (Easley, S.C.: Southern Historical Press, 1977), 101.

6.22.80 The fording place, known as "Island Ford" or "Indian Island Ford," was on the line later established between Laurens and Newberry counties about one-quarter mile above the falls in the Saluda River. Newberry District map, *Mills' Atlas*; Cooper and McCord, *Statutes at Large of South Carolina,* 9:259; Pope, *History of Newberry County,* 69.

Ninety Six is located west of the Saluda River in present-day Greenwood County. The area was surveyed for a trading post in 1738, and by 1750 a small village had grown up in the vicinity. From November 19 to 21, 1775, a battle at Ninety Six between Whigs and Tories produced the first casualties of the Revolution in South Carolina. Marvin L. Cann, *Ninety Six: A Historical Guide; Old Ninety Six in the South Carolina Backcountry, 1700–1781* (Troy, S.C.: Sleepy Creek Publishing, 1996). Later Gen. Nathanael Greene (11.26.80 below) laid siege to the British post at

Ninety Six from May 22 to June 19, 1781. Although he failed to take the fort, the British evacuated both it and the town shortly thereafter. Selesky, *Encyclopedia of the American Revolution,* 2:838–40; Stephanie L. Holschlag, Michael J. Rodeffer, and Marvin L. Cann, *Ninety Six: The Jail* (Ninety Six, S.C.: Star Fort Historical Commission, 1978).

For the origin of the name, see David P. George Jr., "Ninety Six Decoded: Origins of a Community's Name," *South Carolina Historical Magazine* 92 (April 1991): 69–84.

The Ninety Six District, frequently mentioned in these notes, was composed of modern Abbeville, Anderson, Cherokee, Edgefield, Greenville, Greenwood, Laurens, McCormick, Newberry, Oconee, Pickens, Saluda, Spartanburg, and Union counties. The Ninety Six National Historic Site is operated by the National Park Service about two miles south of the present-day town along S.C. Route 248.

Johnson referred to the aftermath of "Boyd's Uprising" in Ninety Six District during early 1779. At the battle of Kettle Creek, Georgia, on February 14, patriot soldiers under Andrew Pickens defeated a force of Loyalists that had been recruited by Col. James [?] Boyd in North and South Carolina. Imprisoning approximately 150 Loyalists at Ninety Six, Whigs tried many of them between March 22 and April 12, 1779. Half of the prisoners were released, and fifty were convicted but pardoned. The remaining twenty-two were condemned to death, but British threats and patriot fears kept all but five from being executed. Lambert, *South Carolina Loyalists,* 82–85; Robert Scott Davis Jr., "The Loyalist Trials at Ninety Six in 1779," *South Carolina Historical Magazine* 80 (April 1979): 172–81.

6.23.80 Tuckasegee Ford was on the main branch of the Catawba River approximately ten to fifteen miles north of the South Carolina boundary; the engagement to which Johnson referred, however, was the battle of Ramsour's Mill, which occurred on the south branch of the Catawba River, near present-day Lincolnton, North Carolina, approximately twenty miles west of Tuckasegee Ford. Jonathan Price and John Strother, "This First Actual Survey of the State of North Carolina" (1808); William S. Powell, ed., *The North Carolina Gazetteer* (Chapel Hill: University of North Carolina Press, 1968), 282; William Tryon, *The Correspondence of William Tryon and Other Selected Papers,* ed. William S. Powell (Raleigh: North Carolina Division of Archaeology and History, 1980–81), 1:490–91.

Gen. Griffith Rutherford (c. 1731–1800) immigrated to North Carolina from Ireland as a child. In 1776 he served in the North Carolina Provincial Congress and became a brigadier general in the state militia. In August 1780 he would command militia at the battle of Camden, where he was wounded and captured. After the war he served in the North Carolina Senate and later moved to Tennessee. Rutherford County, North Carolina, was named for him. Powell, *Dictionary of North Carolina Biography,* 5:275–76.

Johnson was describing the battle of Ramsour's Mill in North Carolina. About thirteen hundred Loyalists, buoyed by the British capture of Charles Town, assembled under Col. John Moore and encamped at Ramsour's Mill in June 1780. General Rutherford, who planned to combine his force of about one thousand militiamen with another four hundred men commanded by Col. Francis Locke, intended to attack Moore's force. But Locke reached Ramsour's before Rutherford. Beginning the attack around daybreak on June 20, 1780, Locke dispersed the larger Loyalist force. Robert O. DeMond, *The Loyalists in North Carolina during the American Revolution* (1940; repr., Baltimore: Genealogical Publishing Co., 1979), 124–27; William L. Sherrill, *Annals of Lincoln County, North Carolina* (1937; repr., Baltimore: Regional Publishing Co., 1967, 1972), 36–40; John Buchanan, *The Road to Guilford Courthouse: The American Revolution in the Carolinas* (New York: John Wiley & Sons, 1997), 106–10.

6.24.80 Allaire, whose quarters provided a view of the jail, gloated over the fate of the American prisoners there. "Diary of Allaire," in Draper, *King's Mountain*, 499.

7.9.80 Capt. Abraham DePeyster. See 3.10.80 above.

The mill was probably Anderson's Mill on Wilson's Creek, which is thought to antedate the Revolution. John A. Chapman, *A History of Edgefield County from the Earliest Settlements to 1897* (1897; repr., Spartanburg, S.C.: Reprint Co., 1980), 112.

Allaire's similar entry for this date included information about their encounter with two "country women." "Diary of Allaire," in Draper, *King's Mountain*, 499.

7.10.80 Col. James Williams (d. 1780), a Virginian, moved to the Ninety Six District of South Carolina in 1772. He served in the Provincial Congress and General Assembly from 1775 to 1778 and became a colonel of militia in 1779. He would be mortally wounded at the battle of Kings Mountain. His wife, Mary (Wallace), was the mother of eight children. Bailey and Cooper, *Biographical Directory of the South Carolina House of Representatives,* 3:766–68.

7.11.80 Indian Creek is north-northeast of Island Ford. Laurens District map, *Mills' Atlas.*

Ryan was doubtless John Ryan, whose one hundred acres was bisected by Indian Creek. Plat, December 21, 1769, Series S213184, Colonial Plat Books (Copy Series), vol. 20, p. 247, South Carolina Department of Archives and History.

Duncan Creek is ten miles northeast from Indian Creek along the Old Ninety Six Road on the Laurens District map, *Mills' Atlas.*

Because numerous Browns lived in the Duncan Creek area during the late eighteenth century, the editors have been unable to identify this Mrs. Brown. Our best guess is that she was the widow of Nathan Brown (1731–June 28, 1779), who was buried in the cemetery of King's Creek Presbyterian Church, Newberry County, which was ten plus miles from where Johnson was on this date. Works Progress Administration, Historical Records Survey, South Carolina Genealogical Society alphabetical card file of Works Progress Administration cemetery inscriptions, microfiche, South Carolina Department of Archives and History.

7.12.80 Enoree River is about three miles northeast of Dunkin Creek on the Laurens District map, *Mills' Atlas.*

Capt. Frost on Padget Creek may have been Maj. Jonathan Frost. He served in Maj. Daniel Plummer's (Tory) Regiment of the Fair Forest militia from June 1780 until his death in December 1780. Jonathan's widow, Mary, received his back pay in 1782. M. J. Clark, *Loyalists in the Southern Campaign,* 1:322, 326.

Padget Creek flows into the Tyger River five to six miles upstream from the confluence of the Tyger and Peters Creek. Maps of Union and Newberry districts, *Mills' Atlas.*

Col. William Bratton (1742–1815), born in Ireland, came to Pennsylvania with his parents and by 1776 had settled in the area that became York County, South Carolina. He served in the South Carolina General Assembly from 1785 to 1790 and the South Carolina Senate from 1791 to 1795. As a militia colonel, he participated in at least five skirmishes and battles during 1780, including the action mentioned here, Hanging Rock (8.10.80 below), and Mobley's Meeting House (8.15.80 below). Bailey and Cooper, *Biographical Directory of the South Carolina House of Representatives,* 3:88–89. For a recent account of the battle at Fishing Creek, to which Johnson referred, see Walter B. Edgar, *Partisans and Redcoats: The Southern Conflict That Turned the Tide of the American Revolution* (New York: William Morrow, 2001), 66–87.

7.13.80 Lieutenant Hunt was probably Benjamin Hunt, who served in Emmerich's Chasseurs in 1778 and then the British Legion Cavalry. However, Col. Richard Winn, one of the American commanders in the battle, noted that a Lieutenant Hunt of the British cavalry had been wounded, surrendered, and was paroled. Raymond, "Roll of Officers," 253; Richard Winn, "General Richard Winn's Notes—1780," ed. Samuel C. Williams, *South Carolina Historical and Genealogical Magazine* 43 (October 1942): 206. For Winn, see 8.17.80 below.

Capt. Christian Huck was a Loyalist from Pennsylvania who had served with the Bucks County Light Dragoons, which were later attached to the British Legion. While serving in Tarleton's unit, Huck led a raid that destroyed the Aera Ironworks belonging to William Hill and Isaac Hayne on Alison Creek in present-day York County. Shortly thereafter, Huck and a detachment of the British Legion, New York Volunteers, and militia arrived at the home of Whig colonel William Bratton on the evening of July 11, 1780. They had an encounter with Bratton's wife and then proceeded to the neighboring plantation of James Williamson, where they camped. During the night, a Whig force commanded by Cols. Bratton, William Hill, Edward Lacey, and Andrew Neel and Capt. James McClure surrounded Huck's force. They attacked at daybreak and routed the Loyalists. The area of Williamson's plantation, now known as Brattonsville, is located in York County.

Katcher, *Encyclopedia of British, Provincial, and German Army Units,* 83–84; Lipscomb, "South Carolina Battles," 22:33–35; Thomas Cowan, "William Hill and the Aera Ironworks," *Journal of Early Southern Decorative Arts* 13 (November 1987): 3.

Col. Edward Lacey (1742–1813) was a native of Pennsylvania whose first service was in the Seven Years' War. In 1758 he moved to South Carolina and later became an active Whig. By 1780 he was a colonel in the state militia and as such participated in at least seven important battles. During much of the time from 1782 to 1791 he served in the General Assembly. He moved to Tennessee in 1797, however, and then to Kentucky. Bailey and Cooper, *Biographical Directory of the South Carolina House of Representatives,* 3:410–11.

The origin of the name Tiger [or Tyger] River is a bit of a puzzle. One possibility is that the name came from Tygert, a Frenchman who traded in the area during the 1750s; a David Tyger also lived in the Enoree-Tyger settlement in 1760. In addition, "tygers," or cougars, roamed all of the southeastern colonies during the seventeenth and eighteenth centuries. The Tyger River flows into the Broad River in what is now Union County. *Names in South Carolina,* 9:23, 11:47, 13:12; James B. Meriwether, *The Expansion of South Carolina, 1729–1765* (Kingsport, Tenn.: Southern Publishers, 1940), 150n13; John Lawson, *A New Voyage to Carolina,* ed. Hugh Lefler (Chapel Hill: University of North Carolina Press, 1967), 123; Union District map, *Mills' Atlas.*

Sugar Creek empties into Fair Forest Creek in present-day Union County. Fair Forest Creek flows into the Enoree River, which in turn empties into the Broad River. The area around Fair Forest Creek proved to be one of the strongholds of loyalism in South Carolina, perhaps partly by chance and partly because influential Loyalist leaders lived in the vicinity. Union District map, *Mills' Atlas*; Lambert, *South Carolina Loyalists,* 35, 111.

Worn-out, abandoned fields were known as "old fields"; the owner in this case may have been Col. William Wofford (1728–c. 1823), who in the 1760s came to South Carolina from Maryland. He served in the Seven Years' War and as a patriot officer earlier in the Revolution. He moved to North Carolina in 1780 and later to Georgia. Bailey and Cooper, *Biographical Directory of the South Carolina House of Representatives,* 3:785–86.

William's brother John—about whom "very little is known"—had three hundred acres on Sugar Creek surveyed for himself in 1772. Jane Wofford Wait, ed., *The History of the Wofford Family* (1928; repr., Spartanburg, S.C.: Reprint Co., 1993), 50; Plat, Nov. 15, 1772, Series S213184, Colonial Plat Books (Copy Series), vol. 20, p. 486, item 3, South Carolina Department of Archives and History. See also 8.26.80 below.

Maj. Daniel Plummer, who was originally from Pennsylvania, commanded a regiment from Fair Forest in the Ninety Six militia. After being seriously wounded at Kings Mountain, he went to East Florida. Lambert, *S.C. Loyalists,* 111, 265; Palmer, *Biographical Sketches of Loyalists,* 697.

Maj. Zachariah Gibbs was born in Virginia but moved to the Fair Forest Creek area of South Carolina before the Revolution. He fought in the battle of Kettle Creek, after which he was captured, imprisoned, tried, and condemned at Ninety Six but was later reprieved. Raising about 150 men, he joined Ferguson. Gibbs's men would fight at Kings Mountain, but he himself was on another assignment. At the end of the war, he went to Canada. Moss, *Roster of the Loyalists in the Battle of Kings Mountain,* 33; Palmer, *Biographical Sketches of Loyalists,* 312.

The Catawba Nation was a small but important Indian group that could field two hundred warriors in 1756. After the Seven Years' War, the treaty of Augusta provided a 144,000-acre reservation for them on the North and South Carolina border at the confluence of Twelve Mile Creek and the Catawba River. Walter B. Edgar, *South Carolina: A History* (Columbia: University of South Carolina Press, 1998), 208; James H. Merrell, *The Indians' New World: Catawbas and Their Neighbors from European Contact through the Era of Removal* (Chapel Hill: University of North Carolina Press, 1989), 163, 198.

The American commander, Col. Richard Winn, later recalled that "when we took the field after the fall of Charles Town, we often encamped on their [the Catawba's] lands for days together. Those friendly Indians drove us beef from their own stocks and several times brought out their whole force and encamped near us. . . ." Winn, "Notes—1780," 7.

The Broad River, which arises in western North Carolina, flows southeastwardly about twenty miles west of the Catawba Indians' territory. Powell, *North Carolina Gazetteer,* 64; Merrell, *Indians' New World,* 199.

7.15.80 Col. Thomas Fletchall (b. 1725) arrived in South Carolina about 1760 and established himself on Fair Forest Creek, where he became a person of consequence. By 1770 he owned approximately sixteen hundred acres and had been commissioned colonel of the Upper Regiment of the colonial militia from the Ninety Six District, which contained many men who declined to join the Whigs in 1775. Fletchall declared, "I am resolved, and do utterly refuse to take up arms against my King." Arrested in December 1775, he was imprisoned until July 1776. In 1780 he joined the British in Charles Town and later fled to Jamaica when they withdrew from South Carolina. Lambert, *South Carolina Loyalists,* 35–36, 256; Palmer, *Biographical Sketches of Loyalists,* 278.

A mill of this type was described by Oliver Evans in *The Young Mill-Wright and Miller's Guide,* 9th ed. (Philadelphia: Carey, Lea & Blanchard, 1836), 159–64, as "a tub mill," having "a horizontal water wheel" with a vertical shaft that was connected directly to the grindstone. The falling water "is shot on the upper side of the wheel at a tangent to its circumference." Although relatively inefficient, this configuration had several advantages, including "exceeding simplicity and cheapness," little friction, and few bearing parts to wear out. Where sufficient water could be made to fall more than eight feet, a tub mill was therefore the preferred design. A

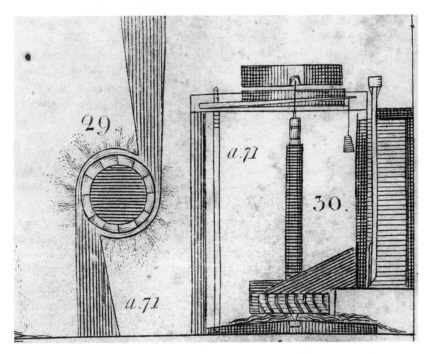

Diagram of a vertical grist mill such as Johnson inspected on July 15, 1780. Oliver Evans, *The Young Mill-Wright and Miller's Guide* . . . (Philadelphia: Carey, Lea & Blanchard, 1836). Courtesy of Rare Books and Special Collections, University of South Carolina Libraries

twenty-foot fall, as at Fletchall's mill, could drive a four-foot millstone at 122 revolutions per minute.

Fair Forest Creek, which featured a shoal with a drop of thirty-six feet over a short distance, would attract many millers in the early nineteenth century. Robert Mills, *Statistics of South Carolina* (1826; repr., Spartanburg, S.C.: Reprint Co., 1972), 758.

Capt. James Dunlap (d. 1781) became a captain in the Queen's Rangers in 1776 and fought with the unit at Brandywine, Philadelphia, Monmouth, and elsewhere in New Jersey. Dunlap later survived several battles in the South Carolina backcountry but was wounded, captured while leading a foraging party, and murdered in the spring of 1781. Draper, *King's Mountain,* 156–64; Bobby G. Moss, *The Loyalists in the Siege of Ninety-Six* (Blacksburg, S.C.: Scotia Hibernia Press, 1999), 40; Greene, *Papers,* 8:71n2; Johnson, *Loyalist Surgeon: War Diary,* 132–33.

Prince's Fort, named for a nearby landowner, had been built during the Cherokee War of 1759–1762. Located on the west side of modern-day Spartanburg, the fort was a circular structure of heavy timbers surrounded by an abatis and a ditch. Lt. Col. Alexander Innes commanded there. Edgar, *Partisans and Redcoats,* 94–97;

McCrady, *South Carolina in the Revolution, 1775–1780*, 613–15. For Innes, see 3.5.80 above.

James McElwain (d.1807) emigrated from Pennsylvania in the early 1750s and received land on Fair Forest Creek in 1755. William A Feaster, *A History of Union County* (Greenville, S.C.: A Press, 1977), 1, 19; Brent Holcomb, ed., *North Carolina Land Grants in South Carolina, 1745–1773* (Greenville, S.C.: A Press, 1980), 25.

McElwain's Creek runs into Fair Forest Creek. Union District map, *Mills' Atlas.*

Allaire and Johnson each gave details that the other omitted. "Diary of Allaire," in Draper, *King's Mountain,* 500–501.

7.16.80 Stephen White purchased this land, where Mitchell Creek (7.31.80 below) joins Fair Forest Creek, in 1773. In 1780 White served in Col. Thomas Brandon's (Whig) regiment, which was composed mostly of men from Union District. White also served for a time under Thomas Sumter. White was dead by March 16, 1782. Brent Holcomb, *Union County, South Carolina, Deed Abstracts,* vol. 1, *Deed Books A–F* (Columbia: SCMAR, 1998), 51; Feaster, *History of Union County,* 22; Bobby G. Moss, *Roster of South Carolina Patriots in the American Revolution* (Baltimore: Genealogical Publishing Co., 1983), 986.

Allaire identified the plantation as Stephen White's and provided slightly more detail. Ferguson would write to Cornwallis from Mitchell Creek on July 21 giving information about commodity prices. "Diary of Allaire," in Draper, *King's Mountain,* 501; Cornwallis Papers, PRO 30/11/2, f. 360–61, South Carolina Department of Archives and History.

7.20.80 Fair Forest Ford was probably five miles southwest of Unionville, where the Union District map, *Mills' Atlas,* shows a bridge in the 1820s.

7.22.80 Lawson's Fork Creek joins the main branch of the Pacolet River one and one-half miles west of the border between Spartanburg and Union districts. Maps of Union and Spartanburg districts, *Mills' Atlas.*

James Woods was granted 250 acres along Fair Forest Creek in 1773. A Whig, he served in the General Assembly from 1776 to 1780 before being murdered on May 10, 1781. Bailey and Cooper, *Biographical Directory of the South Carolina House of Representatives,* 3:786.

Greene River, which originates in Henderson County, North Carolina, turns southeast and empties into the Broad River about five miles north of the South Carolina line in Polk County, North Carolina. Powell, *North Carolina Gazetteer,* 203; *DeLorme North Carolina Atlas and Gazetteer,* 7th ed. (Yarmouth, Maine: DeLorme, 2006), 54.

7.28.80 Col. William Henderson (1748–1788) lived beside the Pacolet River in Ninety Six District. Joining the patriot cause in 1775, he was appointed lieutenant colonel of Continental troops in 1776. Captured at the fall of Charles Town, he was held at Haddrell's Point until he was exchanged several months later. Henderson served in the Second Provincial Congress in 1775–1776 and the General Assembly in 1776, 1779–1780, and 1782–1784; he was also brigadier general of state troops between February 1782 and November 1783. Bailey and Cooper, *Biographical Directory of the South Carolina House of Representatives*, 3:328–29.

7.29.80 Thicketty River or Creek begins in Spartanburg District and runs through Union District into Gilky Creek, which flows into the Broad River. Maps of Spartanburg and Union districts, *Mills' Atlas*.

Allaire termed the rattlesnake "a 'Continental' rattle-snake." "Diary of Allaire," in Draper, *King's Mountain*, 502.

7.30.80 Armstrong Creek flows southwest for about ten miles to empty into Fair Forest Creek approximately thirty miles above its confluence with the Tyger River. Mouzon, "Accurate Map of North and South Carolina," 1775.

The British post at Anderson's Fort, also known as Thicketty Fort, was about 450 yards north of Goucher Creek, some two and one-half miles upriver from the junction of Goucher and Thicketty creeks in present-day Cherokee County. A Whig force under Cols. Isaac Shelby (9.29.80 below), Elijah Clarke (9.25.80 below), Andrew Hampton (10.7.80 below), and Maj. Charles Robertson (10.7.80 below) surrounded the fort on July 30, 1780. The British commander, Col. Patrick Moore (8.5.30 below), initially refused to surrender but soon capitulated. The fort was both well situated and well stocked, and Draper asserts that had "a Ferguson, a Dunlap, or a DePeyster" been in command, the garrison of ninety-three could have resisted "double the number of their assailants." Draper, *King's Mountain*, 86–89; Lipscomb, "South Carolina Battles," 22:36.

Capt. John Cook was born in northern Ireland, immigrated to America in 1745, and settled on Goucher Creek between the Pacolet River and Thicketty Creek. A Loyalist, he served in various capacities in addition to being a member of Maj. Daniel Plummer's Fair Forest regiment of militia. He saw action in several engagements, including the battle of Kings Mountain, and returned to England when the British evacuated Charles Town. By 1807 he was apparently living in Upper Canada. Loyalist Claim Transcript, AO 12/48/247, American Loyalist Claims, National Archives, Kew, Richmond, Surrey, United Kingdom; Carole Troxler, "The Migration of Carolina and Georgia Loyalists to Nova Scotia and New Brunswick" (Ph.D. diss., University of North Carolina, 1974), 265.

7.31.80 Mitchell Creek, a tributary of Fair Forest Creek, is about twelve miles southwest of Armstrong Creek. Union District map, *Mills' Atlas*.

8.1.80 Rocky Mount, near present-day Great Falls on the Catawba River in South Carolina, was a substantial fort garrisoned by 150 local militia and about 150 New York Volunteers. Lt. Col. George Turnbull (3.5.80 above) commanded there on

July 30 when Gen. Thomas Sumter moved against it with some six hundred men. Richard Winn, who was in command of part of the American force, remembered that his men rushed forward, "with bullets in their mouths and powder in their pockets," firing as they charged. The battle lasted for eight hours and produced about a dozen casualties on each side, but the post held out. Rocky Mount was thirty miles northwest of Camden or about fifty miles east of where Johnson was on Mitchell Creek. Winn, "Notes—1780," 211; Selesky, *Encyclopedia of the American Revolution,* 2:997; Peckham, *Toll of Independence,* 73.

8.2.80 Capt. Lewis Bobo was born in Virginia in 1736 and died in the Union District of South Carolina before March 7, 1808, when his will was proved. Bobo served as a captain in Col. Thomas Brandon's Regiment during the Revolution. The Union District map of *Mills' Atlas* identifies a "Bobo's Ford" along the Tyger River and "Capt. Bobo's Plantation House" not far south of the ford. Holcomb, *Union County Deed Abstracts,* 76; *DAR Patriot Index, Centennial Edition,* vol. 1 (Washington, D.C.: National Society of the Daughters of the American Revolution, 1994), 293; Feaster, *History of Union County,* 19; Moss, *South Carolina Patriots,* 79.

Capt. Thomas Hewlett (d. 1780) was the son of Col. Richard Hewlett (d. 1789) of New York. The younger Hewlett served as a captain in the New York Volunteers and was killed at Hanging Rock. Sabine, *Biographical Sketches of Loyalists,* 1:532.

Gen. Thomas Sumter (1734–1832) was born in Virginia, the son of a former indentured servant. After service in the local militia during the Seven Years' War and a trip to London, he was imprisoned for debt, escaped, and absconded to South Carolina, where he married a wealthy widow. From 1775 to 1780 he served in the First and Second Provincial Congresses and the General Assembly. Eventually becoming a colonel, he also participated in several battles, including the defense of Fort Moultrie in June 1776. In 1778 he retired from active service, but the British burned some of his property in May 1780, and he resumed the field. During that summer he led the only really organized resistance movement. Aggressiveness and some success in numerous military engagements during 1780–1781, plus the ability to keep a partisan force in the field, earned him a brigadier general's commission in October 1780 and the nickname "The Gamecock." After the war he again served in the South Carolina Assembly (1783–1790) before becoming a member of the U.S. House of Representatives (1789–1801) and the U.S. Senate (1801–1810). Walter B. Edgar, ed., *The South Carolina Encyclopedia* (Columbia: University of South Carolina Press, 2006), 940–41.

8.5.80 Sgt. Asa Blacksley served under Col. Edmund Fanning in the New York Provincials of the King's American Regiment. He was detached to Ferguson's corps and evidently fought and was captured at Kings Mountain. He returned to active duty in 1781 and was still a sergeant in 1783. That same year, he moved to St. John, New Brunswick, and died there in 1843 at the age of eighty-seven. Moss, *Roster of* *the Loyalists in the Battle of Kings Mountain,* 7; Sabine, *Biographical Sketches of Loyalists,* 1:231.

Capt. Patrick Moore, the Tory commander of Thicketty Fort, was one of Ferguson's captains but may have been elsewhere during the battle of Kings Mountain. Draper's research for *King's Mountain and Its Heroes* yielded contradictory details about Moore's later life (p. 298): some sources said he died at Fort Ninety Six; another claimed he settled in England. Moss, *Roster of the Loyalists in the Battle of Kings Mountain,* 59.

8.6.80 Philip Ford had 150 acres, surveyed in 1769 by William Gist (8.23.80 below), on Gilders Creek, a branch of the Enoree River. Series S213184, Colonial Plat Books (Copy Series), vol. 11, p. 29, South Carolina Department of Archives and History.

Ford's Mill appears on the south side of Gilders Creek on the Greenville District map, *Mills' Atlas.* Colonel Fletchall's (7.15.80 above) regiment of militia mustered "at Ford's," presumably the mill. J. B. O. Landrum, *The Colonial and Revolutionary History of Upper South Carolina* (1897; repr., Spartanburg, S.C.: Reprint Co., 1977), 45.

Jemmy's Creek appears as James Creek on the Spartanburg District map, *Mills' Atlas,* but is identified as Jimmies Creek in Julian J. Petty's "South Carolina Gazetteer Alphabetical Card File," Map Department, Thomas Cooper Library, University of South Carolina, Columbia. The creek was approximately thirteen miles westnorthwest of Bobo's.

8.8.80 Cedar Springs was located south of modern-day Spartanburg at a site which now serves as the campus for the South Carolina School for the Deaf and the Blind. Lipscomb, "South Carolina Battles," 22:35.

The skirmish on August 8, 1780, occurred over a wide area and is known both as the battle of Wofford's Iron Works and the second battle of Cedar Springs. The initial fighting began when Loyalists under Maj. James Dunlap (7.15.80 above) attacked a Whig force near Cedar Springs commanded by Cols. Isaac Shelby, Elijah Clarke (9.25.80 below), and William Graham (10.2.80 below). After a sharp battle, Dunlap was repulsed, but when the main Tory force under Ferguson arrived later, the Whigs withdrew toward Wofford's Iron Works and Lawson's Fork Creek. Ferguson engaged the rear guard of the retreating Whigs until they reached a more defensible position on the north side of the Pacolet River. The definitive account of this affair is found in Draper, *King's Mountain,* 89–102. For summaries and locations, see Lipscomb, "South Carolina Battles," 22:36–37, and Edgar, *Partisans and Redcoats,* 106–7.

Ens. William McFarland [or McFarlane] served in the Second Battalion of Delancey's Brigade. Later promoted to lieutenant, he would drown in the wreck of the transport ship *Martha* in September 1783. M. J. Clark, *Loyalists in the Southern Campaign,* 3:351, 363, 428; Sabine, *Biographical Sketches of Loyalists,* 2:62.

Maj. Burwell Smith and Capt. John Potts were Georgia Whigs. Draper notes that Smith, whose fall was "deeply lamented by Colonel Clarke and his associates," was serving as a major in the Georgia militia at the time. An experienced Indian fighter, he had been active in the settlement of the Georgia frontier. Potts was a captain in the Georgia militia. Draper, *King's Mountain,* 97; Heitman, *Historical Register,* 501, 449.

Ironworks were developed by William Wofford (7.13.80 above) and John Buffington on Lawson's Fork before the Revolution. The South Carolina Assembly subsidized their efforts during 1777. Although the owners sold the property to Simon Berwick in 1779 or 1780, it continued to be known as Wofford's Iron Works. Tories, allegedly under the command of William (Bloody Bill) Cunningham, destroyed the facility in November 1781. Bailey and Cooper, *Biographical Directory of the South Carolina House of Representatives,* 3:785–86; Landrum, *History of Upper South Carolina,* 356; Laurens, *Papers,* 10:338n; Cowan, "William Hill and the Aera Ironworks," 8.

Allaire's account differed in details and added that "Col[s]. Clarke [and] Johnson" and twenty privates were seen wounded. Draper believed that Johnson was actually Maj. Charles Robertson. "Diary of Allaire," in Draper, *King's Mountain,* 503. For Robertson, see 10.7.80 below.

8.10.80 About two hundred Loyalists were stationed at Musgrove's Mill, a post on the Enoree River; their mission was to guard the nearby ford (see the Laurens District map, *Mills' Atlas*). Maj. Edward Musgrove (d. 1792) was one of the earliest settlers in this area near the convergence of Laurens, Spartanburg, and Union counties. It is now Musgrove Mill State Historic Site, approximately twenty-two miles south of Cedar Springs. Draper, *King's Mountain,* 103, 105, 123–24.

Dr. Ross was probably the William Ross who served as "Doctor of Refugees" on Johns Island under Col. Zachariah Gibbs of Ninety Six District between August 20 and November 9, 1781. M. J. Clark, *Loyalists in the Southern Campaign,* 1:533.

Josiah Culbertson was born between 1742 and 1748 in Lancaster County, Pennsylvania. He moved to North Carolina sometime before 1770 and later settled in the Ninety Six District of South Carolina along Fair Forest Creek. After enlisting in the fall of 1775, he participated in expeditions against Loyalists and the Cherokee Indians. He also fought at the battles of Stono, Ramsour's Mill, Cedar Springs, Musgrove's Mill, Kings Mountain, and Cowpens. Culbertson later moved to Indiana, where he died in 1839. Bobby G. Moss, *The Patriots at the Battle of Cowpens,* rev. ed. (Blacksburg, S.C.: Scotia-Hibernia Press, 1985), 73–74. Draper preserves several traditions concerning Culbertson's exploits during the war. See Draper, *King's Mountain,* 91–95, 136–39, 252–53.

Allaire correctly identified Culverson as Culbertson. "Diary of Allaire," in Draper, *King's Mountain,* 503.

The battle of Hanging Rock occurred August 6. Gen. Thomas Sumter may have had eight hundred men; the British commander, Maj. John Carden of the Prince of Wales Regiment, perhaps eight hundred, including contingents from the North Carolina Royalists and the British Legion (the numbers in various accounts differ widely). During the battle, which lasted longer than five hours, at least twenty Americans were killed and forty wounded; the British may have suffered two hundred casualties. The partisans nevertheless withdrew before consolidating their victory after discipline broke down while they plundered British supplies. Boatner, *Landmarks of the American Revolution*, 347–48; Edgar, *Partisans and Redcoats*, 106; Peckham, *Toll of Independence*, 74.

Hanging Rock, which was almost due north of Camden, was east of the Catawba River approximately seventy-five miles east-southeast of Cedar Springs. Maps of Kershaw and Lancaster districts, *Mills' Atlas*.

Browne's Corps was the Prince of Wales's American Volunteers. Gen. Montforte Browne raised this regiment, which came south in 1779. Browne's Corps should not be confused with Thomas Brown's South Carolina Rangers, some of whom also fought at Hanging Rock. Katcher, *Encyclopedia of British, Provincial, and German Army Units*, 95; C. Ward, *War of the Revolution*, 2:709–11.

8.11.80 Maj. Zachariah Gibbs. See 7.13.80 above.

8.12.80 Capt. Thomas Stribling Jr. was born in Virginia in 1730 and served under Col. Thomas Brandon during the Revolution. He was sheriff of Union District in 1791 and moved to Pendleton District sometime later. Elizabeth, the wife of "Capt. Thomas Stribling," died there in May 1807, and he was buried at nearby Anderson in 1818. Allan D. Charles, *The Narrative History of Union County* (Spartanburg, S.C.: Reprint Co., 1987), 453; *DAR Patriot Index*, 3:2841; Patricia Law Hatcher, ed., *Abstract of Graves of Revolutionary Patriots* (Dallas, Tex.: Pioneer Heritage Press, 1988), 4:85; J. M. Lesesne, comp., "Marriage and Death Notices from the *Pendleton Messenger* of Pendleton, South Carolina," *South Carolina Historical and Genealogical Magazine* 47 (January 1946): 29; Moss, *South Carolina Patriots*, 903.

Allaire added that Stribling, having taken protection, "as yet has not broken his promise." "Diary of Allaire," in Draper, *King's Mountain*, 503.

Maj. John Rutherford (d. 1781), a son of Gen. Griffith Rutherford, served as a major in the North Carolina militia. He fought at Ramsour's Mill and was killed at Eutaw Springs. Draper, *King's Mountain*, 503n; Heitman, *Historical Register*, 478.

8.13.80 Tinker Creek, about twenty-two miles southeast of Cedar Springs, flows into the Tyger River from the northwest approximately twelve miles upstream from the confluence of the Tyger and the Broad rivers. Maps of Union and Spartanburg districts, *Mills' Atlas*.

Smith's Mills on Swift Creek doubtless belonged to the William Smith, who on May 6, 1773, filed a memorial recording a chain of title to two hundred acres on

Swift Creek originally granted to John Winn September, 29, 1769. Series S111001, Memorial Books (Copy Series), vol. 12, p. 177, item 3; An Unrecorded Plat for Land Not Granted to William Orr identified Swift Run Branch as a tributary of Tinker Creek, Tyger River, Series S213197, box 4, item 962. Both items at South Carolina Department of Archives and History.

8.14.80 The editors have been unable to identify Quaker Ford on the Tyger River, but *Mills' Atlas,* Newberry District map, locates Greenshaw's Ford on the Tyger River west of Lyles Ford (8.15.80 below) on the Broad River. By road, the two fords were approximately seven miles apart on Mills's map, which corresponds fairly well with Johnson's belief that the distance was six miles.

Regarding the plantation of Col. James Lisles [or Lyles], to quote Bailey and Cooper, *Biographical Directory of the South Carolina House of Representatives,* 3:448n34, "as with other members of the large Lyles clan, existing records were too vague to identify various individuals with certainty." That said, on May 9, 1770, a James Lyles filed a plat for 150 acres in the vicinity of the Broad and Tyger rivers; a James Liles also served as a captain and colonel and was with General Sumter when Johnson's unit was at the plantation of the Lisles. Series S213184, Colonial Plat Books (Copy Series), vol. 11, p.552, item 3, South Carolina Department of Archives and History; Moss, *South Carolina Patriots,* 369; Draper, *King's Mountain,* 75.

8.15.80 Lisles [or Lyles] Ford crossed the Broad River between Newberry and Fairfield districts approximately one mile upriver from the convergence of the Enoree and Broad rivers. Ephraim Liles acquired land on the Fairfield side of the ford in the 1750s and his brother John was granted land to the west shortly thereafter. The small settlement of Lyles Ford, which developed around this crossing, appears on Mills's Newberry District map. Sharon Avery, "Place Names in Fairfield County," *Names in South Carolina* 30 (Winter 1983): 31.

In December 1780 Tarleton described the crossing as "very good." Quoted in Fred B. Newby, "The Use of Maps by the British Army in the Carolinas, 1780–1781," p. 22, manuscript in possession of the editors.

Francis Coleman on September 1, 1772, filed a memorial tracing the recent title for 350 acres on the Broad River next to Clement Mobberly. Two months later 150 acres on Beaver Creek were platted for him. Johnson would have crossed Beaver Creek earlier on this day's march. Series S111001, Memorial Books (Copy Series), vol. 11, p. 388, item 3; Series S213184, Colonial Plat Books (Copy Series), vol. 14, p. 139, item 1. Both at South Carolina Department of Archives and History.

Edward Mobley and his six sons with their families arrived from Virginia and Maryland around 1758 and settled on Beaver Creek in what became known as the Mobley [or Moberley] Settlement, located on the south fork of Little River about six miles west of modern-day Winnsboro. Tradition holds that, although the family was Anglican, the local meetinghouse was open to all denominations. One of the first battles between patriots and Loyalists after the fall of Charles Town occurred there, perhaps as early as May 26, 1780, although some accounts appear to place it in June. Col. Charles Coleman commanded the Loyalists, who, Gen. Richard Winn (one of the American commanders) later wrote, were "in a few minuits" driven "from a strong house, . . . and totally defeated with a small loss of killed and wounded." Fairfield District, *Mills' Atlas*; Fitz Hugh McMaster, *A History of Fairfield County, South Carolina, from "Before the White Man Came" to 1942* (1946; repr., Spartanburg, S.C.: Reprint Co., 1980), 74, 205; Lipscomb, "South Carolina Battles," 22:33; Winn, "Notes—1780," 202.

Y. Vols. was Johnson's abbreviation for the New York Volunteers. See Katcher, *Encyclopedia of British, Provincial, and German Army Units*, 93, 95.

Gen. Horatio Gates (1728?–1806) was born in England and served in the British army in America during the Seven Years' War. But in 1772 he sold his commission and moved to Virginia. The Second Continental Congress commissioned him brigadier general in 1775. Two years later he commanded the forces that defeated Gen. John Burgoyne at Saratoga in a battle that was one of the great turning points of the war. Congress subsequently made him commander of the Southern Department, where he suffered a major defeat at the battle of Camden, South Carolina (8.19.80 below). Garraty and Carnes, *American National Biography*, 8:788–91. See also Paul David Nelson, *General Horatio Gates: A Biography* (Baton Rouge: Louisiana State University Press, 1976).

Lord Rawdon, the British commander in the area, ordered Lt. Col. George Turnbull to evacuate Rocky Mount prior to the battle of Camden. Cornwallis to Lord George Germain, Aug. 20, 1780, in K. G. Davies, ed., *Documents of the American Revolution, 1770–1783*, vol. 18, *Transcripts 1780* (Shannon: Irish University Press, 1972), 148. Also see 8.1.80 above for Turnbull and Rocky Mount.

8.17.80 This Winn plantation belonged to Col. John Winn (b. c. 1727), not his more famous brother Col. Richard Winn (1750–1818). John moved from Virginia to South Carolina sometime before 1766, when he is known to have been a practicing surveyor. By the time of the Revolution he owned some three thousand acres in the upcountry and represented the district between the Broad and Catawba rivers at the Provincial Congress. Winn was commissioned a lieutenant colonel in the militia and evidently served in South Carolina between 1778 and 1780, although little is known of his activities. He was captured by the British and paroled to one of the Sea Islands in June 1780. In December 1780 Richard Winn apparently learned that his brother was to be executed for violating the terms of his parole. Richard later recalled that he informed Cornwallis that he would execute a hundred British captives if his brother were put to death. John apparently remained a prisoner on parole until the end of the war and spent most of his remaining years developing the town of Winnsboro. Buford S. Chappell, *The Winns of Fairfield County* (Columbia, S.C.: R. L. Bryan, 1975), 9, 12, 19–22; John Winn, Parole June 8, 1780, Cornwallis Papers, PRO 30/11/2, no. 103, South Carolina Department of Archives and History; Winn, "Notes—1780," 8.

Allaire specified that Winn was at James Island as a prisoner. "Diary of Allaire," in Draper, *King's Mountain,* 504.

8.19.80 The battle of Camden began at daybreak on August 16, 1780, when Gen. Horatio Gates's army met Cornwallis's force composed of Loyalist militia, provincial units, and British regulars eight miles north of Camden. The British were heavily outnumbered, but Gates's left wing quickly collapsed and the Continentals under Johann Baron DeKalb were left exposed. The Whigs were thoroughly routed and Gates was forced to retreat toward North Carolina. British casualties were listed as 324; the American loss was estimated at 250 killed and 800 wounded. Peckham, *Toll of Independence,* 74. The battle has been frequently described, but see especially Nelson, *General Horatio Gates* and Wickwire and Wickwire, *Cornwallis.* Lipscomb provides a summary and location in "South Carolina Battles," 22:37.

Johnson listed Generals DeKalb, Gregory, and Rutherford as among the Whig casualties at Camden. A native of Bavaria, Baron DeKalb was commissioned a major general in the Continental army in September 1777. He was wounded eight times at Camden and died on August 19, 1780. Brig. Gen. Isaac Gregory (c. 1737–1800) of the North Carolina militia was born in Pasquotank County, North Carolina. He was appointed sheriff of the county eight times and served in the colonial legislature in 1775 and the Provincial Congresses of 1775 and 1776. He was commissioned colonel in 1776 and brigadier general on May 12, 1779. He later served in the North Carolina House of Commons and in the North Carolina Senate from 1782 to 1795. Heitman, *Historical Register,* 192, 262; Powell, *Dictionary of North Carolina Biography,* 2:367. For General Griffith Rutherford, see 6.23.80 above.

Lt. Col. Alexander Innes. See 3.5.80 above.

The battle of Musgrove's Mill occurred on August 18. Elijah Clarke (9.25.80 below), Isaac Shelby (9.29.80 below), and James Williams commanded Georgians and over-mountain men, 11 of whom were killed and wounded; British casualties were 150—including Lt. Col. Alexander Innes, who was severely wounded—and 70 prisoners. This battle, which occurred about forty miles northwest of Johnson's location, was a fateful prelude to the battle of Kings Mountain. Peckham, *Toll of Independence,* 74.

Maj. Thomas Fraser served under Alexander Innes and commanded a company of the South Carolina Royalists. He was a native of Scotland and worked as a merchant in Virginia prior to his seven years of service with the provincial corps. M. J. Clark, *Loyalists in the Southern Campaign,* 1:465, 3:368.

Capt. Peter Campbell (c. 1756–1822), from Trenton, New Jersey, served as a captain in the Second New Jersey Volunteers. A prisoner in 1777–1778, he was released in time to join Archibald Campbell's expedition against Georgia in 1779. He served in the Southern Campaign through the battle of Eutaw Springs in September 1781. Campbell settled in New Brunswick following the war. Palmer, *Biographical Sketches of Loyalists,* 135; Edward Alfred Jones, *The Loyalists of New Jersey: Their Memorials, Petitions, Claims, etc., from English Records* (Boston: Gregg Press, 1972), 40.

Lt. William Chew served in the Second and Third New Jersey Volunteers from 1777 to 1782. He later became one of the lieutenants in the King's New Brunswick Regiment, which was established in 1793; he would die at Fredericton around 1812. E. A. Jones, *Loyalists of New Jersey,* 106, 68, 266.

Lt. John Camp served as an ensign in the Third New Jersey Volunteers in 1777. He was wounded and discharged in 1778. By late 1779 he appears to have been back in service as an ensign under Lt. William Chew. E. A. Jones, *Loyalists of New Jersey,* 265; M. J. Clark, *Loyalists in the Southern Campaign,* 3:130, 140.

Lt. Col. Isaac Allen (d. 1806) had been a lawyer in Trenton, New Jersey, before the war. Joining the British under Gen. William Howe in 1776, he raised the Second New Jersey Volunteers, which he commanded as a lieutenant colonel. Active duty in New Jersey, New York, and the Southern Campaign followed. From July 1782 until the British evacuation of Charles Town in December, he would serve as the commandant of occupied Charles Town. After the war, he settled in Canada, where he became a member of the council and judge of the supreme court in New Brunswick. McCowen, *British Occupation of Charleston,* 13, 144; E. A. Jones, *Loyalists of New Jersey,* 9–10.

Peters Creek joins the Tyger River three miles upriver from the junction of the Tyger and the Broad rivers. Newberry District map, *Mills' Atlas.*

[Mr] Smith. Although Cornwallis pardoned three men who had taken British protection and then been captured in arms at the battle of Camden, such clemency represented an exception to his general policy, for on August 18 he informed his commander at Ninety Six—and presumably other officers—that "I have ordered in the most positive manner, that every militiaman who had borne arms with us and had afterwards joined the enemy should be immediately hanged." Accordingly David Ramsay later asserted that "at or near Camden" five named individuals, including Eleazer Smith, were "hung without any ceremony." Anthony Allaire, who was on the spot, noted that "a Mr Smith" was executed at Colonel Winn's. Wickwire and Wickwire, *Cornwallis,* 174, quote 179; David Ramsay, *The History of the Revolution of South Carolina, from a British Province to an Independent State* (Trenton, N.J.: Isaac Collins, 1785), 2:157; "Diary of Allaire," in Draper, *King's Mountain,* 505.

8.21.80 Capt. Frederic Lapham was a "commissary of purchases" for Gen. Thomas Sumter during 1780 and 1782. Moss, *South Carolina Patriots,* 572.

Padget Creek. See 7.12.80 above.

Mr. Duncan was probably Captain William Duncan, who was listed as a captain in Lt. Col. Zachariah Gibbs's Regiment of the Loyalist Spartan Militia, Ninety Six Brigade, in August 1781. By June 10, 1783, Col. Benjamin Roebuck of the Whig Spartan Regiment reported a William Duncan among the dead Loyalists. M. J. Clark, *Loyalists in the Southern Campaign,* 1:278; Robert W. Barnwell Jr., ed., "Reports on Loyalist Exiles from South Carolina, 1783," *Proceedings of the South Carolina Historical Association,* 1937, p. 43.

Contrary to Johnson's report, this battle occurred on the eighteenth of August. Tarleton fell on Sumter's encampment at Fishing Creek north of modern-day Great Falls, Chester County, South Carolina, completely surprising and routing the Whigs. For details and summaries of the battle, see Tarleton, *History of the Campaigns of 1780 and 1781,* 110–16; Anne King Gregorie, *Thomas Sumter* (Columbia, S.C.: R. L. Bryan, 1931), 100–102; and Lipscomb, "South Carolina Battles," 22:37.

Allaire gave somewhat larger figures for Tarleton's casualties; American losses have been estimated as 50 killed, 100 wounded, and 310 captured. "Diary of Allaire," in Draper, *King's Mountain,* 505; Peckham, *Toll of Independence,* 74.

8.22.80 James Harrison (1748–1815), a native of Virginia, settled in the Ninety Six District on Fair Forest Creek (7.13.80 above) in 1778. Harrison, an active Whig, fought in several battles, including Cowpens and Eutaw Springs; his home was evidently burned during the Revolution. He served in numerous local offices and intermittently in the General Assembly and state senate, 1783–1786, 1794–1795. Bailey and Cooper, *Biographical Directory of the South Carolina House of Representatives,* 3:321–22.

8.23.80 John Blasingham was a Union District planter who was granted 200 acres near Sugar Creek (7.13.80 above) in 1771; during the next twenty years he would receive an additional 786 acres around Sugar and Fair Forest creeks. His military service during the Revolution was in the militia; later he became sheriff of Union District and a member of the General Assembly, 1783–1787, 1791, and 1794–1795. Bailey and Cooper, *Biographical Directory of the South Carolina House of Representatives,* 3:74–75.

Sarah was Capt. William Gist's wife. A magistrate and land surveyor in Ninety Six District at the beginning of the Revolution, he was arrested on three occasions for his Loyalist sympathies. Gist, who was Ferguson's primary scout, would be captured at the battle of Kings Mountain. On November 5, 1780, he escaped with Lts. Anthony Allaire, William Stevenson, and John Taylor and eventually reached Charles Town, where he served until 1782. His estate was later confiscated, but the South Carolina legislature restored 500 acres of the unsold land to his wife and children. Brent Holcomb, *Union County, South Carolina, Minutes of the County Court, 1785–1799* (Easley, S.C.: Southern Historical Press, 1979), 46; Draper, *King's Mountain,* 355, 483, 513; Palmer, *Biographical Sketches of Loyalists,* 318; Michael E. Stevens, ed., *Journals of the House of Representatives, 1789–1790* (Columbia: University of South Carolina Press, 1984), 355.

Allaire identified Blasingham as "Blasingame" and ends his entry with Ferguson "set out for Camden." "Diary of Allaire," in Draper, *King's Mountain,* 505.

8.26.80 John Wofford was one of the five Wofford brothers of the prominent Spartanburg County family. Most of the brothers settled on the Tyger River. Little information is available on John Wofford except that he fathered eleven children and that he may have been an enlisted soldier during the Revolution, although there is some indication that he was a Quaker. His audited account appears to request that payment for supplies furnished to American troops be delivered through John "Blasingame" (8.23.80 above). J. B. O. Landrum, *History of Spartanburg County* (1900; repr., Spartanburg, S.C.: Reprint Co., 1985), 220, 224; Wait, *History of the Wofford Family*, 50; Account Audited of Claims 8705, South Carolina Department of Archives and History.

Cluers Creek appears on Mouzon's map (1775) as a tributary of Fair Forest Creek on the south side approximately thirteen miles upstream from the Tyger River in present-day Union County.

The battle of Cedar Springs. See 8.8.80 above.

Allaire moved at 6 A.M. to Wofford's plantation on McCluers [*sic*] Creek and omitted Johnson's medical errand. "Diary of Allaire," in Draper, *King's Mountain*, 505.

8.28.80 Josiah Culbertson. See 8.10.80 above.

8.29.80 Browne's Corps. See 8.10.80 above.

Allaire lumped Tuesday the 29th through Thursday the 31st, during which he wrote only that they "Lay at Culbertson's; nothing extra." "Diary of Allaire," in Draper, *King's Mountain*, 505.

9.2.80 Iron Works, Lawson's Fork. See 8.8.80 above for Wofford's Iron Works.

Frost, a blacksmith in the vicinity of Cedar Springs or the iron works on Lawson's Fork. Unfortunately the editors could not identify this blacksmith. Some of Johnson's text for this entry is difficult to read, but there is probably a "W" before the word "Oak." This suggests that the blacksmith used the fungus of either a white oak, *Quercus alba*, or a water oak, *Quercus nigra*, both of which are found in the area.

Allaire stated that they forded Fair Forest Creek and specified that the wounded man was "a Rebel militia-man," that he was wounded in the right arm, and "the bone was very much shattered." "Diary of Allaire," in Draper, *King's Mountain*, 506.

9.4.80 Cases [or Casey] Creek, which appears at 35°04'46 N, 81°52'37 W on the United States Geological Survey, South Carolina, Spartanburg, Valley Falls map, is an eastward-flowing tributary of the Pacolet River.

9.5.80 The editors have been unable to identify the Colemans on the Pacolet River. Alexander Innes's Corps, the South Carolina Royalists, included the following Colemans: Sgt. Stephen, Pvt. Prince, and Maj. Christopher. Ens. Robert Coleman, who was on half pay in Savannah during 1780, may also have been attached to the unit. Major Coleman was sent to the backcountry of South Carolina in the spring of 1780, which suggests that he was considered a person of influence in the area. William Tennant, who had been attempting to encourage support for the

Whigs in 1775, also encountered a Captain Colman, apparently an incipient Tory, in the Thicketty Creek area. M. J. Clark, *Loyalists in the Southern Campaign*, 1:7, 40, 47; Tennant Journal, in R. W. Gibbes, *Documents of the American Revolution: Consisting of Letters and Papers Relating to the Contest for Liberty, Chiefly in South Carolina. . . .* vol. 1, *1764–76* (1855; repr., Spartanburg, S.C.: Reprint Co., 1972), 229–30.

Allaire, who omitted the fact that two of Coleman's sons were in the South Carolina Royalists corps, gave more attention to Coleman as the head of the household than did Johnson. "Diary of Allaire," in Draper, *King's Mountain*, 506.

9.6.80 Buck Creek runs into the Pacolet River from the northwest approximately six miles downstream from the confluence of the north and south forks of the Pacolet. Spartanburg District map, *Mills' Atlas.*

Neilson was probably Robert Neilson, who owned land on Buck Creek in Tryon County, North Carolina, just above John Kirkconnel's holdings. John Kirkconnel Memorial, 1776, S111001, Memorial Books (Copy Series), vol. 2, p. 481, item 2, South Carolina Department of Archives and History.

William Case may have been the individual for whom two hundred acres on the south side of the Tyger River at its confluence with the Broad River were laid out in 1762. S111001, Memorial Books (Copy Series), vol. 14, p. 207, item 3, South Carolina Department of Archives and History.

9.7.80 North Carolina–South Carolina line. In 1772 North and South Carolina appointed commissioners to extend the boundary line westward from the Catawba River to the Cherokee Indian line of 1767, and during late May and early June they completed work. William Moultrie, one of the commissioners for South Carolina, kept a slim but interesting journal of their activities. See William Moultrie, "The Journal of William Moultrie While a Commissioner on the North and South Carolina Boundary Survey, 1772," ed. Charles S. Davis, *Journal of Southern History* 8 (November 1942): 551–55; William S. Powell, *North Carolina through Four Centuries* (Chapel Hill: University of North Carolina Press, 1989), 95.

This boundary line, which Uzal Johnson crossed, put perhaps as many as five thousand former North Carolinians in South Carolina, many of whom had received grants from North Carolina for land subsequently situated in South Carolina. For the procedures used to validate their titles, see Charles Lee, "Lands Granted by North Carolina below the 1772 Line: Validation of Titles," *South Carolina Historical Magazine* 69 (October 1968): 284–89.

William Gilbert (1735–1790), a prominent patriot who began to purchase land in Tryon County (renamed Rutherford in 1779) in 1769, became the largest property holder in the area. His farms and home, known as Gilbert Town, which were about a mile north of present-day Rutherfordton, would serve as the county seat from 1781 to 1785. Gilbert's career included membership in the Tryon Committee of Public Safety and the state general assembly in 1779, 1780, 1782, and 1783; he and his wife also used their home to store arms. Ferguson, who was aware of the Gilberts' politics, at times intentionally quartered his troops at the plantations of rebels. Powell, *Dictionary of North Carolina Biography,* 2:296–97; Powell, *North Carolina Gazetteer,* 190; John L. Cheney Jr., ed., *North Carolina Government, 1585– 1974: A Narrative and Statistical History* (Raleigh: North Carolina Department of the Secretary of State, 1975), 203, 207, 210, 212.

Gilbert Town, which on September 23 Allaire described as containing "one dwelling house, one barn, a blacksmith's shop, and some out-houses," was approximately fourteen miles north of the North and South Carolina boundary. "Diary of Allaire," in Draper, *King's Mountain,* 508.

Allaire, who termed Ferguson "Maj." and omitted Johnson, noted that Captain DePeyster and he remained where they were "with the remainder of the American Volunteers and militia." Allaire continued to refer to Ferguson as "Maj." in the next several entries, which was technically correct. Ferguson had been appointed major in the Seventy-first Regiment in late 1778; his appointment as lieutenant colonel "in America" occurred on December 1, 1778, but news of it arrived in America after his death. "Diary of Allaire," in Draper, *King's Mountain,* 506; Selesky, *Encyclopedia of the American Revolution,* 1:355.

9.8.80 Allaire noted they were at Denards Ford, which was located at or near present-day Twitty Bridge as shown on the 7.5 minute North Carolina Pea Ridge quadrangle map of the United States Geological Survey. It was about eight miles from Gilbert Town. "Diary of Allaire," in Draper, *King's Mountain,* 506; Clarence W. Griffin, *The History of Old Tryon and Rutherford Counties, North Carolina, 1730–1936* (1937; repr., Spartanburg, S.C.: Reprint Co., 1977), 57.

9.9.80 After the battle of Musgrove's Mill, in which they participated on August 19, Elijah Clarke (9.25.80 below) and his Georgians moved south and prepared to lay siege to Augusta. Their abortive attack lasted from September 14 to 18. Cashin, *King's Ranger,* 114–18.

9.11.80 In January 1775 James Adair was appointed overseer of the road from Col. John Walker's (9.12.80 below) past William Gilbert's; eleven years later he sold fifty acres to the commissioners appointed for selecting a site for the new county seat. As a result the present business district of Rutherfordton is on what was part of Adair's plantation. Brent Holcomb, comp., *Tryon County, North Carolina: Minutes of the Court of Pleas and Quarter Sessions, 1769–1779* (Columbia, S.C.: SCMAR, 1994), 149; Griffin, *History of Old Tryon and Rutherford Counties,* 109.

9.12.80 Cane Creek. See below in this note.

Capt. Samuel Ryerse. See 4.21.80 above.

Duncan Fletcher first appeared in 1777 as a lieutenant in the Loyal American Regiment, which had been raised in New York during the previous year. He was later assigned to the American Volunteers with Ferguson and would fight in the battle of Kings Mountain. Eventually becoming a captain, he went to Nova Scotia at the end of the war. Raymond, "Roll of Officers," 252; Katcher, *Encyclopedia of British, Provincial, and German Army Units,* 91; Draper, *King's Mountain,* 480–81.

Col. John Walker (1728–96) was born in New Castle County, Delaware. He moved first to Virginia and then to North Carolina, eventually settling near the mouth of Cane Creek where it joins the Second Broad River in present-day Rutherford County. This is approximately five miles northeast of Rutherfordton. At the beginning of the Revolution he was appointed chairman of the Tryon Committee of Safety, and in 1775 he also served in the Third Provincial Congress for Tryon County. A captain and then major (1777) in the First Regiment of North Carolina Continental Troops, he resigned his commission shortly thereafter because of age. After Rutherford County was organized in April 1779, he was appointed a justice of the peace, and the first session of the county court was held at his house. Powell, *Dictionary of North Carolina Biography,* 6:113.

Burke County was established in 1777 from part of Rowan County and named in honor of Thomas Burke (1747–1783), later a delegate to the Continental Congress and governor of North Carolina. Powell, *North Carolina Gazetteer,* 75; David T. Morgan and William J. Schmidt, *North Carolinians in the Continental Congress* (Winston-Salem, N.C.: John F. Blair, 1976), 35. The county seat was established in 1777 at what was incorporated in 1784 as Morgantown (now Morganton), named after Gen. Daniel Morgan. It is approximately thirty miles northeast of Rutherfordton. Powell, *North Carolina Gazetteer,* 334.

The skirmish at Cane's Creek involved Whigs under Col. Charles McDowell (9.29.80 below) and Ferguson's Tory detachment. Draper describes the location as "some three miles southwest of Brindletown, in the south-eastern corner of McDowell County, and something like fifteen miles from Gilbert Town." Draper, *King's Mountain,* 148.

Joseph White (d. 1790 or 1791) was actually a major who had first been commissioned in the Rowan County militia in late 1775 or early 1776. Having served in the expedition against the Cherokee Indians in 1776, he became a major in the Burke County militia when that district was created from Rowan County in 1777. Although wounded in this skirmish, White would be present at the battle of Kings Mountain. Bobby G. Moss, *The Patriots at Kings Mountain* (Blacksburg, S.C.: Scotia-Hibernia Press, 1990), 267.

Allaire's longer entry supplies additional detail and some sarcasm aimed at the Americans. "Diary of Allaire," in Draper, *King's Mountain,* 507.

9.13.80 For Capt. James Dunlap, see 7.15.80 above.

The ilium is the top of the pelvic bone where the femur joins the hip. Henry Gray, *Anatomy, Descriptive and Surgical* (1858; New York: Gramercy Books, 1977), 172.

Allaire supplied additional details about the location of various detachments. "Diary of Allaire," in Draper, *King's Mountain,* 507.

9.14.80 Sir Henry Clinton, the British commander in chief, issued a number of proclamations, but Johnson probably referred to the one of June 1, 1780, which was published in Charles Town as a broadside that promised amnesty to the king's "deluded Subjects" who would "still be received with Mercy and Forgiveness, if they immediately return to their Allegiance. . . ." Early American Imprints, Series 1: Evans, 1639–1800, Readex Digital Collections No. 16790.

9.15.80 Capt. James Chitwood served in the Loyalist militia from Tryon (later Rutherford) County, North Carolina. Born c. 1720 in Northumberland County, Virginia, he moved to Tryon County about 1772. He would be captured at the battle of Kings Mountain and executed a week later. William B. Bynum, ed., *The Heritage of Rutherford County, North Carolina* (Winston-Salem, N.C.: Hunter, 1984), 157–58; Holcomb, *Tryon County Minutes of the Court of Pleas and Quarter Sessions*, 203–4; Draper, *King's Mountain*, 340; DeMond, *Loyalists in North Carolina*, 132.

An "abbitees" [abatis] is "a defense constructed by placing felled trees lengthwise one over the other with their branches towards the enemy's line"; a worm snake fence consisted of rails or poles piled on each other in a zigzag fashion. *Oxford English Dictionary*, 2nd ed., s.v. "abatis," "snake-fence."

Allaire's long entry, which encompasses September 15 and 16, while he was with Ferguson pursuing Whigs who eventually eluded them, is quite different from Johnson's. Allaire's group reached Pleasant Garden, North Carolina, which he termed "a very handsome place." It was "composed of the most violent Rebels I ever saw, particularly the young ladies." "Diary of Allaire," in Draper, *King's Mountain*, 507–8.

From Sunday the seventeenth through Thursday the twenty-first, Allaire marched and countermarched, usually quartering at the plantations of "Rebels." "Diary of Allaire," in Draper, *King's Mountain*, 508.

9.22.80 Captain Turner was perhaps Michael Turner, whom Bobby Moss plausibly locates on Cane Creek. The present editors, however, have been unable to confirm this identification. Johnson, *Loyalist Surgeon: War Diary*, 66.

Allaire returned to Colonel Walker's on this date. "Diary of Allaire," in Draper, *King's Mountain*, 508.

9.23.80 Allaire's contingent marched three miles to Gilbert Town. For his description of the town, see 9.7.80 above.

9.24.80 The Gilbert house remained standing for nearly a century, during which tradition held that Dunlap's blood was visible on the floor. Perhaps so; Dunlap was apparently murdered there some five months later. "Declaration respecting the murder of Captn. Dunlap Qs Rangers, 28 Mar. 1781," in Johnson, *Loyalist Surgeon: War Diary*, 132–33. See the sketch of Dunlap at 7.15.80 above as well as Draper's account of the incident in *King's Mountain*, 156–64.

Allaire's longer entry recorded that five hundred subjects "came in, also a number of ladies" and summarized a report of Elijah Clarke's (9.25.80 below) unsuccessful attack on the British at Augusta, Georgia. He failed to mention the hanging of American captives, which Johnson noted on the twenty-fifth. "Diary of Allaire," in Draper, *King's Mountain,* 508.

9.25.80 Col. Elijah Clarke (c. 1733 or 1742–1799) was born in North Carolina. In the 1760s he moved to western South Carolina and by the early 1770s to newly opened lands in Georgia. Although illiterate, he became a captain in the militia and a noted Indian fighter who quickly rose to lieutenant colonel of the Wilkes County militia. After the British captured Georgia, he led about thirty men to North Carolina, from which he continued to operate as an effective partisan leader, most notably in the recapture of Augusta in June 1781. During most of the 1780s he served in the state legislature. During the 1790s he led abortive incursions into Spanish Florida and Indian lands. Coleman and Gurr, *Dictionary of Georgia Biography,* 1:10–12. See also the introduction to the present volume.

Johnson's description of the siege of Augusta is a bit muddled. The fight began on September 14, when about 250 Creek Indians were attacked at their camp outside Augusta by Whigs under Col. Elijah Clarke. As the Indians retreated toward Augusta, they encountered Thomas Brown and his rangers, who were hurrying toward the sound of the fighting. The Tories then took refuge in a stone house belonging to Robert Mackay, which was located near the Savannah River. But before the Whigs completely surrounded them, Brown was able to send two messages to Lt. Col. John Harris Cruger (9.25.80 below) at Ninety Six requesting assistance. The siege at Mackay's lasted until the morning of September 18, when Cruger arrived with a large reinforcement and forced Clarke to retreat. Cashin, *King's Ranger,* 113–20.

Thomas Brown (d. 1825) immigrated to Georgia from England in 1774 with seventy-four indentured servants, whom he used to develop his extensive lands. A staunch supporter of the Crown, he was tarred and feathered by Whigs in August 1775. He later went to Florida, where he raised a regiment of rangers, of which he became lieutenant colonel. In 1779 he was also appointed as a superintendent of the Southern Indian Department. At the end of the war he went to the West Indies after having participated in enough battles to have been wounded fourteen times. Coleman and Gurr, *Dictionary of Georgia Biography,* 1:123–24.

The prisoners taken "with protections in their pockets" were mainly paroled Georgia militiamen from Wilkes County. Clarke had threatened to shoot them if they refused to join him in the expedition against Augusta. Only thirteen of them were officially executed, a surprisingly small number, according to Brown's biographer, "considering the extent of the British outrage." Cashin, *King's Ranger,* 114; quote 118.

Lt. Col. John Harris Cruger (1738–1807), a Loyalist from a prominent New York family, had been part of Archibald Campbell's force that captured Savannah in

1778. Beginning in August 1780, he was in charge at Ninety Six, which withstood a siege by Gen. Nathanael Greene's forces in the spring of 1781. Cruger would also command Loyalists at the battle of Eutaw Springs later that year. After the war he moved to London. Palmer, *Biographical Sketches of Loyalists*, 191; Greene, *Papers*, 8:340n1.

Allaire lumped Monday the 25th and Tuesday the 26th in a single entry: "lay at Gilbert Town; nothing extra." "Diary of Allaire," in Draper, *King's Mountain*, 509.

9.26.80 Lt. William Stevenson (c. 1758–1818), from Monmouth County, New Jersey, who first served as a Loyalist militia officer, was commissioned as a lieutenant in 1776 and later transferred to the Third Battalion of the New Jersey Volunteers, where he served as a lieutenant under Capt. Samuel Ryerse (4.21.80 above). Stevenson fought at Charles Town, Moncks Corner, and Musgrove's Mill. Attached to Ferguson's corps, he was later wounded and captured at Kings Mountain but escaped on November 5, 1780. At the end of the war he settled in Nova Scotia. Moss, *Roster of the Loyalists in the Battle of Kings Mountain*, 78.

9.27.80 Capt. Turner's. See 9.22.80 above.

James Adair. See 9.11.80 above.

Johnson misplaced his description of Hillsborough here. See 11.22.80 below.

Allaire moved at five o'clock in the morning three miles to Rucker's Mill. "Diary of Allaire," in Draper, *King's Mountain*, 509.

9.28.80 Lt. John Taylor. See 5.2.80 above.

Lt. Duncan Fletcher. See 9.12.80 above.

White Oak was a well-known spring in the vicinity of modern Brindletown on the road from Gilbert Town to what became Morganton. Draper, *King's Mountain*, 148.

Allaire's servant could not be identified, but officers were authorized to provide themselves with "Negro servants" at the rate of two per company. According to Draper, an African American was with Ferguson's cook when both were captured. The African American, who was on horseback, soon escaped; the cook was later paroled. [Feb.?] 18, 1780, Capt. F. DePeyster's Orderly Book, January–August 1780 and February–June 1782, New-York Historical Society, New York, N.Y.; Draper, *King's Mountain*, 205.

Allaire did not mention the incident.

Col. Veazey Husband, who lived in Rowan County, North Carolina, near the Catawba River, was among the individuals who petitioned in the early 1770s that their area be made a separate jurisdiction. Their request was answered when Burke County was created in 1777. This Husband is thought to have been a relation of Hermon Husband, a leading Regulator, and to have been killed with Ferguson at the battle of Kings Mountain. Draper, *King's Mountain*, 276, 294, 482; William L. Saunders, ed., *Colonial Records of North Carolina*, vol. 9, *1771–1775* (1890; repr., Wilmington, N.C.: Broadfoot, 1993), 91.

Allaire, who was elsewhere on this date, recorded the unit's progress across Green River. "Diary of Allaire," in Draper, *King's Mountain,* 509.

9.29.80 For Burke Court House, see 9.12.80 above.

Col. Isaac Shelby (1750–1826) was born in Maryland and moved with his parents to Virginia about 1773. In 1776 he became captain of a company of Virginia minutemen and in 1780 colonel of militia in Sullivan County, North Carolina. He took part in the battles of Thicketty Fort, Cedar Springs, Musgrove's Mill, and Kings Mountain. In 1781 and 1782 he served in the North Carolina legislature before moving to Kentucky in 1783, where he would become the first—and a two-term—governor of the state (1792–1796, 1812–1816). During the War of 1812 he also commanded troops. Selesky, *Encyclopedia of the American Revolution,* 2:1053–54; Powell, *Dictionary of North Carolina Biography,* 5:326–27. Also see the introduction to this edited diary.

Col. Charles McDowell (1743–1815) was born in Virginia but settled at Quaker Meadows in Burke County, North Carolina, at the outbreak of the Revolution. In 1776 he became lieutenant colonel of the local militia and in the early 1780s a brigadier general. His brother, Joseph McDowell (1756–1801), known as "Quaker Meadows Joe" to distinguish him from the many other McDowells in western North Carolina, was a major at the time Uzal Johnson mentioned him (see 10.15.80 below). Prior to the battle of Kings Mountain, the senior American officers involved chose Col. William Campbell (10.7.80 below) as their nominal commander, thereby passing over Charles McDowell, the most senior officer present. Charles accordingly relinquished the command of his regiment either to his brother, Joseph, or—as some scholars believe—to his cousin Joseph (from Pleasant Gardens, North Carolina) and departed for Hillsborough carrying messages to General Gates. The brothers McDowell also served in the state legislature, the conventions to ratify the U.S. Constitution, and, in Joseph's case, the U.S. Congress. Buchanan, *Road to Guilford Courthouse,* 218; Powell, *Dictionary of North Carolina Biography,* 4:142–44.

Col. Benjamin Cleveland (1738–1806) was a frontiersman, physically big and temperamentally reckless. Born in Virginia, he and his family moved to western North Carolina when he was thirty-one. In 1775 he became chairman of the Committee of Safety for Surry County, and in 1776 he served as a captain of militia in an expedition against the Cherokee Indians. Two years later, when Wilkes County was created from Surry, Cleveland headed the commission of justices and became colonel of the militia. As such, he made war on Loyalists to the extent that when some of his men summarily hanged two Tories in 1779, he was indicted for murder, but he was later pardoned by the governor. He would figure prominently in the battle of Kings Mountain and its aftermath. After the war he moved to South Carolina. Powell, *Dictionary of North Carolina Biography,* 1:385–86.

Allaire moved to a plantation that had been raided by the Indians about a year earlier. His account supplies details of this attack and its aftermath. "Diary of Allaire," in Draper, *King's Mountain,* 509.

9.30.80 Richard Boyle, a native of Ireland, served as ensign in the First Battalion of DeLancey's Brigade. He was present at the siege of Savannah and was captured at Kings Mountain but was later paroled. Raymond, "Roll of Officers," 263; Katcher, *Encyclopedia of British, Provincial, and German Army Units,* 84–85; Johnson, *Loyalist Surgeon: War Diary,* 70n.

Denard's Ford. See 9.8.80 above. Draper, *King's Mountain,* 203.

The editors have been unable to positively identify Mr. Powers, Broad River. The only Powers we located in Rutherford County was John Powers, who sold land in 1803. However, several Bowers appear earlier in adjacent Lincoln County (conceivably Johnson misunderstood the name; because the mouth forms *b* and *p* similarly, those consonants are frequently confused). Rutherford County Grantor Index and "Minutes of the Court of Common Pleas and Quarter Sessions, Lincoln County, North Carolina, April 1779–January 1789," comp. Anne W. McAllister and Kathy G. Sullivan, 1988, both items at North Carolina State Archives, Raleigh; Daniel Jones, *An Outline of English Phonetics,* 9th ed. (London: Cambridge University Press, 1972), 49.

Allaire remained where he was. The attempt to intercept Elijah Clarke failed. "Diary of Allaire," in Draper, *King's Mountain,* 509.

10.1.80 White Oak. See 9.28.80 above.

Allaire's contingent returned to Denard's Ford, where they had been on September 8. "Diary of Allaire," in Draper, *King's Mountain,* 509.

10.2.80 Col. Greyms was probably William Graham (1742–1835), the commanding colonel of the Lincoln County militia at this time. He was born in Virginia but moved to North Carolina before the Revolution. He was a member of the Provincial Congresses in 1775–1776. Becoming colonel of the Tryon County militia, he served in campaigns against North and South Carolina Loyalists early in the war and in the defense of Charles Town during 1780, as well as in several later skirmishes. Visiting his sick wife, he missed most of the battle of Kings Mountain. Nathanael Greene, *The Papers of General Nathanael Greene,* vol. 6, *1 June 1780–25 December 1780,* ed. Dennis M. Conrad (Chapel Hill: University of North Carolina Press, 1991), 566 and n; Draper, *King's Mountain,* 476.

Thicketty River. See 7.29.80 above.

Allaire accompanied Ferguson on this march. "Diary of Allaire," in Draper, *King's Mountain,* 509.

10.3.80 Buck Creek. See 9.6.80 above.

Cases [or Casey] Creek. See 9.4.80 above.

Case's House. See 9.6.80 above.

William Abbot owned land near the confluence of Buck Creek and the Pacolet River. In 1802 the road from Spartanburg to Island Ford on the Broad River bisected this property perhaps ten miles south of the North Carolina border. Plat of Isaac Young, October 22, 1802, for 295 acres in Spartanburg County, Series S213292, State Plat Books (Columbia Series), vol. 39, p. 203, South Carolina Department of Archives and History.

Allaire marched approximately twenty miles on a different route and encountered a hale and hearty man 101 years old. "Diary of Allaire," in Draper, *King's Mountain,* 509.

10.4.80 Several Sharps acquired land in the general area through which Johnson was now traveling. But the editors believe William Sharp was probably the individual mentioned here. He was a surveyor who frequently dealt in land in the Broad River valley on both sides of the North and South Carolina boundary. In particular, in 1767 he acquired three hundred acres on the west side of the Broad River at Suck Creek. The Price-Strother map (Price and Strother, "Survey of North Carolina," 1808) locates this creek approximately twelve miles up the south side of Broad River from the mouth of Buffalo Creek, which Johnson mentions on October 5. It is unclear whether this Sharp was the William Sharp who filed an account from Union County in May 1786 detailing 886 days of military service under Captains Palmer, Jolly, and Hughes of Colonel Brandon's Regiment. Holcomb, *North Carolina Land Grants in South Carolina,* 110, 111; Holcomb, *Tryon County Minutes of the Court of Pleas,* 48, 56, 113, 128, 137, 155, 184; Margaret M. Hoffmann, *Colony of North Carolina: Abstracts of Land Patents,* vol. 2, *1765–1775* (Weldon, N.C.: Roanoke News Co., 1984), 25, 79, 82, 94, 443, 444, 502, 531; Accounts Audited of Claims, 6903, South Carolina Department of Archives and History.

William Tate's Plantation was on the western side of the Broad River opposite the mouth of Buffalo Creek. Tate, on whose land a ferry operated (see 10.5.80 below), came from Virginia and acquired land in both Carolinas. His will, which was probated in September 1792, suggests that his oldest son, William, was an adult at the time his father devised property to him. Whether the William Tate who served as a captain in the Fourth Regiment of Continental Artillery was William Sr. or William Jr. is unclear, although the most recent treatment of the captain's extraordinary later career—which involved an attack on Wales at the head of French troops in 1797—rather implausibly suggests that William Sr. was a septuagenarian soldier. Ethel S. Updike, *Tate Families of the South* (Salt Lake City, Utah: Hobby Press, 1971), 19–20; John D. Ahlstrom, "Captain and Chef de Brigade William Tate: South Carolina Adventurer," *South Carolina Historical Magazine* 88 (October 1987): 183–91, quote 186. See also Bailey and Cooper, *Biographical Directory of the South Carolina House of Representatives,* 3:699.

Kemp's over Broad River was perhaps the plantation of Moses Kemp, which lay northwest of the three hundred acres on Buffalo Creek platted for Vardry McBee in 1773. Plat, Sept. 6, 1773, Series S213184, Colonial Plat Books (Copy Series), vol. 18, p. 108, South Carolina Department of Archives and History.

10.5.80 Tate's Ferry became Dare's Ferry in 1813. *The Papers of General Nathanael Greene*, vol. 7, *26 December 1780–29 March 1781*, ed. Dennis M. Conrad (Chapel Hill: University of North Carolina Press, 1994), map 212; York District map, *Mills' Atlas*; Cooper and McCord, *Statutes at Large of South Carolina*, 9:462.

Buffalo Creek empties into the Broad River from the east about one-half mile north of Dare's Ferry. York District map, *Mills' Atlas*.

Allaire omitted an entry for this date.

10.6.80 Kings Mountain, according to William Moultrie (3.12.80 above), was named for "a person who first settled about this place." Moultrie also noted that a wagon road ran from this area to Charles Town, "about 180 miles" away. Moultrie, "Journal," 554.

Kings Mountain National Military Park and Kings Mountain State Park straddle Cherokee and York counties, South Carolina. However, the present-day town of Kings Mountain is in North Carolina.

Allaire moved at 4 A.M.; otherwise, the entries are substantially similar. "Diary of Allaire," in Draper, *King's Mountain*, 510.

10.7.80 Gen. James Williams. See 7.10.80 above.

Col. William Campbell (1745–1781) was born in Virginia. In 1769 he settled on the Holston River and five years later served as a militia captain in Dunmore's War, a campaign against the Indians. In February 1776 he became a captain in the First Virginia Regiment in the Continental army but resigned late in the year to defend his home, which was exposed to Indian attack. Four years later he became colonel of the local militia and as such inflicted summary justice on local Loyalists. On October 2, 1780, he was chosen to command the militias that would defeat Ferguson's force five days later. In March 1781 he and his men performed well at the battle of Guilford Court House, North Carolina. Although his riflemen were in the campaign against Cornwallis in Virginia, Campbell died, presumably of a heart attack, before the British surrender at Yorktown. Garraty and Carnes, *American National Biography*, 4:304–5.

Col. Isaac Shelby. See 9.29.80 above.

Col. Edward Lacey. See 7.13.80 above.

Col. Thomas Brandon (1741–1802) was born in Pennsylvania and moved to South Carolina in the mid-1750s. By the time of the Revolution he was a captain in the militia, soon a major, and then in 1779 a colonel. As well as this battle at Kings Mountain, he was in several significant skirmishes and the battle of Cowpens (January 1781). In 1797 he became brigadier general of the state militia. Beginning in 1776 he also served periodically in the General Assembly and the state senate (1791–1799), representing Union District. Draper, *King's Mountain*, 469; Bailey and Cooper, *Biographical Directory of the South Carolina House of Representatives*, 3:86–88.

Col. Andrew Hampton (d. 1805) moved south from Virginia in the mid–eighteenth century and established himself in North Carolina on the Catawba River. Sometime before the outbreak of the Revolution he moved west to present-day Rutherford County. A militia captain in 1775, he became a colonel by 1779. He served during the siege of Charles Town in 1780 and fought in several battles in the backcountry thereafter, the most important being Kings Mountain. In 1781 he was chosen sheriff of Rutherford County. (He should not be confused with the Hamptons of South Carolina, who also came from Virginia.) Griffin, *History of Old Tryon and Rutherford Counties,* 89n6; Johnson, *Loyalist Surgeon: War Diary,* 73.

Col. William Graham. See 10.2.80 above.

Col. John Sevier (1745–1815) was born in the Shenandoah Valley of Virginia, the oldest of seven children, and received only a spotty education. He married at sixteen, farmed, ran a tavern, and traded in land. In 1773 he and his family moved to western North Carolina (now Tennessee) and settled on the Holston River. Renowned for his ability as an Indian fighter, he soon became a colonel in the state militia and proved to be one of the key figures in the battle of Kings Mountain. During the next thirty-five years he would be elected to the governorship of what became Tennessee six times and to the U.S. Congress four times. Powell, *Dictionary of North Carolina Biography,* 5:317–18. See also the introduction to this edited diary.

Col. Benjamin Cleveland. See 9.29.80 above.

Col. John Thomas Jr. (1751–1819), the son of John Thomas Sr. (1720–1811), was born in Pennsylvania. When John Jr. was about four, his family moved to South Carolina and eventually settled in the Fair Forest Creek area. John Sr. supported the American cause and became colonel of the Spartan Regiment of militia in 1775. After the fall of Charles Town he accepted protection from the British but somehow ran afoul of British authorities and was imprisoned for fourteen months beginning in the summer of 1780. So it was his son, John Jr., to whom Johnson referred. However, John Jr., who became colonel of the regiment after his father's imprisonment, was probably in or near Hillsborough, North Carolina, at this time. On January 17, 1781, he would command a unit at the battle of Cowpens. In the 1780s he served as sheriff of the Ninety Six District and as a member of the General Assembly before moving to Illinois about 1807 and becoming the first treasurer of that state. Robert D. Bass, *Gamecock: The Life and Campaigns of General Thomas Sumter* (New York: Holt, Rinehart and Winston, 1961), 88; Bailey and Cooper, *Biographical Directory of the South Carolina House of Representatives,* 3:708–11.

Col. Robinson was actually Maj. Charles Robertson (1740–1797?), who fought at the battles of Wofford's Iron Works and Musgrove's Mill as well as Kings Mountain. Draper's account suggests that he was Sevier's right-hand man. He served in the fifth North Carolina Provincial Congress in 1776 for Anson County and may have also represented Washington County. In 1778 he was in the Senate for Washington

County. Between 1781 and 1785 he served in the lower house for Washington (now in Tennessee), Richmond, and Montgomery counties, and in 1788–1789 he represented Richmond County as a delegate to the state convention to ratify the U.S. Constitution. Draper, *King's Mountain,* 84, 87, 97–98, 118–19, 421, 503; Cheney, *North Carolina Government, 1585–1974,* 157, 159, 202, 207, 208, 213, 215–16, 767, 1296.

Colonel Chandler was probably William Candler (1738–1789), who was a major when he commanded the small group of Georgians at Kings Mountain. He was born in Ireland, grew up in Virginia, and moved to Georgia in 1762. Serving under Elijah Clarke (9.25.80 above), he was in several battles and eventually became a colonel. After the war, he would also sit in the Georgia state legislature during 1784–1785. Draper, *King's Mountain,* 469.

Alternatively Johnson might have intended to refer to Major William Chronicle (1755–1780). Born in North Carolina, Chronicle served in South Carolina and Georgia during the early part of the war as well as at the defense of Charles Town in 1780. He would be killed at the battle of Kings Mountain while leading militia from Lincoln County, North Carolina. Powell, *Dictionary of North Carolina Biography,* 1:370.

Johnson exaggerated the size of the American force, which was probably about 1,550; the British had approximately 1,000 men. Peckham, *Toll of Independence,* 76.

Capt. Abraham DePeyster. See 3.10.80 above.

Ensign Richard McGinnis was in the West Jersey Volunteers in 1778; by the following year he had been shifted to the Third Battalion of the New Jersey Volunteers, commanded by Lt. Col. Isaac Allen (8.19.80 above). McGinnis was promoted to lieutenant in 1780. E. A. Jones, *Loyalists of New Jersey,* 292; Raymond, "Roll of Officers," 268; Katcher, *Encyclopedia of British, Provincial, and German Army Units,* 93.

Johnson's figures for British casualties are higher than some consensus estimates, which put them at about 150 killed and 160 wounded, but he may well have been in the best position to know. His tally of the American losses is also higher than most conventional estimates, but official reports by both sides often omitted the militia. See notes above for Johnson's entry on May 7, 1780, and Lawrence E. Babits, *A Devil of a Whipping: The Battle of Cowpens* (Chapel Hill: University of North Carolina Press, 1998), 151–52, which demonstrates that Daniel Morgan failed to count the militia in recording his casualties at the battle of Cowpens. American losses at the battle of Kings Mountain have commonly been numbered at 28 killed and 62 wounded. Peckham, *Toll of Independence,* 76.

Their own surgeon may have been Francis Whelchel Sr., an American surgeon who is known to have been at the battle. Moss, *Patriots at Kings Mountain,* 265–66.

Allaire, whose description of the battle differed considerably from Johnson's, included a much lower estimate of the losses among the Loyalist militia and a gracious tribute to Ferguson. "Diary of Allaire," in Draper, *King's Mountain,* 510.

10.8.80 Johnson was apparently traveling northwest toward the Gilbert Town area until October 11.

Allaire's entry was substantially different. "Diary of Allaire," in Draper, *King's Mountain,* 510.

10.9.80 Allaire's entry was again substantially different. "Diary of Allaire," in Draper, *King's Mountain,* 510.

10.10.80 For the phrase "contented with our lot," see 4.26.80 above.

10.11.80 Col. John Walker. See 9.12.80 above. Johnson wrote that Walker's land, which was near the mouth of Cane Creek, was in Tryon County, but by 1780 this area was actually in Lincoln County.

10.13.80 Bickerstaff's plantation, located about nine miles northeast of present-day Rutherfordton, North Carolina, was known as Bickerstaff's Old Fields and, later, Red or Burnt Chimneys. On modern maps the Sunshine community encompasses it. This plantation belonged to Aaron Bickerstaff (or Biggerstaff), a Loyalist militia captain who was mortally wounded at the battle of Kings Mountain. Draper, *King's Mountain,* 328, 483; Griffin, *History of Old Tryon and Rutherford Counties,* 68; Landrum, *Colonial and Revolutionary History of Upper S.C.,* 216.

The personnel of the flag detail were detained "Pro certis causes bene Nemine Notis." The Latin phrase can be translated as "for certain things which are well known, no one needs the reasons." (For assistance with the rather elliptical phrasing, the editors thank University of South Carolina professors Robert Patterson and John Basil.)

Capt. Samuel Ryerse. See 4.21.80 above.

"Would not hemp do the business [better]." Johnson may have meant no more than that a rope binds better than mere words, but, given the context, he probably alluded to a hangman's noose. "To wag hemp in the wind" was, for example, a colloquial expression meaning "to be hanged." John S. Farmer and W. E. Henley, *Slang and Its Analogues, Past and Present,* 7 vols. in 3 (1890; repr., New York: Kraus Reprint Corp., 1965), 3:302.

10.14.80 Rumors that Banastre Tarleton was in the vicinity caused the hangings to be stopped at nine. Lambert, *South Carolina Loyalists,* 143.

The victims not mentioned by Johnson were Captain Grimes, Lieutenant Lafferty, John McFall, John Bibby, and Augustine Hobbs. Draper, *King's Mountain,* 340.

Col. Ambrose Mills (c. 1722–1780) was born in England and moved to Maryland while still a child. He later settled on the South Carolina frontier, where his first wife was killed by Indians during the Seven Years' War of 1756–1763. He subsequently married Ann Brown (see next paragraph) and established their home along the Green River in Rutherford County, North Carolina. He was twice jailed for his Loyalist activities, first in August 1776 for purportedly instigating people to ally with the Indians and join the British. After posting a bond and swearing allegiance to the state, he was discharged in September. Two years later Mills cooperated with David Fanning in raising five hundred men with the intention of joining the British at St. Augustine. However, Mills and several others were apprehended and jailed. Following his release, he joined Ferguson's corps. He was executed for allegedly prompting the Cherokee to attack the South Carolina frontier early in the Revolution. Draper, *King's Mountain,* 481–82, 340; Saunders, *Colonial Records of North Carolina,* vol. 10, *1775–1776* (1890; repr., Wilmington, N.C.: Broadfoot Publishing Co., 1993), 730, 827; Carole Troxler, "Refuge, Resistance, and Reward: The Southern Loyalists' Claim on East Florida," *Journal of Southern History* 55 (November 1989): 574.

Mrs. Mills was Ann Brown, a sister-in-law of Col. Thomas Fletchall of South Carolina (7.15.80 above). In September 1783 Ann Mills witnessed the sale of 150 acres of land on Green River, Rutherford County, North Carolina, by William Mills, who had acquired the property by "heirship." An Ann Mills also appears among Rutherford County taxpayers in 1785. Draper, *King's Mountain,* 481; Brent Holcomb, comp., *Deed Abstracts of Tryon, Lincoln and Rutherford Counties, North Carolina, 1769–1786: Tryon County Wills and Estates* (Easley, S.C.: Southern Historical Press, 1977), 146; Brent Holcomb, comp., *1785 Tax List, Rutherford County, North Carolina* (Chapel Hill, N.C.: Holcomb, 1974), 2.

Capt. Robert Wilson served in the Fair Forest militia under Col. Daniel Plummer (7.13.80 above). He resided in the Ninety Six District of South Carolina, and his widow received his final pay in 1782. Draper, *King's Mountain,* 340n; Moss, *Roster of the Loyalists in the Battle of Kings Mountain,* 90.

Capt. James Chitwood was buried one-half mile away at Benjamin Bickerstaff's. Draper, *King's Mountain,* 344–45. Also see 9.15.80 above for Chitwood.

The daughters of Capt. James Chitwood and his wife, Alice, were probably Elizabeth Chitwood Whiteside and Catherine Chitwood Burts, both of whom were born in Virginia around 1750, moved with their parents to North Carolina, and later settled in Missouri. C. Kenyon Withrow, "Notes on the Chitwood Family Tree," *Forest City This Week,* Oct. 24, 1973; Bynum, *Heritage of Rutherford County,* 157–58; Chitwood Family Genealogy Forum, http://genforum.com/chitwood/, posted online by Caroline Fairall, September 19, 1999; letter from Thomas Thomson to James Chitwood, *St. Louis Genealogical Society Quarterly* 12 (Summer 1979): 102.

Allaire does not mention the women. "Diary of Allaire," in Draper, *King's Mountain,* 510–11.

Isaac Baldwin of Burke County was about to be hanged when his brother cut his bonds and the two escaped. However, he was murdered by Whigs not long after this incident. Draper, *King's Mountain,* 341–42 and n.

Walter Gilkey was executed for wounding a young boy even though Gilkey's father offered a horse, saddle, and equipment plus "a hundred dollars" as ransom for his son. Draper, *King's Mountain,* 332–33.

10.15.80 Cane Creek. See 9.12.80 above as well as Price-Strother map (1808) for the wandering route of this creek.

Johnson may have added "Burk County" to distinguish this crossing at the head-waters of the Catawba River from the more well-known Island Ford on the Catawba River between present-day Catawba and Iredell counties. Powell, *North Carolina Gazetteer,* 247.

The arduous forced march was designed to put the group beyond the reach of Tarleton's dragoons as quickly as possible. Draper, *King's Mountain,* 344.

Colonel McDowell's house could have belonged to either Charles or Joseph McDowell; both lived at Quaker Meadows. See 9.29.80 above for the McDowells.

Allaire indicated that about one hundred prisoners escaped. Other details also differ, but Allaire's version is otherwise substantially similar, although less informative. "Diary of Allaire," in Draper, *King's Mountain,* 511.

10.16.80 Johns River—otherwise known as Mulberry Fork of Middle Creek—was named for John Perkins, an African American landowner in the vicinity. The river flows generally south for about thirty miles before emptying into the Catawba River in Burke County. Gen. Griffith Rutherford to Gov. Caswell, February 17, 1780, in Walter Clark, ed., *State Records of North Carolina,* vol. 15, *1780–1781* (Goldsboro, N.C.: Nash Brothers Printers, 1898), 340; Powell, *North Carolina Gazetteer,* 255.

10.17.80 Joseph Holt, who was a resident of Wilkes County in 1782, was probably the owner of this plantation, although Allaire in the printed version of his diary called him "Hatt." Clarence E. Ratcliff, comp., *North Carolina Taxpayers,* vol. 2, *1679–1790* (Baltimore: Genealogical Publishing Co., 1987), 98; "Diary of Allaire," in Draper, *King's Mountain,* 511. For other Holts, see William S. Powell, James K. Huhta, and Thomas J. Farnham, eds., *The Regulators in North Carolina: A Documentary History, 1759–1776* (Raleigh, N.C.: State Department of Archives and History, 1971), 135, and Greene, *Papers,* 7:383.

10.18.80 Moravian Creek flows northeast to join the northern branch of the Yadkin River northwest of the Wilkes County Court House. The creek's name derives from the Moravians who settled in the area. Price-Strother map (1808); Powell, *North Carolina Gazetteer,* 334.

Wilkes County was formed in 1778 from Surry County and was named for John Wilkes, a British member of Parliament regarded as a champion of liberty by Americans. Powell, *North Carolina Gazetteer,* 535.

Allaire noted that the prisoner was hanged at about five o'clock in the morning. "Diary of Allaire," in Draper, *King's Mountain*, 511.

10.19.80 A Bird Hogwood and a Partin Hogwood were living in Wilkes County in 1782, but the editors have been unable to locate them more precisely. Ratcliff, *North Carolina Taxpayers*, 2:82.

10.20.80 There were several Sales in the area through which Johnson was traveling, roughly the land below the Yadkin River and east of modern-day Wilkesboro, which was Capt. Alexander Gordon's militia district in Wilkes County. The 1782 tax list for this district includes Cornelius, John, Leonard, Thomas, and William Sale. The latter may have been the principal progenitor of the family. His will, executed in September 1787, mentioned his sons Cornelius, William, James, and Robert. Cornelius, perhaps the most prominent among his generation, received a grant of four hundred acres "on the south side of Shallowford Road" (see 10.22.80 below). Cornelius Sale also appears frequently in the Wilkes County court minutes: he served periodically as an overseer of new roads and was appointed a constable between 1779 and 1780. The will of Cornelius was probated in February 1811. Ratcliff, *North Carolina Taxpayers*, 2:177; Johnson J. Hayes, *The Land of Wilkes* (Wilkesboro, N.C.: Wilkes County Historical Society, 1962), 20–21; Minutes for June 10, 1779, March 9, 1780, and April 28, 1784, Wilkes County Court of Pleas and Quarter Sessions; Wilkes County Deed Books A-1:278 and 356, B-1:57 and 136; Wilkes County Will Books 1:245–46 and 2:320. All unpublished records are in the North Carolina State Archives.

10.21.80 HeadPiths Plantation was probably Headpath, Hedgepeth, Hudspeth, Hedgspeth, or Hedgepith's. Numerous individuals with these surnames appear in local records about this time; which one Johnson referred to is unclear. John Hudspeth, who was evidently a lawyer, appears frequently in Jo White Linn, comp., "Surry County, North Carolina, Will Abstracts," 1974, North Carolina State Archives. See the following for examples of variant spellings: Walter Clark, ed., *State Records of North Carolina*, vol. 14, *1779–1780* (Winston, N.C.: M. I. and J. C. Stewart Printers, 1896), 667; Gertrude S. Hay, ed., *Roster of Soldiers from North Carolina in the American Revolution* (Durham: North Carolina Daughters of the American Revolution, 1932), 533; Brent Holcomb, comp., *Marriages of Surry County, North Carolina, 1779–1868* (Baltimore: Genealogical Publications Co., 1982), 100.

Edward Clanton does not appear on a 1774 tax list for Surry County, but he is included in a 1785 list of taxpayers living in Captain Wright's District of Surry County. This district included the area around Deep Creek. Clanton executed a deed for 225 acres along the south fork of Deep Creek in 1797, and he appears frequently in the Surry County court minutes from the early 1790s. Minutes of Feb. 15, 1791, Feb. 15, 1792, May 14, 1793, and Feb. 22, 1794, Surry County Court of Pleas and Quarter Sessions; Surry County Deeds, Book G:37; Luther N. Byrd, comp., "Tax Lists for Surry County, North Carolina, 1774 and 1785," 1947; all at North Carolina State Archives.

10.22.80 Shallow Ford crossed the northern fork of the Yadkin River in Surry County. Greene, *Papers,* 7:maps 212–13 and 356–57.

Salem was a Moravian town whose name signified peace; it was established in 1766 and joined with Winston to become Winston-Salem in 1913. Powell, *North Carolina Gazetteer,* 434.

Much emphasis was put on music by the Moravians, or the "Renewed Unitas Fratrum," a pietistic offshoot from the Lutheran Church. Their great leader Count von Zinzendorf of Saxony (1700–1760) believed that "in the Bible one sees how God speaks to Men . . . and in the song book how Men speak to God." Daniel B. Thorp, *The Moravian Community in Colonial North Carolina: Pluralism on the Southern Frontier* (Knoxville: University of Tennessee Press, 1989), 14, 12, quotes 18.

"Friends to government or hard Money" referred to Moravians, whose principles precluded the taking of oaths and service in the military. Beginning in 1777, the North Carolina legislature exempted them from the portion of the oath of allegiance that required citizens to "defend the independent Government" of North Carolina. In return, the Moravians paid substantial fines and triple taxes. Still, combatants often regarded those who sought to remain neutral as sympathetic to their enemies, and the Moravians frequently suffered accordingly. DeMond, *Loyalists in North Carolina,* 55, quote 155.

Mechanicks. Persons "having a manual occupation" or "working at a trade." *Oxford English Dictionary,* 2nd ed., s.v. "mechanic."

The Moravian towns Bethabara and Bethania, north of Salem, were predominantly agricultural villages, although Bethabara had a somewhat more complex economy. Together, the Moravian settlements were an important source of supplies for the patriots of Surry County and, to a lesser extent, for the British army. Thorp, *Moravian Community in Colonial North Carolina,* x, 31, 109, 114; Adelaide L. Fries, ed., *Records of the Moravians in North Carolina,* vol. 4, *1780–1783* (Raleigh, N.C.: Edwards & Broughton, 1930).

Allaire indicated the total distance traveled this day was twenty-four miles, not twenty-eight, and he omitted Johnson's supposition about the allure of money. Otherwise, the differences in their entries are insubstantial. "Diary of Allaire," in Draper, *King's Mountain,* 511.

10.23.80 One of the Continental officers Johnson mentioned was, according to Allaire, "Mr. Simons." He was probably Lt. Richard Simons of Col. William Washington's (4.13.80 above) Third Continental Dragoons, who would be killed at the battle of Eutaw Springs on September 8, 1781. "Diary of Allaire," in Draper, *King's Mountain,* 511–12; Heitman, *Historical Register,* 498; Gibbes, *Documentary History of the American Revolution,* 3:158; Haller, *William Washington,* 66.

Allaire considered him to be "exceeding polite." The other officer could not be identified.

10.24.80 Capt. Campbel may have been Capt. John Campbell (1743–1808) of the Washington County, Virginia, militia, which was commanded by Col. William Campbell (10.7.80 above). Moss, *Patriots at Kings Mountain*, 38.

The editors have been unable to identify Joseph Ridgeway, despite extensive searching. That Allaire did not mention him suggests that he was not a well-known literary character. However, several Joseph Ridgeways—or perhaps their namesakes—appear in the records of eighteenth-century New Jersey and New York. See *A Catalogue of Books, Belonging to the Library Company of Bridge-Town (commonly called Mount-Holly) in New-Jersey* (Philadelphia: William Goddard, 1768), 5, Early American Imprints, Series 1: Evans, 1639–1800, Readex Digital Collections No. 41849; *Pennsylvania Gazette*, May 7, 1783; and U.S. Congress, *Biographical Directory of the United States Congress, 1774–2005* (Washington, D.C.: Government Printing Office, 2005), 1810. Johnson would also develop a remote family relationship with some of the Ridgeways when his daughter married into the Boudinot family, which was related to the Ridgeways through the Stocktons. George A. Boyd, *Elias Boudinot, Patriot and Statesman, 1740–1821* (Princeton, N.J.: Princeton University Press, 1952), 289; Joseph R. Klett, ed., *Genealogies of New Jersey Families from the Genealogical Magazine of New Jersey*, vol. 2, *A Genealogical Dictionary of New Jersey Bible Records and Other Family Records* (Baltimore: Genealogical Publishing Co., 1996), 443.

Allaire noted that Bethabara was six miles from Salem and that its inhabitants were "very kind to all the prisoners." "Diary of Allaire," in Draper, *King's Mountain*, 512.

10.25.80 Allaire observed that the men of their detachment were permitted "to go into the houses in the town without a guard" because Captain DePeyster gave his word for their good behavior. "Diary of Allaire," in Draper, *King's Mountain*, 512.

10.28.80 Allaire's entry for Thursday the twenty-sixth to Saturday the twenty-eighth was "nothing extra," although the official Moravian diarist at Salem recorded an eclipse of the sun on the 27th. "Diary of Allaire," in Draper, *King's Mountain*, 512; Fries, *Records of the Moravians in North Carolina*, 4:1574.

10.29.80 Johnson, being ill, was not present at a religious service that other prisoners were forced to attend. Allaire gave the particulars: "Col. Cleveland waited on Capt. DePeyster and the rest of the officers, and asked us if we, with our men, would come and hear a sermon at ten o'clock. He marched the militia prisoners from their encampment to the town, and halted them: and sent an officer to our quarters to acquaint us they were waiting for us. We then ordered our men to fall in; marched to the front of the prisoners; the whole then proceeded on to a height about one-half mile from the town. Here we heard a Presbyterian sermon, truly adapted to their principles and the times; or, rather, stuffed as full of Republicanism as their camp is of horse thieves." "Diary of Allaire," in Draper, *King's Mountain,* 512.

The Moravian diarists had somewhat different versions of the event. The writer at Salem mentioned that several of the Moravian Brethren "attended the thanksgiving sermon which Mr. Hill preached in Bethabara in view of the victory over the Tories." The Bethabara diarist was more detailed: "In the afternoon there was preaching in the woods between Ranke's and the big meadow. A great crowd of soldiers had gathered, and most of our Brethren; it was estimated that about two thousand were present, to whom Mr. Hill preached earnestly on the 63rd chapter of Isaiah." Fries, *Records of the Moravians in North Carolina,* 4:1574, 1632.

10.30.80 Allaire recorded that a man was about to be executed for responding to a taunt from an American that the prisoners would "be hanged" with "nevermind that, it will be your turn next." Col. Benjamin Cleveland (9.29.80 above), however, reprieved the offender. "Diary of Allaire," in Draper, *King's Mountain,* 512.

10.31.80 James Supple, a native of Ireland, served in DeLancey's First Brigade as an ensign and lieutenant. Raymond, "Roll of Officers," 271, 258; M. J. Clark, *Loyalists in the Southern Campaign,* 3:20–26, 350, 362.

Allaire estimated the ice to be one-quarter-inch thick. "Diary of Allaire," in Draper, *King's Mountain,* 512.

11.1.80 Col. Benjamin Cleveland. See 9.29.80 above.

The editors have been unable to identify McCatchum.

Col. Martin Armstrong (c. 1739–1808), who was originally from Augusta County, Virginia, moved to North Carolina and eventually settled in Surry County, where he became colonel of the local militia. Disobeying orders to join Gen. Horatio Gates, he led his unit against Ferguson at Kings Mountain. Repeated insubordination eventually caused him to be stripped of his command in 1781, but he retained his rank in the militia and eventually became a brigadier general. In addition, Armstrong served in numerous local offices as well as in the North Carolina Senate (1783–1784) and the House of Commons (1799). Despite possible fraud in his conduct of the land office, he ended his career as surveyor general of Tennessee. Powell, *Dictionary of North Carolina Biography,* 1:46; Cheney, *North Carolina Government,* 156, 211, 212, 240; Greene, *Papers,* 6:546n16.

11.2.80 Bethania. See 10.22.80 above.

Lt. John Taylor. See 5.2.80 above.

11.3.80 Allaire noted that he had heard that Gen. Alexander Leslie had landed in Virginia. "Diary of Allaire," in Draper, *King's Mountain,* 513.

11.4.80 Major James Read, a Continental army officer, served as an assistant to Col. Thomas Polk, the commissary in charge of supplying General Greene's army in North Carolina. Read later commanded a volunteer corps of mounted men from Halifax County, North Carolina. Greene, *Papers,* 6:574–75 and n5; 7:431n1.

Gen. Horatio Gates. See 8.15.80 above.

The Moravians had heard the prisoners were to be taken to Virginia. Like many rumors, this one grew from a kernel of fact, but Johnson's confusion may have reflected some of the uncertainty among American authorities over the matter. General Gates, who was still in charge of the Southern Department, ordered that the prisoners taken at Kings Mountain be marched to Fincastle Court House in western Virginia, where he believed a stockade for them could be built in "good Whig country, and well stored with provisions," remote from British incursion. Thomas Jefferson, who was then governor of Virginia, was not enthused about this plan. Although he thought that regular soldiers (including presumably those from the Loyalist provincial units) might be sent to Winchester to join British prisoners already there, he considered the "Tories" (the Loyalist militiamen) to be more of a problem. The Fincastle Court House area (renamed Montgomery County) was, he believed, the "most disaffected" part of the state and vulnerable to British incursions. Moreover, the important lead mines that supplied American troops were located in this area. To increase the number of prisoners near them would be to risk "vital injury." Jefferson therefore favored a plan suggested by Col. William Campbell, who thought that the "spirit of this part of the Captives is so absolutely broken" that they would be willing "to enlist in our armies for the war or to do anything else which shall be required of them." Jefferson referred the matter to the Continental Congress, obviously hoping that the prisoners would be sent as far north as possible. Fries, *Records of the Moravians in North Carolina,* 4:1632–33; Gates to Jefferson, Nov. 1, 1780, and Jefferson to Samuel Huntington, Nov. 7, 1780, in Jefferson, *The Papers of Thomas Jefferson,* vol. 4, *1 October 1780 to 24 February 1781,* ed. Julian P. Boyd (Princeton, N.J.: Princeton University Press, 1951), 86–87 and n, 98–99.

The Continental Congress, however, had other plans. On November 21, it recommended that the prisoners be held how and where Jefferson thought proper and that a list of the Tory prisoners be sent to the chief executives in their respective home states for whatever action seemed appropriate. Huntington to Jefferson, Nov. 21, 1780, in Paul H. Smith, ed., *Letters of Delegates to Congress, 1774–1789,* vol. 16, *Sept. 1, 1780–Feb. 28, 1781* (Washington, D.C.: Library of Congress, 1989), 369–70.

Much of this planning turned out to be superfluous. Armstrong, who commanded the militia of Surry County, North Carolina, where the prisoners then were, proceeded to dismiss, parole, or enlist most of them in the Whig militia. Both Generals Gates and Greene, who had hoped to exchange these prisoners for the Americans being held by the British in Charles Town, were appalled at Armstrong's action. Gates reprimanded him, and Greene noted that "we have lost by the folly, not to say anything worse, of those who had them in charge upwards of six hundred men." After suspending Armstrong from his command, the North Carolina legislature launched an investigation. Armstrong's defense was that he had too few men and too little equipment to guard the prisoners and to have sent them west was to have doomed them because the over-mountain men had threatened to kill them. Jefferson, *Papers,* 4:178n; Greene to Washington, Dec. 7, 1780, Greene, *Papers,* 6:544; Journals of the Senate, Feb. 3, 1781, in Walter Clark, ed., *State Records of North Carolina,* vol. 17, *1781–1785* (Goldsboro, N.C.: Nash Brothers Printers, 1899), 668. The letter dated November 19, 1788, from Armstrong to Gates in which he justified his actions is included in W. Clark, *State Records of North Carolina* (14:744–45), where it is attributed to Maj. Mark Armstrong. The internal evidence and surrounding circumstances suggest, however, that it was written by Col. Martin Armstrong.

The remaining prisoners apparently wound up in different places: Greene planned a sturdy stockade for them at Salisbury, North Carolina, which was never completed; some were to be tried for treason at Halifax; others were held in Virginia; and a few, including Johnson, went to Hillsborough. Patrick Lockhart to Jefferson, Dec. 4, 1780, Jefferson, *Papers,* 4:177–78; Greene to Capt. Joseph Marbury, Dec. 4, 1780, Greene, *Papers,* 6:521–22 and n6; Ensign Richard Boyle to Greene, Feb. 17, 1781, Greene, *Papers,* 7:305. See also Draper, *King's Mountain,* 357–60.

Allaire merely noted that he had dined at a country house. "Diary of Allaire," in Draper, *King's Mountain,* 513.

11.5.80 Allaire and the two other officers—along with Capt. William Gist of the South Carolina Loyalist militia—made good their escape and fifteen days later reached the British post at Ninety Six. Being "told we could not get paroles to return within the British lines; neither were we to have any till we were moved over the mountains in the back parts of Virginia, where we were to live on hoe cake and milk" was, according to Allaire, what prompted their escape. Extract of a Letter from an Officer, dated Charleston, Jan. 30, 1781, in Draper, *King's Mountain,* 519.

Lt. William Stevenson. See 9.26.80 above.

Lt. John Taylor. See 5.2.80 above.

From this date onward, Allaire's diary no longer parallels Johnson's. See Armstrong to Gates, Nov. 7, 1780, and postscript of Nov. 11, 1780, in W. Clark, *State Records of North Carolina,* 14:727–78, for his report of the escape of Allaire, Stevenson, Taylor and others wherein he remained confident that the remaining captive officers would not escape because "they Show every mark of Uneasiness for the Ungentlemanlike Conduct of Those absent."

11.6.80 The British had landed at Plymouth in Virginia. Actually some 2,200 British troops under Maj. Gen. Alexander Leslie (5.12.80) had landed at Portsmouth, Newport News, and Hampton on October 20 and 21. They remained only a month, however, before (as a result of the Whig victory at Kings Mountain) being ordered to reinforce Cornwallis in the Carolinas. John E. Selby, *The Revolution in Virginia, 1775–1783* (Williamsburg, Va.: Colonial Williamsburg Foundation, 1988), 216–17, 221, and *A Chronology of Virginia and the War of Independence, 1763–1783* (Charlottesville: University Press of Virginia, 1973), 40.

11.8.80 Johnson, identified as the "English Doctor," was present at the bandaging of a severely wounded man. Fries, *Records of the Moravians in North Carolina,* 4:1633.

11.9.80 Perhaps the Mountain Road was the one that went northwest from Salem to Bethabara, Bethania, and Pilot Mountain. Price-Strother map (1808).

Regarding the Branch Plantation, a Moravian chronicler recorded that the remaining Tory and British prisoners "went as far as Ranke's." A list of "Men Resident in Wachovia, 1775 to 1783" compiled from church registers contains John Rank (Bethabara, b. 1737), Gottlob Ranke (Bethania, b. 1761), and Michael Ranke (Bethania, b. 1729), as well as a Johann Ranke later identified as being from Bethania (October 15, 1781). John was therefore probably the owner of "The Branch," which was within a mile of Bethabara, where the prisoners had been held. Fries, *Records of the Moravians in North Carolina,* 4:1633, 1923, 1764, 1772.

11.12.80 Maj. Joseph Winston (1746–1815), who was born in Louisa County, Virginia, settled along the Dan River in North Carolina about 1769. In 1776 he was appointed major of the Surry County militia and served in the campaign against the Cherokee Indians. In addition, he participated in several expeditions against North Carolina Tories between 1776 and 1781. At the battle of Kings Mountain he commanded a portion of the force, for which he was commended by the North Carolina legislature. He later joined Gen. Nathanael Greene and fought at the battle of Guilford Court House. He served in the North Carolina Senate in 1790–1791, 1802, 1807, and 1812 and in the U.S. Congress from 1793 to 1795 and 1803 to 1807. Draper, *King's Mountain,* 454–56; U. S. Congress, *Biographical Directory of the United States Congress, 1774–2005,* 2187.

11.16.80 Perhaps this was Archey Smith, who lived near Ninety Six in the vicinity of a British outpost that Moses Kirkland commanded. Allaire stayed a night at Smith's after his escape from the Whigs. "Diary of Allaire," in Draper, *King's Mountain,* 515.

Col. Moses Kirkland (1725?–1787), a man of shady character and questionable deals, had settled in South Carolina by 1752 and became a prominent planter and mill owner. He was active in the Regulator movement and was commissioned a captain of militia in 1775. He deserted the patriot cause soon after and took his entire unit over to the British. Captured and imprisoned in 1776, Kirkland escaped and was appointed deputy superintendent of the Seminole Indians for the British. In July 1780 he resumed command of a Loyalist regiment in the Ninety Six District and eventually rose to the rank of lieutenant colonel. After the war he moved to Jamaica and later died at sea. Edgar and Bailey, *Biographical Directory of the South Carolina House of Representatives,* 2:380–81. See also 6.15.80 above for his ferry on the Saluda River.

Lt. Col. John Cruger. See 9.25.80 above.

11.18.80 Capt. Samuel Wood (1735–1825) of the North Carolina militia was born in Albemarle County, Virginia. A resident of Burke County, North Carolina, during the Revolution, he fought in the battles of Kings Mountain and Cowpens. After the war he moved to Lincoln County, Kentucky. Moss, *Patriots at Kings Mountain,* 274–75.

For Hillsborough, see 11.22.80 below, when Johnson arrived there.

11.20.80 The editors could not conclusively identify Lieutenant Ashbourne, but among the Ashburns who resided in the area toward which Johnson was headed were Anderson and John, both of whom appeared on lists of Caswell County taxpayers in 1777, 1784, and 1786. Clarence E. Ratcliff, comp., *North Carolina Taxpayers,* vol. 1, *1701–1786* (Baltimore: Genealogical Publishing Co., 1984), 7; vol. 2, *1679–1790,* 6.

Because Johnson had probably just crossed into Guilford County, this Bullock may have been the Edward Bullock who died in 1813 in Guilford County, leaving a large family, including his wife, Ann. Irene Webster, *Guilford County, North Carolina, Will Abstracts, 1771–1841* (Madison, N.C.: Irene Webster, 1979), 5, 6.

Anthanks [or probably Unthanks] were a prominent extended family of Quakers who lived in the area. Allen, John, and Joseph were adult men who might have been hospitable to Johnson in 1780. Allen's taxes were remitted in 1782 because he was "a balloted man" doing duty in the Continental service for nine months. Francis C. Anscombe, *I Have Called You Friends: The Story of Quakerism in North Carolina* (Boston: Christopher Publishing House, 1959), 300; Webster, *Guilford County Will Abstracts,* 205; Minute Packet of the Court of Pleas and Quarter Sessions, 1782–1788, in Sallie W. Stockard, *History of Guilford County, North Carolina* (Knoxville, Tenn.: Gaut-Ogden Co., 1902), 32.

Guilford Court House was the county seat of Guilford County, established in 1774. The name was changed to Martinsville in 1785, but in 1808 the site was abandoned when the county seat was moved to Greensboro. Powell, *North Carolina Gazetteer,* 206.

The editors were unable to identify Mr. Logan with certainty because most of the first ten years of Guilford County records were lost during the battle of Guilford Court House on March 15, 1781. He may have been the David Logan whose goods were to be "sold by the sheriff" in May 1782. Guilford County, North Carolina, Court Minutes, August 1781–May 1788, p. 32, transcribed by Jane S. Hill, 1999, North Carolina State Archives.

Nonse is an archaic form of *nonce,* meaning "for the occasion . . . or temporarily." The Latin *ipse* can be translated as "master of the house." *Oxford English Dictionary,*

2nd ed., s.v. "nonse," "nonce"; *Oxford Latin Dictionary* (Oxford: Clarendon Press, 1968), 2:965.

11.21.80 Col. John Paceley [or Paisley] (d. 1811)] of Guilford County was appointed major of the local minutemen on September 9, 1775, and promoted to lieutenant colonel on April 22, 1776. According to various reports, his plantation was from three to ten miles east of Guilford Court House; it appears on the Price-Strother map (1808) and a map in the *Papers of Nathanael Greene,* 7:356. Walter Clark, ed., *State Records of North Carolina,* vol. 22, *Miscellaneous* (Goldsboro, N.C.: Nash Brothers Printers, 1907), 144–46; Saunders, *Colonial Records of North Carolina,* 10:206, 531; Greene, *Papers,* 7:356; Webster, *Guilford County Will Abstracts,* 48–49. See Eli W. Caruthers, *Revolutionary Incidents; and Sketches of Character, Chiefly in the "Old North State"* (Philadelphia: Hayes and Zell, 1854), 340, for a tale of one of his exploits during the Revolution.

Maj. William O'Neal lived west of the Haw River and was responsible for drafting local militia in Orange County. Reportedly corrupt, he allegedly took bribes from those wishing to avoid military service. Banastre Tarleton used O'Neal's plantation as a campsite, and O'Neal himself was later wounded and captured by the British. In attempting to obtain his release, Gen. Nathanael Greene used his wife, Elizabeth, as an intermediary. Price-Strother map (1808); Hugh F. Rankin, *The North Carolina Continentals* (Chapel Hill: University of North Carolina Press, 1971), 288; Greene, *Papers,* 7:350 and n, 383 and n, and map, 356; Alma Cheek Redden, ed., *Abstracts of the Minutes of the Inferior Court of Pleas and Quarter Sessions of Orange County, North Carolina, 1777–1788* (Charlotte, N.C.: Artistic Letter Shop, 1966), pt. 1:5–9, 25–51.

11.22.80 This is probably Trollinger's Ford, which was due east of O'Neal's on the road to Hillsborough. O'Neal served as an overseer of this road at times. Buchanan, *Road to Guilford Courthouse,* 361; Price-Strother map (1808); Powell, *North Carolina Gazetteer,* 218; Redden, *Minutes of Court of Pleas and Quarter Sessions of Orange County,* pt. 1:28.

William Courtney was a prominent Quaker. In 1777 he became one of the five commissioners who constituted the governing body of Hillsborough, and in the following year the North Carolina legislature designated him to supervise the construction of a new county courthouse. For much of the time from 1778 to 1790 he served as a justice of the peace; in 1777–1778 and 1780 he also represented Hillsborough in the General Assembly. In addition he operated a tavern in his house that contained a room large enough to accommodate two hundred people. Ruth Blackwelder, *The Age of Orange: Political and Intellectual Leadership in North Carolina, 1752–1861* (Charlotte, N.C.: William Loftin, 1961), 24; Hugh Lefler and Paul Wager, eds., *Orange County, 1752–1952* (Chapel Hill, N.C.: The Orange Printshop, 1953), 16, 46, 48, 173; Redden, *Minutes of Court of Pleas and Quarter Sessions of Orange County,* pt. 1:5, 13, 15, 49; Asbury, *Journal and Letters of Francis Asbury,* 1:371.

General "Stevenson" was probably a slip of the pen for Maj. Gen. Edward Stevens (1745–1820) of the Virginia militia. His troops crumbled at the battle of Camden in August 1780 but would fight well at the battle of Guilford Court House in 1781. Although wounded at the latter, Stevens took part in the siege of Yorktown and would serve in the Virginia Senate from 1782 to 1790. Greene, *Papers*, 6:512–514 and n1; 7:316n1, 184; Horatio Gates to Thomas Jefferson, Nov. 1, 1780, Jefferson, *Papers*, 4:86. After the battle of Camden, he joined the southern army at Hillsborough, where he would be in charge of prisoners. Greene, *Papers*, 7:195–96.

Col. Abishai Thomas, D. Q. G., identifying himself as an "assistant deputy quartermaster," wrote Gen. Nathanael Greene from Hillsborough on December 24, 1780. He was commissioned deputy quartermaster general in the First Regiment of the North Carolina Continental line on May 1, 1777. Greene, *Papers*, 6:611; W. Clark, ed., *State Records of North Carolina*, vol. 16, *1782–1783* (Goldsboro, N.C.: Nash Brothers Printers, 1899) 1168.

In 1782 Benjamin Leonard was granted a license to keep an ordinary or tavern in his house in Hillsborough; he may have died shortly thereafter, however, for John Allison, the administrator of a Benjamin Leonard's estate, filed an inventory of it on February 26, 1783. Redden, *Minutes of Court of Pleas and Quarter Sessions of Orange County*, pt. 2:2, 11.

During the late 1760s Col. James Thackston was a partner of William Johnson in the mercantile business and an associate of the leading men of Hillsborough. A captain of the local militia during the Regulator uprising, he supported royal governor William Tryon but became a Whig during the American Revolution. As such, he was appointed colonel of the Hillsborough District minutemen in 1775 and eventually lieutenant colonel of the Fourth Regiment of North Carolina Continentals. After serving in the North Carolina House of Commons during 1787, he died sometime before April 11, 1792. Powell, *Dictionary of North Carolina Biography*, 6:18–19; Tryon, *Correspondence*, 2:82n5.

Under British rule, Francis Corbin (d. 1767) was successively a member of the Royal Council and the lower house of the legislature, as well as Lord Granville's principal land agent. The latter position gave him considerable power over the disposition of land in the Granville District, the large area adjacent to Virginia that Granville retained after the other Carolina proprietors surrendered their holdings to the Crown in the 1720s. Corbin was also deeply involved in local factional infighting and proved to be, in the words of a recent scholar, "thoroughly untrustworthy." The town of Hillsborough, which was founded in 1754, was first named for Corbin, but five years later the assembly incorporated it as Childsburgh in honor of the attorney general of North Carolina, Thomas Childs. In 1766, however, its name was again changed, this time to honor the current British secretary of state for the colonies, Lord Hillsborough. The revolutionary state legislature met there in 1778, 1780, and 1782–1784. H. Roy Merrens, *Colonial North Carolina in the Eighteenth Century: A Study in Historical Geography* (Chapel Hill: University of North Carolina Press, 1964), 24; A. Roger Ekirch, *"Poor Carolina": Politics and*

Society in Colonial North Carolina, 1729–1776 (Chapel Hill: University of North Carolina Press, 1981), 135; Powell, *Dictionary of North Carolina Biography*, 1:431–32; Work Projects Administration for the State of North Carolina, Federal Writers' Project of the Federal Works Agency, *North Carolina: The WPA Guide to the Old North State* (Columbia: University of South Carolina, 1988), 367–68; Powell, *North Carolina Gazetteer*, 228.

11.24.80 Col. John Gunby (1745–1807) was a Continental officer from Maryland who rose from captain in 1776 to brigadier general in 1783, shortly before he retired from the army. He was at the first and second battles of Camden (August 16, 1780, and April 25, 1781) and served with distinction at the battle of Guilford Court House (March 15, 1781). Selesky, *Encyclopedia of the American Revolution*, 2:474.

11.25.80 In April 1777 William Newman received a license to maintain a tavern in his house in Hillsborough. The license was renewed in 1780 (when his property was valued at £1,223), 1782, 1783, 1784, as well as 1785. William Newman was also a juror in the court of quarter sessions in 1783 and 1785. Redden, *Minutes of Court of Pleas and Quarter Sessions of Orange County*, pt. 1:7; pt. 2:3, 17, 30; Orange County Tax Lists, 1780, folder 4, North Carolina State Archives.

Benjamin Chapman provided the bond necessary for Newman to acquire his tavern license in 1782, and Chapman himself received a similar license in 1784. In August 1782 Chapman served on the grand jury; and a man of the same name became the master of William Edwards, age fifteen, who was bound to him until he became twenty-one to "learn the art of stocking weaver." Whether William Chapman, age eleven, who was bound out as an orphan in 1788, was one of the children that Johnson inoculated in 1780 is unclear. Redden, *Minutes of Court of Pleas and Quarter Sessions of Orange County*, pt. 2:3, 30; pt. 1:59; pt. 3:45.

Inoculation, which used live virus and usually produced a real but milder case of smallpox than that acquired by natural contagion, was standard procedure in the British army; Washington adopted it in 1777. Elizabeth A. Fenn, *Pox Americana: The Great Smallpox Epidemic of 1775–82* (New York: Hill and Wang, 2001), 92–95.

Newman and Chapman were prescient. By early 1781 smallpox had broken out in the Moravian communities and among the prisoners of war being held at Salisbury, North Carolina. The epidemic would reach Hillsborough by May. For a good, short description of inoculation and its history in the American colonies, see Fenn, *Pox Americana*, 31–43, 123–25.

11.26.80 On November 27 Gen. Nathanael Greene wrote Baron Steuben from Hillsborough that he had "arrived at this place last evening" and would leave in about an hour. General Greene (1742–1786), a fighting Quaker, had been a merchant in Rhode Island, a private in a state army unit, and quartermaster general of the Continental army from 1778 to 1780 before being appointed to head the southern army. He assumed command of the troops at Charlotte, North Carolina, on December 2, 1780, and would perform so well that he is considered the "strategist of the Revolution." Greene, *Papers,* 6:506; Garraty and Carnes, *American National Biography,* 9:528, 530.

Col. Lewis Morris Jr. was the son of Lewis Morris Sr. (d. 1798), a prominent militia general and signer of the Declaration of Independence from New York. Lewis Jr. was made lieutenant colonel in 1778 and served as Nathanael Greene's aide-de-camp from June 1779 until the end of the war. Heitman, *Historical Register,* 403; Nathanael Greene, *The Papers of General Nathanael Greene,* vol. 3, *18 October 1778–10 May 1779,* ed. Richard K. Showman (Chapel Hill: University of North Carolina Press, 1983), 269n1.

Maj. Ichabod Burnet (c. 1756–1783), like Morris, was an aide to General Greene who accompanied him southward from the northern theater. The son of Dr. William Burnet, who served as a delegate to the Continental Congress from New Jersey, Ichabod attended Princeton University before serving for a short time as the secretary of the Essex County, New Jersey, Committee of Safety. He was formally appointed as Greene's aide on March 23, 1778. He resigned from the army in 1783 and died on a business trip to Havana, Cuba, shortly thereafter. Nathanael Greene, *The Papers of General Nathanael Greene,* vol. 5, *1 November 1779–31 May 1780,* ed. Richard K. Showman (Chapel Hill: University of North Carolina Press, 1989), 110n1; 6:431n4.

11.28.80 The name Samuel Allen appears frequently enough in diverse records that it is difficult to be certain that one is dealing with the same Samuel Allen, but Johnson's landlord was probably a tax official for Hillsborough District in 1777 and 1778 and one of several men appointed by the county court in 1778 to open a road north of town from the Hawfield Meeting House to James Clark's on Little River. During the same session of the court he was also appointed foreman of the grand jury. In addition, his name appears on petitions requesting clemency for two different men, one a Regulator [in 1771?] and the other a Loyalist [c. 1782]. He may also have been the individual who received licenses to operate a tavern in 1785 and 1786. Redden, *Minutes of Court of Pleas and Quarter Sessions of Orange County,* pt. 1:6, 19, 15, 12; pt. 3:2, 29; Saunders, *Colonial Records of North Carolina,* 9:26–27; Walter Clark, ed., *State Records of North Carolina,* vol. 19, *1782–1784, with Supplement, 1771–1782* (Goldsboro, N.C.: Nash Brothers Printers, 1901), 932.

12.2.80 At least Aaron, George, Henry, Isaac, Jesse, John, Joseph, Peter, and Thomas were among the Sharps living in Orange County during the Revolutionary era. Joseph, who owned two lots in Hillsborough in 1790, was perhaps the most likely to have been a resident of the town. He or one of the other Sharps apparently operated an establishment referred to as "Sharp[']s Grinery's" [*sic,* a tannery or commissariat?] that supplied hides to the British while they occupied the town. Ratcliff, *North Carolina Taxpayers,* 2:182; Walter Clark, ed., *State Records of North*

Carolina, vol. 26, *Census, 1790 and Names of Heads of Families* (Goldsboro, N.C.: Nash Brothers Printers, 1905), 1313; Lefler and Wager, *Orange County, 1752–1952,* 15; Francis Nash, *Hillsboro, Colonial and Revolutionary* (1903; repr., Chapel Hill, N.C.: The Orange Printshop, 1953), 71; Saunders, *Colonial Records of North Carolina,* 9:371; A. R. Newsome, ed., "A British Orderly Book, 1780–1781, Part IV," *North Carolina Historical Review* 9 (October 1932): 371.

12.3.80 Col. Gunby's objection to Johnson's inoculating the inhabitants, as Johnson surmised, may well have been at least partly the result of personal pique. But because inoculation produced a contagious case of smallpox, many people feared the procedure and some colonies banned it. Nevertheless, since its results were generally beneficial, it was popular in some areas, such as lowcountry South Carolina, where a knowledgeable British officer reported that almost every family was inoculated. Thus, Gunby may also have been wary of the potential political implications of allowing a Loyalist to perform what many inhabitants would have regarded as a good deed. Alexander Innes to John Andre, May 21, 1780, Clinton Papers, William L. Clements Library, University of Michigan, Ann Arbor; Fenn, *Pox Americana,* 33, 36–40.

Regarding the magistrates of the town, Johnson could have meant either the commissioners of the town, who were the elected governing body after 1777, or the justices of the peace for Orange County. Most likely, however, he referred to William Courtney in particular, who held both offices and with whom he was already acquainted. For Courtney, see 11.22.80 above. Blackwelder, *Age of Orange,* 16ff. For the names of other justices, consult Redden, *Minutes of Court of Pleas and Quarter Sessions of Orange County,* pt. 1, and Lefler and Wager, *Orange County, 1752–1952,* 173.

12.4.80 Dr. John L. Elbert was listed as a junior surgeon on a roster of medical officers compiled at the hospital in Hillsborough on November 5, 1780, by Dr. James Browne, chief physician and surgeon of the Southern Department. Elbert became surgeon's mate of the Fifth Maryland Regiment on January 1, 1782, before retiring in April 1783. Louis C. Duncan, *Medical Men in the American Revolution, 1775–1783* (1931; repr., New York: Augustus M. Kelley, 1970), 321; Heitman, *Historical Register,* 213.

12.5.80 Because Brickell was a fairly common name in the eighteenth-century South, identification of this individual is difficult, but the editors believe that Johnson referred to Dr. John Brickell (1749–1809), who for thirty years practiced medicine in Savannah, Georgia, where he arrived about 1779. He had been born in Ireland and may have lived in Virginia for some time. Like Johnson, he attended King's College medical school, although he did not graduate; perhaps old school ties accounted for his willingness to trust Johnson with his horse. Like many other Whigs, he may have left Georgia during the latter part of the British occupation.

In 1786 the Georgia legislature would name Brickell as one of two men designated to compile a list of veterans who had been disabled in the service of the United States. Victor H. Bassett, *Voices from the Past,* reprinted from the Bulletin of the Georgia Medical Society (Savannah, 1937), 26; June 17 and 24, 1784, *Gazette of the State of Georgia*; Allen D. Candler, ed., *Colonial Records of the State of Georgia* (1904–1910; repr., New York: AMS Press, 1970), 19:518–24; Daniel Turner, "Letters and Papers of Dr. Daniel Turner: A Rhode Islander in South Georgia," part 1, ed. Richard K. Murdoch, *Georgia Historical Quarterly* 53 (September 1969): 382n6.

More than a decade later, Brickell wrote "Observations on the Medical Treatment of General Washington in his [last] Illness," which was highly critical of the excessive bleeding prescribed by his physicians. John Brickell, "Medical Treatment of General Washington," *Transactions of the College of Physicians of Philadelphia,* 25 (1903): 90–94.

12.6.80 William Johnson was a prominent Scots merchant who with James Thackston (11.22.80 above) operated a store at Hillsborough. In 1779 the court of quarter sessions appointed him and two other merchants to examine the returns of the tax assessors, and in 1780 he was named as one of several individuals to inspect the local currency. His will was probated in May 1785. Marjoleine Kars, *Breaking Loose Together: The Regulator Rebellion in Pre-Revolutionary North Carolina* (Chapel Hill: University of North Carolina Press, 2002), 62; Redden, *Minutes of the Court of Pleas and Quarter Sessions of Orange County,* pt. 1:38, 48; pt. 3:4.

12.7.80 James Munro was another prominent Scots merchant, who, along with others trading to Britain, Ireland, and the West Indies, was ordered in August 1777 to take the oath of allegiance to the state. Because he refused to do so, he was banished from North Carolina. Thereupon he went to New York but later returned and became a citizen. During the British occupation of Hillsborough in 1781, he and "Persons deputed by him" had permission to pass British checkpoints without hindrance. When the British left the town, he "seized and buried the county records, which destroyed many of them." With the American victory, he left the state and applied for compensation from the British government for his losses as a Loyalist. In 1780 his property, which had been estimated to be worth £20,788, included more than thirteen hundred acres and several lots with buildings in Hillsborough. Redden, *Minutes of the Court of Pleas and Quarter Sessions of Orange County,* pt. 1:5, 20; pt. 3:16–17; A. R. Newsome, ed., "A British Orderly Book, 1780–81, Part 4," *North Carolina Historical Review,* 9 (October 1932): 372; William D. Bennett, ed., *Orange County Records* (Raleigh, N.C.: privately published, 1987), 2:vii–viii; Palmer, *Biographical Sketches of Loyalists,* 636; Orange County Tax Lists, 1780, folder 4, North Carolina State Archives.

12.11.80 Captain Brown was probably John Brown (d. 1812), who received an ensign's commission in the First North Carolina Regiment of Continental troops.

In 1776 he became a second lieutenant and a captain in 1777 before transferring to a regiment of North Carolina dragoons. A brother-in-law of Charles and Joseph McDowell (9.29.80 above), he commanded a company under Col. Benjamin Cleveland at the battle of Kings Mountain. He also served in the North Carolina Senate in 1778 and 1780 and in the House of Commons in 1786–89, as well as in the state conventions of 1788 and 1789 called to ratify the U.S. Constitution. Draper, *King's Mountain,* 460; Heitman, *Historical Register,* 125; Cheney, *North Carolina Government, 1585–1974,* 202, 206, 218–223, 767, 770.

Because a plethora of Turners populate relevant records, the editors have been unable to identify this Mr. Turner with certainty. One of the two most likely individuals, however, is Edward Turner, a prominent resident of Orange County who in 1777 and 1779 served as the overseer of roads out of Hillsborough as well as a member of the grand jury. Redden, *Minutes of the Court of Pleas and Quarter Sessions of Orange County,* pt. 1:8, 39, 33.

The other promising possibility is Robert Turner, a Loyalist captain who was entitled to pay from February 1776 to October 27, 1778. This same man may also have joined Col. David Fanning's unit as a captain in the summer of 1781. M. J. Clark, *Loyalists in the Southern Campaign,* 1:346; W. Clark, *State Records of North Carolina,* 22:195–96.

James Supple. See 10.31.80 above.

12.17.80 Halifax, North Carolina, was incorporated in 1760 and named for Lord Halifax, then president of the British Board of Trade. From 1779 to 1781 it was the seat of the North Carolina legislature. Powell, *North Carolina Gazetteer,* 209.

12.25.80 It is interesting that Johnson made no mention of Christmas, although the holiday was sufficiently celebrated in the South for some commanders to mark the day. Col. Richardson to Hon. H. Laurens, January 2, 1776, Gibbes, *Documents of the American Revolution,* vol. 1, *1764–76,* 247; Nathanael Greene, *The Papers of General Nathanael Greene,* vol. 10, *3 December 1781–6 April 1782,* ed. Dennis M. Conrad (Chapel Hill: University of North Carolina Press, 1998), 102.

1.1.81 Maj. Ichabod Burnet. See 11.26.80 above.

Johnson's request to be paroled does not appear in the *Papers of General Nathanael Greene,* but negotiations about paroles and a possible general exchange continued throughout much of the spring of 1781. On January 12 Greene indicated he would try "to promote a general exchange and to grant paroles where exchanges cannot be had." Greene's instructions to Col. Edward Carrington on March 11, 1781, stipulated his terms for such an exchange, but the cartel governing the process was not signed until May 3, 1781. Greene, *Papers,* 7:113 (quotation), 425–26n3. See also Betsy Knight, "Prisoner Exchange and Parole in the American Revolution," *William and Mary Quarterly* 48 (April 1991): 201–22.

1.2.81 Perhaps this was a child of James Frazier, a Presbyterian minister who had been appointed in 1778 as one of nine trustees of a new school to be known as the Academy of Science Hall. A Loyalist, he spent four months in a Whig jail sometime after Yorktown and eventually went to Canada before returning to Scotland by 1793. In 1780 his property had been valued at £3,540. Ratcliff, *North Carolina Taxpayers,* 2:69; Redden, *Minutes of the Court of Pleas and Quarter Sessions of Orange County,* pt. 1:53; Troxler, "Migration of Carolina and Georgia Loyalists to Nova Scotia and New Brunswick," 243; Orange County Tax Lists, 1780, folder 4, North Carolina State Archives.

Munro's children stayed behind when he was banished from the state (12.7.80 above). During his absence James Hogg (1.21.81 below) acted as their guardian. Redden, *Minutes of the Court of Pleas and Quarter Sessions of Orange County,* pt. 3:16–17.

1.8.81 Sandy Point was approximately five miles above Jamestown on the James River. A British expedition commanded by the erstwhile American general Benedict Arnold sailed into Chesapeake Bay on December 30. By January 5 and 6, 1781, his soldiers had burned much of Richmond. Baron Von Steuben's letters of December 31 (which Greene received on January 13) and January 8 contained news of the attack. Selby, *The Revolution in Virginia,* 65, and *Chronology of Virginia and the War of Independence,* 40; Greene, *Papers,* 7:34, 76–79, 109–11.

1.12.81 From 1778 to 1783 William Whitted served on several juries in the Orange County court and was thrice appointed to supervise road work. His town house still stands at the corner of Churton and East Queen streets. Redden, *Minutes of the Court of Pleas and Quarter Sessions of Orange County,* pt. 1:16, 25, 32, 34, 44, 57; pt. 2:6, 14, 16, 34.

1.14.81 Mr. Lynch was probably Thomas Lynch, who did jury duty in 1778 and 1780. In May 1780 he received a license to keep a tavern at his house. After his death—apparently fighting for the British at the battle of Guilford Court House, March 15, 1781—his wife, Mary, was appointed as his executrix; she would also receive licenses for a tavern from 1782 to 1786. In addition, she petitioned the court in 1785 for permission to build a gristmill on Back Creek, which was approximately fifteen miles west of town. Redden, *Minutes of the Court of Pleas and Quarter Sessions of Orange County,* pt. 1:58, 21, 45, 47; pt. 2:1, 14, 28, 21; pt. 3:4, 30, 7; Greene, *Papers,* 7:356–57; Johnson, *Loyalist Surgeon: War Diary,* 97.

1.20.81 The editors could find no Burd in Orange County during the Revolutionary period. However, there were several Birds, including Emmon, James, James Jr., Richard, and Thomas. A Richard Bird was one of many petitioners who sought clemency for an outlawed Regulator, John Fruit, in the early 1770s, and he or another Richard Bird accepted a British commission as a lieutenant about July 1781. More likely, however, the individual who requested that Johnson inoculate his family was James or James Sr.; in February 1779 the former received £4 for repairs to the jail in Hillsborough, and the latter served on the grand jury in August 1778. W. Clark, *State Records of North Carolina,* 26:1286; 22:195–96; Saunders, *Colonial Records of North Carolina,* 9:94; Redden, *Minutes of the Court of Pleas and Quarter Sessions of Orange County,* pt. 1:22, 30.

1.21.81 James Hogg (1729–1804), who was born in Scotland, was a merchant-planter. After immigrating to America he moved to Hillsborough in 1775, where he established himself on 1,163 acres along the Eno River. He served on the revolutionary Hillsborough Committee of Safety, but in August 1777 he—along with other Scots merchants—was ordered by the county court to swear allegiance to the state. Having apparently satisfied his Whig compatriots, he was briefly a captive of the British in 1781; two years later his house reputedly became the site at which Revolutionary War officers founded the North Carolina Society of the Cincinnati (one of the state branches of the national veterans organization established by the officers of the Continental army in 1783). He would also be active in the Transylvania Company, which sought to develop western lands, and as a trustee and benefactor of the University of North Carolina. Powell, *Dictionary of North Carolina Biography,* 3:160–61; Orange County Tax Lists, 1780, folder 4, North Carolina State Archives; Redden, *Minutes of the Court of Pleas and Quarter Sessions of Orange County,* pt. 1:5; Curtis C. Davis, *Revolution's Godchild: The Birth, Death, and Regeneration of the Society of the Cincinnati in North Carolina* (Chapel Hill: University of North Carolina Press, 1976), 6.

An intriguing but perhaps apocryphal description of some of Hogg's activities during the war appears in "Reminiscences of Dr. William Read." Read, a physician from Georgia, was in North Carolina about the time of the battle of Camden, South Carolina (August 15–16, 1780). According to Read, both the British and the Americans then granted Hogg de facto neutrality, which permitted him to supply General Gates's troops; and the doctor claimed to have seen "a hundred mules and horses, loaded with corn, ascending the rocky heights near Hillsborough, and he understood that they were in motion all night," headed for Hogg's gristmills and the American army. Gibbes, *Documentary History of the American Revolution,* 2:272.

Among several Farmers, Samuel Farmer appeared on the Orange County tax lists for 1755, Job Farmer in 1779, and Othniel Farmer in 1790. Thomas Farmer, however, was listed in both 1779 and 1790, and he was the only Farmer specifically identified as being a resident of "Hillsboro Town." He also represented that area in the North Carolina General Assembly in 1782 and 1783. He was therefore probably the proprietor of the house where Johnson stayed, although Johnson's diary failed to mention that this Farmer was an American militia colonel, then at Salisbury, North Carolina, preparing to join Gen. William Davidson. Ratcliff, *North Carolina Taxpayers,* vol. 1, *1701–1786,* 67; vol. 2, *1679–1790,* 65; W. Clark, *State Records of North Carolina,* 26:1301, 1313; Cheney, *North Carolina Government, 1585–1974,* 210, 212; Greene, *Papers,* 7:169–70, 120n1.

1.23.81 At least eight Kellys appear in the records as residing in or around Hillsborough during the revolutionary era: Chanler, Charles, David, James, two Johns, Robert, and William. James was the only one listed in the Hillsborough District of Orange County in 1780. Johnson, however, may well have gone to see one of the Johns, who appear to have been the most prominent members of the group. In February 1783 one of them was part of a jury named to lay out a road from the Caswell County line to the Eno River near Abercrombies Mill. His appointment suggests that he resided along this route and therefore out of town. By May 1783 one John was dead, and Jean Kelley was the administratrix of his estate. But the other John continued to appear prominently in the court records at least through November 1786. Orange County Tax Lists, 1780, folder 4, North Carolina State Archives; Redden, *Minutes of the Court of Pleas and Quarter Sessions of Orange County,* esp. pt. 2:12, 16.

1.24.81 Jacob Branton, who owned 330 acres of land in 1780, was a member of the jury pool for the county court in 1779 and 1782 as well as a grand juror in 1786; Jacob Brinton (who could have been the same man) served as a grand juror in May 1779 and with a group to lay out a road in 1783. Orange County Tax Lists, 1780, folder 4, North Carolina State Archives; Redden, *Minutes of the Court of Pleas and Quarter Sessions of Orange County,* pt. 1:32, 33; pt. 2:10; pt. 3:16.

1.30.81 Reports of a battle between Gens. Alexander Leslie (5.12.80) and Daniel Morgan were muddled. It was actually the battle of Cowpens on January 17 when Morgan's forces defeated the British under Banastre Tarleton, who lost approximately 110 men killed, 200 wounded, and 527 captured. Cowpens National Battlefield is located in northwestern Cherokee County, South Carolina. Peckham, *Toll of Independence,* 79; Don Higginbotham, *Daniel Morgan, Revolutionary Rifleman* (Chapel Hill: University of North Carolina Press, 1961), 136–44.
   Col. John Gunby. See 11.24.80 above.

1.31.81 Capt. Abraham DePeyster. See 3.10.80 above.
   Commissary of Prisoners. "One to whom a special duty or charge is committed by a superior power." *Oxford English Dictionary,* 2nd ed., s.v. "commissary."

2.3.81 Mrs. Samuel Allen. See 11.28.80 above.

2.4.81 Williams was then a common name in the vicinity, and it has been impossible to positively identify this individual. However, DePeyster and Johnson enjoyed enough prestige as officers, despite their status as prisoners, to associate with the local elite. Mrs. Williams may therefore have been Agnes, the wife of John

Williams (1731–1799). He was a lawyer, deputy attorney general for the Hillsborough District, and in 1778 Speaker of the North Carolina Commons House. He also served briefly as a delegate to the Continental Congress. He was, like James Hogg (see 1.21.81 above), a speculator in western lands through the Transylvania Company and a trustee of the University of North Carolina. From 1779 until he died, he was a judge of the Superior Court of North Carolina. Powell, *Dictionary of North Carolina Biography*, 6:209.

Mrs. Thomas Lynch. See 1.14.81 above.

2.5.81 James Munro. See 12.7.80 above.

On January 19, two days after Tarleton's defeat at Cowpens, Cornwallis set out in pursuit of Morgan and Greene; on January 25 he tried to speed his progress by burning much of the army's baggage at Ramsour's Mill. But Greene's force crossed the Dan River ahead of the British, and Cornwallis gave up the chase, falling back to Hillsborough, where on February 22 he would futilely invite "loyal subjects" to join his forces. Wickwire and Wickwire, *Cornwallis*, 274–85, 443.

2.7.81 Presumably Johnson was to join the prisoners taken at Cowpens, for on January 25 Greene ordered that all prisoners of war were to be sent to Virginia. Although the privates were to be "well guarded," the officers were to be paroled. Greene to Maj. Edmund M. Hyrne, Jan. 25, 1781, and Greene to Gen. Edward Stevens, Jan. 25, 1781, Greene, *Papers*, 7:194–95.

Dix's Ferry was an important crossing of the Dan River approximately five miles north of the North Carolina border on the road from Hillsborough to Halifax Court House, Virginia. Four miles down river from "Great Falls," the area contained buildings that could be used as storehouses. Capt. John Smith to Greene, Dec. 25, 1780, Greene, *Papers*, 6:614 and end paper map; 7:213.

From 1771 to 1781 at least seven Rileys appear in the records of Orange County and immediately adjacent areas: Edward, Edward Jr., Jacob, James, John, John Sr., and William. The editors have therefore been unable to identify which Riley Johnson is referring to, but given the distance and direction that Johnson went this day, the most likely possibility is Jacob, who in 1779 was an overseer of the road from Hillsborough to Six Mile Tree. In 1777, however, James Riley received permission from the Caswell County Court to build a mill on land that he owned on Country Line Creek (2.8.81 below). Ratcliff, *North Carolina Taxpayers*, vol. 1, *1701–1786*, 171; vol. 2, *1679–1790*, 172; Orange County Tax Lists, 1780, folder 4, North Carolina State Archives; Redden, *Minutes of the Court of Pleas and Quarter Sessions of Orange County*, pt. 1:38; pt. 3:40; William S. Powell, *When the Past Refused to Die: A History of Caswell County, North Carolina, 1777–1977* (Durham, N.C.: Moore, 1977), 64.

2.8.81 Col. William Moore's Plantation on Country Line Creek was about six miles south of the Virginia border. A lieutenant colonel in the militia, Moore would also be elected commissioner of confiscated estates for Hillsborough District in 1783. General Greene would stop at his place five days after Johnson did. Greene, *Papers,* 7:284–85, 298n1, and map on 356–57; Lefler and Wager, *Orange County, 1752–1952,* 44, 63.

Country Line Creek, which flows generally north through Caswell County, North Carolina, to empty into the Dan River at Mill Town on the provincial border, probably received its name from the propensity of eighteenth-century settlers to consider Virginia and North Carolina separate countries. Powell, *History of Caswell County,* 3, 9.

2.9.81 Mr. Arnold was perhaps Ambrose Arnold, who was granted a tavern license by the Caswell County court in 1787 and had been appointed a constable in 1782. Jeannine D. Whitlow, ed., *Heritage of Caswell County, North Carolina* (Yanceyville, N.C.: Hunter, 1985), 94.

Peter Hart was a resident of Orange County in 1779 and 1800. In 1779 he served as a juror in the Court of Quarter Sessions; in 1785 Stephen Madden's duty as a road overseer extended from the Caswell County line to Peter Hart's plantation. This plantation should not be confused with Hartsford, an elaborate complex near Hillsborough that Thomas Hart described in detail when he offered it for sale in 1779. Ratcliff, *North Carolina Taxpayers,* vol. 2, *1679–1790,* 89; Ronald V. Jackson, ed., *North Carolina 1800 Census Index* (North Salt Lake, Utah: Accelerated Indexing Systems, 1974), 98; Redden, *Minutes of the Court of Pleas and Quarter Sessions of Orange County,* pt. 1:41; pt. 3:2; *Gazette of the State of South Carolina,* Sept. 15, 1779.

2.10.81 Upon assuming command of the Southern Department, Greene proposed a general exchange to Cornwallis, but the latter showed limited interest in the matter until the battle of Cowpens on January 17 added more than five hundred prisoners to those already held by the Americans. "Serious talks" began in March, and on May 3, 1781, British and American negotiators signed a general agreement. In the interim, however, some officers were paroled or exchanged on a case-by-case basis. DePeyster and Johnson were among the lucky ones, for on February 8, 1781, Greene directed Col. John Gunby (11.24.80 above) to parole two British officers at Hillsborough to Charles Town. A list of American officers being held in the Charles Town area with dates of their exchanges indicates that four American surgeons were exchanged in March 1781. A reciprocal arrangement may have benefited Johnson. Knight, "Prisoner Exchange and Parole," 209–10; Philip Ranlet, "In the Hands of the British: The Treatment of American POWs during the War of Independence," *The Historian* 62 (Summer 2000): 750–51; Greene, *Papers,* 7:256; "Roll of the Continental Officers, Prisoners of War in South Carolina, as They Stand for Exchange," *Yearbook, City of Charleston, South Carolina,* 1897, 417–25.

2.14.81 The virtually illegible name may have been Decon or Deiken. The editors suspect that Johnson meant Deiken and that, acting as an employee of James

Munro (12.7.80 above), he served as a guide for DePeyster and Johnson on the way to Charles Town; for in granting them paroles, General Greene stipulated that a "carefull person must attend them." Seven years later a six-year-old orphan, William Deiken, was bound out by the Orange County court to Robert McCracken until he reached the age of twenty-one. Greene to Col. John Gunby, Feb. 8, 1781, in *Papers of Nathanael Greene,* 7:256; Redden, *Minutes of the Court of Pleas and Quarter Sessions of Orange County,* pt. 3:45.

2.16.81 There were several Tennens, Tinnens, and Tinnings in the Hillsborough area at this time: Cairns, Hugh, James, John, and Robert, at least one of whom (Hugh) was a prominent justice of the peace. Johnson, however, probably encountered James Tinning, who in 1777 was an overseer of a road terminating at Woody's Ferry (see below in this note) as well as a court-appointed appraiser of a site for a projected gristmill on the Haw River. Both duties suggest that he lived in the vicinity. Redden, *Minutes of the Court of Pleas and Quarter Sessions of Orange County,* esp. pt. 1:1, 4, 17.

Woody's Ferry crossed the Haw River approximately two miles above the mouth of Cane Creek; the operator may have been James Woody, who in 1778 was appointed overseer of a section of road that terminated at the Haw River. Greene, *Papers,* 7:357 (map); Redden, *Minutes of the Court of Pleas and Quarter Sessions of Orange County,* pt. 1:23.

There were probably two or more William Lindleys alive at this time; which one Johnson referred to is unclear. The most well-known figure was a descendant of Thomas Lindley (1706–1781), a Quaker who moved from Chester County, Pennsylvania, to the Cane Creek area of Orange County, North Carolina, by 1759 and became a substantial landowner. His grandson William was a captain of the Chatham County Loyalist militia in July 1781 and an active partisan. As British fortunes waned in the area, Captain Lindley moved across the mountains to western North Carolina, where he was murdered in January 1782. However, in November 1782 the Orange County court accepted a William "Linley" as surety for two other men. Moreover, according to Orange County tax records, the estate of a William Lindley was still being administered in 1790. The decedent, who appears to have died on September 29, 1784, was probably the individual to whom Johnson referred. Powell, *Dictionary of North Carolina Biography,* 4:67; Redden, *Minutes of the Court of Pleas and Quarter Sessions of Orange County,* pt. 2:10; W. Clark, *State Records of North Carolina,* 26:1293; William W. Hinshaw, *Encyclopedia of American Quaker Genealogy,* vol. 1, *North Carolina* (Ann Arbor, Mich.: Edwards Brothers, 1936), 359.

2.17.81 The Widow McCarrol was Frances McCarrol, the sister of Mary Freeman, who in 1770 married the future Revolutionary War governor of North Carolina, Thomas Burke. Frances's late husband was doubtless James McCarrol, who was appointed a justice of the peace in Chatham County on August 12, 1774. By 1779, when she was listed as a taxpayer in Orange County, she had apparently become a widow. As Cornwallis approached Hillsborough in early 1781, Burke arranged for the successful evacuation of his wife and sister-in-law, although McCarrol, who had great faith in Greene's army, went most reluctantly. John S. Watterson, *Thomas Burke, Restless Revolutionary* (Washington, D.C.: University Press of America, 1980), 168, 12; Robert J. Cain, ed., *Colonial Records of North Carolina [Second Series]: Records of the Executive Council, 1755–1775* (Raleigh: North Carolina Department of Cultural Resources, 1994), 311; Ratcliff, *North Carolina Taxpayers*, vol. 2, *1679–1790*, 139. For the location of McCarrol's land, see the Price-Strother map (1808).

The east and west forks of Deep River join in southwestern Guilford County, from which the main stream flows generally southeast until it joins the Haw River in Chatham County to become the Cape Fear River. Powell, *North Carolina Gazetteer*, 139.

Searcey's Ferry was located where the road that led southwest from Hillsborough crossed Deep River at the border between Randolph and Chatham counties, as depicted on the Price-Strother map (1808) and described in *Randolph County, 1779–1979* (Asheboro, N.C.: Randolph County Historical Society, 1980), 135–36, 245.

The editors have been unable to identify the Dutch Butcher. It is worth noting, however, that Germans (the Deutsch or "Dutch") began settling in North Carolina during the 1740s and by 1790 constituted more than 5 percent of the total population. Randolph County, through which Johnson was traveling at this time, attracted a number of them. In particular, a congregation of pietistic Dunkers under Jacob Stutzman established themselves near the Uwarrie River at points that came within ten miles of Deep River, which Johnson had just crossed. The Dunker congregation, which constructed no meetinghouse, dispersed after the death of their minister, but the 1790 census continued to reveal numerous German names in the area. See Thomas L. Purvis's Comment in "The Population of the United States, 1790: A Symposium," *William and Mary Quarterly* 41 (January 1984): 125; Roger A. Sappington, "Dunker Beginnings in North Carolina in the Eighteenth Century," *North Carolina Historical Review* 46 (Summer 1969): 217, 221, 224, 228; Roger A. Sappington, "Two Eighteenth Century Congregations in North Carolina," *North Carolina Historical Review* 47 (April 1970): 203.

2.18.81 Apparently beginning in the 1750s, Samuel Parsons bought and sold several parcels of land along the Little River. While this area was still in Anson County, Parsons became involved in the contested election of 1773. His precise role is unclear, but a witness testified that he saw "one Sam Parsons . . . with a bottle in his hand" apparently interrogating voters. The phrasing suggests that at the time Parsons was not yet a prominent figure, but in 1784, after part of Anson County had been split off to form Montgomery County, Parsons represented it in the state senate. Brent Holcomb, *Anson County North Carolina Deed Abstracts, 1749–1766; Abstracts of Wills and Estates, 1749–1795* (Baltimore: Genealogical Publishing Co., 1980), 77; Julian P. Boyd, "The Sheriff in Colonial North Carolina,"

North Carolina Historical Review 5 (April 1928): 177–78 (quote); W. Clark, *State Records of North Carolina,* 19:400. See also Hoffmann, *Colony of North Carolina: Abstracts of Land Patents,* 2.

2.19.81 Capt. John Kimborough held property—including a well-known mill on the Little River, where Johnson was at this time—in both Carolinas and was a prominent figure in each state. Associated with the Regulators, he represented Rowan County in the North Carolina legislature in 1771–1772 and Montgomery County in 1779–1780. Meanwhile, in 1775 he was commissioned a captain in the St. Davids, South Carolina, volunteer militia, and he would later hold the same rank in the North Carolina Loyalist militia.

While the British held Camden, South Carolina, Kimborough took twenty-seven slaves there and went into hiding before surrendering to the Whigs on November 22, 1780. Jailed but subsequently paroled, he petitioned North Carolina authorities for clemency, but the legislature rejected his request in 1782. By 1791, however, he was one of the "substantial planters" who requested that the South Carolina General Assembly improve a road that would facilitate travel from Camden, South Carolina, to Fayetteville, North Carolina.

A devout man, Kimborough was noted for hosting large religious meetings of many sects—Quakers, Baptists, Dunkers, and others. A Baptist, Rev. Evan Pugh, would preach his funeral sermon in September 1796.

Greene, *Papers,* 7:43n, 213 map; Kars, *Breaking Loose Together,* 128; Walter Clark, ed., *State Records of North Carolina,* vol. 13, *1778–1779* (Winston, N.C.: M. I. and J. C. Stewart Printers, 1896), 785; 14:750; 16:163; 19:382, 931; "List of Officers of the Militia of South Carolina Who Took Part in the War of the Revolution, 1775–1783," *Yearbook, City of Charleston, South Carolina,* 1893, p. 232; ——— to Gen. Francis Marion, July 6, 1781, in Gibbes, *Documentary History of the American Revolution,* vol. 3, *1781–1782,* 103–4; George Lloyd Johnson Jr., *The Frontier in the Colonial South: South Carolina Backcountry, 1736–1800* (Westport, Conn.: Greenwood Press, 1997), 100; Evan Pugh, *The Diaries of Evan Pugh, 1762–1801,* trans. Horace F. Rudisill (Florence, S.C.: St. David's Society, 1993), 373.

Cornelius Robinson purchased three hundred acres on the south side of the Pee Dee River in 1759; six years later he acquired part of his brother's six-hundred-acre tract. He was appointed justice of the peace for Anson County in 1762 and 1778. Captured by Whigs in 1782, Robinson was subsequently paroled and released. Holcomb, *Anson County Deed Abstracts,* 20, 55; William L. Saunders, ed., *Colonial Records of North Carolina,* vol. 6, *1759–1765* (1888; repr., Wilmington, N.C.: Broadfoot, 1993), 799; Walter Clark, ed., *State Records of North Carolina,* 16:180–81; Clark, *State Records of North Carolina,* vol. 23, *Laws, 1715–1776* (Goldsboro, N.C.: Nash Brothers Printers, 1904), 992.

Charles Robinson acquired six hundred acres on the northeast side of the Pee Dee River in 1746, adjoining the east side of the Little River. He also served as a justice of the peace for Anson County and represented that district in six colonial assemblies between 1751 and 1771. Robinson also served as a member of the Anson County Committee of Correspondence in 1774. Also captured by Whigs in 1782, like his brother Cornelius, he was subsequently paroled and released. Holcomb, *Anson County Deed Abstracts,* 55; William L. Saunders, ed., *Colonial Records of North Carolina,* vol. 4, 1734–1752 (1886; repr., Wilmington, N.C.: Broadfoot, 1993), 1274–75; vol. 5, *1752–1759* (1887; repr., Wilmington, N.C.: Broadfoot, 1993) 42; 6:362; vol. 7, *1765–1768* (1890; repr., Wilmington, N.C.: Broadfoot, 1993), 725; vol. 8, *1769–1771* (1890; repr., Wilmington, N.C.: Broadfoot, 1993), 106; 9:107, 1033.

2.20.81 William Blewitt was in the area at least as early as 1752, when he witnessed a land grant. From then until he made his will in 1790, he accumulated approximately eight hundred acres on both sides of the Pee Dee River in the vicinity of Blewitt Falls, where he operated a ferry and a fishery. A justice of the peace, Blewitt in 1769 signed a petition that recounted the grievances of the Regulators. Interestingly enough, the county court subsidized his ferry so that individuals attending court sessions, elections, and militia musters could have free passage. Holcomb, *Anson County Deed Abstracts,* 25, 65; Mary Wilson McBee, comp., *Anson County, North Carolina, Abstracts of Early Records* (Baltimore: Genealogical Publishing Co., 1980), 93, 123; Saunders, *Colonial Records of North Carolina,* 8:256; Tryon, *Correspondence,* 2:378–82.

Claudius Pegues (1719–1790) emigrated from England to South Carolina in 1736. Between 1755 and 1768 he established himself along the eastern side of the Pee Dee River near Cheraw, South Carolina. Eventually acquiring 3,766 acres, he became "one of the wealthiest and most influential planters in the backcountry." Pegues, "a zealous Whig," served in numerous local offices as well as in the First and Second Provincial Congresses (1775–1776) and the state General Assembly. On May 3, 1781, the cartel for the general exchange of British and American prisoners of war was signed at his house. This structure, which was built about 1760, still stands and is now on the National Register of Historic Places. Edgar and Bailey, *Biographical Directory of the South Carolina House of Representatives,* 2:514–15; Greene, *Papers,* 8:222n1; Johnson, *Frontier in the Colonial South,* 73, 74, 88n33.

2.23.81 The Pee Dee River, formed by the junction of the Uwarrie and Yadkin rivers in Montgomery County, North Carolina, flows into Winyah Bay east of Georgetown, South Carolina. Powell, *North Carolina Gazetteer,* 376.

Cheraw, nine miles south of the boundary between North and South Carolina, was settled in the 1750s at the head of navigation on the Pee Dee River. Mills, *Statistics of South Carolina,* 498. See also Alexander Gregg, *History of the Old Cheraws* (1867; repr., Spartanburg, S.C.: Reprint Co., 1982) and Work Projects Administration, Workers of the Writers' Program of the Work Projects Administration in

South Carolina, *South Carolina: A Guide to the Palmetto State* (1941; repr., Columbia: University of South Carolina Press, 1988), 339.

The area, which was often called "The Cheraws," took its name from the Cheraw (or Saraw) Indians who once inhabited it. Meriwether, *Expansion of South Carolina,* 90.

Johnson erred in thinking this was the Anson Court House. He had crossed into South Carolina north of Pegues's and was now looking at the Cheraws District Court House, which had been built pursuant to the South Carolina Circuit Court Act of 1769. The Anson County, North Carolina, Court House dated from 1755 and was on the west side of the Pee Dee River, just north of the South Carolina border. After the war, a new courthouse was built at what became Wadesboro, which remains the county seat of Anson County, North Carolina. Richard M. Brown, *The South Carolina Regulators* (Cambridge, Mass.: Harvard University Press, 1963), 106; John Collet, "A Compleat Map of North-Carolina from an Actual Survey," (1770); Work Projects Administration for the State of North Carolina, Federal Writers' Project of the Federal Works Agency, *North Carolina: The WPA Guide to the Old North State,* 339–400.

Long Bluff was settled between 1748 and 1752 by planters from the Welsh Neck of the Great Pee Dee River; its name derived from the bluff that extends for approximately three miles along the western side of the river. The courthouse and jail which appear on Henry Mouzon's map of North and South Carolina (1775) at Long Bluff operated from 1772 until 1791. T. E. Wilson, "Names in Darlington County," *Names in South Carolina* 3 (Winter 1956): 8; Brown, *South Carolina Regulators,* 106.

Perhaps this was Jonathan Williamson, who was listed among the Loyalists who were "Distressed Refugees" in Charles Town during the autumn of 1782. That he was issued a coffin for a child of Samuel Millar, who was from the Cheraw District, suggests that Williamson was also from this area. M. J. Clark, *Loyalists in the Southern Campaign,* 1:526, 550.

2.24.81 Maj. John James (1732–1791) was born in Ireland and moved to South Carolina with his parents while still a baby. As a young man, he served as a captain of militia in the Cherokee War (1759–1761) and by the late colonial period had become a prominent landowner in Prince Frederick Parish. On the eve of the Revolution, he resigned his commission in the colonial militia and was elected to the captaincy of a Whig company. He served in Charles Town in 1776 and later fought under Gen. William Moultrie during Gen. Augustine Prevost's invasion of South Carolina in 1779. After the fall of Charles Town, James refused to accept a British parole and joined Francis Marion's unit (2.25.81 below). He was promoted to major during the war but left military service prior to the peace. James represented his parish in the Second Provincial Congress (1775–1776) and the state General Assembly in 1776 and 1782. Bailey and Cooper, *Biographical Directory of the South Carolina House of Representatives,* 3:376–77.

The King's American Regiment had been raised in December 1776 at New York, where, except for an expedition in July 1778 to Newport, Rhode Island, it remained for most of the next three years. It was then sent south, where some of its men served in the battle of Kings Mountain; others occupied Georgetown, where Lt. George Campbell commanded at this time. Johnson probably encountered the twenty-five men that Marion's soldiers had captured on January 21. Katcher, *Encyclopedia of British, Provincial, and German Army Units,* 88, 90; Robert D. Bass, *Swamp Fox: The Life and Campaigns of General Francis Marion* (Columbia, S.C.: Sandlapper Press, 1959), 119; George C. Rogers, *The History of Georgetown County, South Carolina* (Columbia: University of South Carolina Press, 1970), 135–36; Nisbet Balfour to Clinton, Feb. 24, 1781, in New York Public Library, *Calendar of the Emmet Collection of Manuscripts,* 488.

The editors have been unable to find any record of a Jouett in the region through which Johnson was then traveling. Surnames with the closest spelling were Jaudon (in Prince George Parish) and Joulee (in Prince Frederick). However, southern pronunciations of *j* and *d* were sometimes confusing, and there were several DeWitts in the area. William was the most prominent. A captain in the local Whig militia, he was a member of the lower house of the legislature from 1782 to 1783, before he resigned to become sheriff of the Cheraw District. In 1785 he would be elected to the state senate. Three years later he served in the state convention that ratified the U.S. Constitution, which he favored. Moore and Simmons, *Abstracts of Wills of South Carolina,* 212; *The Register Book for the Parish Prince Frederick Winyaw, Ann: Dom: 1713* (1916; repr., Easley, S.C.: Southern Historical Press, 1982) 46; Frederic G. Cassidy, ed., *Dictionary of American Regional English* (Cambridge, Mass.: Harvard University Press, 1985–), 1:lii, 2:57, 3:124; Bailey and Cooper, *Biographical Directory of the South Carolina House of Representatives,* 3:184–85.

Black Creek runs southeastwardly through modern-day Darlington County, roughly parallel to the Pee Dee River, emptying into it in Marlborough District. Maps of Marlborough and Darlington districts, *Mills' Atlas.*

Finkley's was probably Finklia's, presumably the tavern where Henry Laurens, who had served as president of the Continental Congress, also stopped on his way home from Philadelphia to South Carolina in 1779. Food for his horses and breakfast for himself, he noted, were "cheap" there. The Finklia family would become prominent in Florence and Marion counties. Laurens, *Papers,* 15:610; G. Wayne King, *Rise Up So Early: A History of Florence County South Carolina* (Spartanburg, S.C.: Reprint Co., 1981).

Jeffs'n Creek is identified on Mills's maps of Darlington and Marion districts as Jeffrey's Creek, a tributary of the Pee Dee River.

Joseph Burch's plantation was apparently between the west bank of the Pee Dee River and the north side of Willow Creek. His mill, which on June 8, 1782, would be the site of negotiations between Francis Marion and Tory leader Micajah Ganey, is believed to have been somewhat farther south on Mill Branch, a tributary of the Great Pee Dee as identified on the Marion District map, *Mills' Atlas.* King, *Rise Up*

So Early, 27; Lipscomb, "South Carolina Revolutionary War Battles, Part 9," *Names in South Carolina* 28 (Winter 1981): 36; Hugh F. Rankin, *Francis Marion: The Swamp Fox* (New York: Thomas Y. Crowell, 1973), 282.

2.25.81 Lynches Creek rises in the Waxhaws area of North and South Carolina before flowing southeast until it joins the Pee Dee River approximately twenty-five miles from the coast. Snow's Island, which Gen. Francis Marion and his men used as a hiding place, lies adjacent to Lynches Creek on the north and the Pee Dee River to the east. Greene, *Papers,* 10:end map; Rankin, *Francis Marion,* 126.

The editors have been unable to identify this Jones.

Black Mingo Ferry appears on Mouzon's map (1775). For the early history of the surrounding community, see J. W. Nelson Chandler, "Willtown, Black Mingo: The Rise and Fall of an Early Village in the South Carolina Lowcountry," *South Carolina Historical Magazine* 105 (April 2004), 107–34.

Gen. Francis Marion (1732?–1795), born in South Carolina, served in the local militia and a provincial regiment raised during the Cherokee War in 1761. In 1775 he was elected to the First Provincial Congress and chosen as a captain in the Second South Carolina Regiment, which became part of the Continental establishment. By September 1776 Marion had become lieutenant colonel of the unit. In 1780 Gen. Gates put him in charge of the local militia in the area around Georgetown, South Carolina, and for the next two years he waged a successful guerrilla campaign against the British that earned him the nickname "The Swamp Fox." After the war, he would serve in the state Senate for much of the period from 1782 to 1791. Bailey and Cooper, *Biographical Directory of the South Carolina House of Representatives,* 3:477–79; Rankin, *Francis Marion.*

Capt. Alexander Tweed became a vestryman of Prince Frederick Parish church in 1767 and the following year an overseer of the poor. In 1770 he received a grant for one thousand acres on the Pee Dee River, and by 1781 he was a substantial planter whose slaves carried supplies to Francis Marion's camp. His most notable service, however, would be as a member of the state convention that ratified the U.S. Constitution in 1788. As such, although he observed that the "general voice" of his constituents was against ratification, he maintained an open mind, well aware that "we are not acting for ourselves alone, but, to all appearance, for generations unborn." His wife, Elizabeth, died at Black Mingo in 1785, and his own death notice, which appeared in 1803, identified him as "Captain." Laurens, *Papers,* 5:22n; Plat for 1000 acres, Craven County, on Pee Dee River, Jeffrey's Creek, June 5, 1770, Series S213184, Colonial Plat Books (Copy Series), vol. 11, p. 347, South Carolina Department of Archives and History; Rogers, *History of Georgetown County,* 134; Jonathan Elliot, ed., *The Debates in the Several State Conventions on the Adoption of the Federal Constitution as Recommended at Philadelphia in 1787 . . .* (1888; repr., New York: Ayer, 1987), 4:332–33; Elizabeth H. Jervey, ed., "Death Notices from the *State Gazette of South-Carolina* of Charleston, South Carolina," *South Carolina Historical and Genealogical Magazine* 51, (July 1950): 25; Jeannie H. Register, ed.,

"Marriage and Death Notices from the *City Gazette,*" *South Carolina Historical and Genealogical Magazine* 27 (April 1926): 101.

2.26.81 Potato Ferry, located twelve miles south of Black Mingo, crossed the Black River between Williamsburg and Georgetown districts. The name was probably derived from the large crops of sweet potatoes carried over the ferry. Henry Laurens noted that the charge there was one-tenth that of the ferry across the Kent Narrows south of Annapolis, Maryland. *Mills' Atlas*; Nexsen B. Johnson, "Some Williamsburg County Names," *Names in South Carolina,* 16 (Winter 1969): 40; Laurens, *Papers,* 15:610.

Several prominent Fords owned property in the Pee Dee and Black River areas, and Johnson's uncertainty as to where he was at this time makes sorting them out problematic. However, the most likely candidates are Stephen Jr. and George, each of whom inherited land at the juncture of the Black River and Green's Creek from their father, George, who died in 1776. Stephen (1748–1790), who lived in Prince Frederick Parish, provided supplies for Continental troops during the Revolution, and he served in the General Assembly in 1779–1780. Moore and Simmons, *Abstracts of Wills of South Carolina,* 279; Bailey and Cooper, *Biographical Directory of the South Carolina House of Representatives,* 3:239–40.

Georgetown, which was laid out in 1729, became a significant center of trade in the early 1730s after the establishment of a local customs house permitted direct trade within the British Empire, and many of the colony's wealthiest merchants would handle its exports of rice, indigo, and naval stores. Prince George Winyah Episcopal Church, begun in 1745, still stands at the corner of Broad and Highmarket streets. The British, who evacuated the town after Francis Marion's troops approached on May 28, 1781, left much of it in ruins. Rogers, *History of Georgetown County,* 32, 47–48, 82, 166; Rankin, *Francis Marion,* 213–14.

3.1.81 Sampit River and ferry appear on James Cook's "Map of the Province of South Carolina," 1773, and on the Georgetown District Map, *Mills' Atlas*. The name seems to have derived from the Sampa or Sampit Indians, who once lived along its banks. Chapman Milling, *Red Carolinians* (Columbia: University of South Carolina Press, 1969), 220. For the shifting locations of the Sampa, see Eugene Waddell, comp., *Indians of the South Carolina Lowcountry, 1562–1751* (Spartanburg, S.C.: Reprint Co., 1980), esp. 6, 284–85.

North Santee River. The Spanish, who navigated along these shores in 1609, found the Santee Indians living by this river; when Johnson crossed, it was probably 150 to 200 yards wide. John R. Swanton, *Indians of the Southeastern United States* (1946; repr., Washington, D.C.; Smithsonian Institution Press, 1979), 177; Hazard, "View of Coastal South Carolina in 1778," 182.

Lynch's causeway, which was about one and one-fourth miles long, crossed Lynch's land. Opened in March 1741, it was rebuilt in 1771 and improved in 1778, when a traveler recorded that he had seen "a great Number of Negros at work upon it, throwing up Dirt etc." But, he continued, "at present it is impassable" and the old stretches "very little better; travellers frequently get their horses swamped upon it. . . ." Rogers, *History of Georgetown County,* 43–44; Hazard, "View of Coastal South Carolina in 1778," 182.

South Santee River, according to Ebenezer Hazard, was about four hundred yards wide and "so shallow that the scow was set over with a pole." Hazard, "View of Coastal South Carolina in 1778," 182.

Despite repeated attempts, the editors have been unable to identify Mr. Ford.

Baiting was "to give food and drink to (a horse or other beast), especially when upon a journey." *Oxford English Dictionary,* 2nd ed., s.v. "bait."

White's Tavern, which Johnson located seventeen miles north of Hibben's Ferry (which ran between Mount Pleasant and Charles Town, 4.26.80 above), was very close to Wappetaw Independent Church. In 1787 a George White, who may have been the individual to whom Johnson referred, was one of the trustees of this church. After the war, a traveler, who called this tavern "Mrs. White's," arrived at it when "all the white people were away and no one had keys; consequently everything had to be obtained by breaking the doors." Petrona R. McIver, "Early Taverns on the Georgetown Road," *Names in South Carolina* 14 (Winter 1967): 34; Petrona R. McIver, "Wappetaw Congregational Church," *South Carolina Historical Magazine* 58 (January 1957): 84; Joseph B. Martin III, "A Guide to Presbyterian Ecclesiastical Names and Places in South Carolina, 1685–1985," *South Carolina Historical Magazine* 90 (January and April 1989): 200; Francesco dal Verme, *Seeing America and Its Great Men: The Journal and Letters of Count Francesco dal Verme, 1783–1784,* trans. and ed. Elizabeth Cometti (Charlottesville: University Press of Virginia, 1969), 53–54.

3.2.81 Exchange of prisoners. See 2.10.81 above.

After arriving in Charles Town and being informed of his exchange, an officer wrote a letter briefly describing the battle of Kings Mountain, which was published in London and in various Loyalist newspapers in the United States. Draper tentatively attributed the letter to "Capt. Ryerson" (4.21.80 above), but a comparison of Johnson's journal with this letter suggests that Johnson was the writer. Draper, *King's Mountain,* 519; *Rivington's Royal Gazette* (New York), March 21, 1781.

3.6.81 Nelson's Ferry. Johnson's duty at this post was relatively short. On May 15 the British "blew up the Fort at Neilson's Ferry" and evacuated the troops to Moncks Corner. Greene, *Papers,* 8:274. Also see 6.1.80 above for Nelson's Ferry.

Moncks Corner. See 4.13.80 above.

Bibliography

MANUSCRIPTS

Calhoun County Museum and Cultural Center, St. Matthews, South Carolina
Brice, Sarah. "Cave Hall," 1997.

Clements (William L.) Library, University of Michigan, Ann Arbor
Henry Clinton Papers.
Orderly Books, George Wray Papers, 1770–1848.

Dallas Historical Society, Dallas, Texas
British Orderly Books, 1779, Coit Papers.

Filson Library of the Filson Historical Society, Louisville, Kentucky
Journal of William Dells, 1776.

The National Archives, Kew, Richmond, Surrey, United Kingdom
American Loyalist Claims, AO 12 and 13.
Paymaster General, Army Establishment, Miscellaneus Books, PMG 14.
War Office, Judge Advocate General's Office, Courts Martial, Proceedings, WO
    71.

New Brunswick Museum, Saint John, New Brunswick, Canada
Lieutenant Anthony Allaire's Memorandum of Occurrences during the Campaign
    in 1780, Order Book, etc.

New Jersey Archives, Trenton
Card Index, "Loyalists in the King's Army, 1776–1783."
Newark Township, Essex County, 1790 Tax Ratables.
Records of the Commissioners of Forfeited Estates, Essex County, Account Book
    of Sales.

New Jersey Historical Society, Newark
Elias Boudinot Stockton Genealogical Collection.
Genealogy of the Johnson-Kip-Burnet–VanWagenen Families (Newark, New Jer-
    sey), transcribed by Lewis D. Cook in 1960 from the Universal Family Bible.
Minutes of the Medical Society of New Jersey.
Trinity Cathedral Miscellaneous Documents.

New-York Historical Society, New York, New York
Capt. F[rederick] DePeyster's Orderly Book, January–August 1780 and February–June 1782.

North Carolina State Archives, Raleigh
Guilford County, North Carolina, Court Minutes, August 1781–May 1788, transcribed by Jane S. Hill, 1999.
"Minutes of the Court of Common Pleas and Quarter Sessions, Lincoln County, North Carolina, April 1779–January 1789," compiled by Anne W. McAllister and Kathy G. Sullivan, 1988.
Minutes of the Surry County Court of Pleas and Quarter Sessions.
Minutes of the Wilkes County Court of Pleas and Quarter Sessions.
Orange County Tax Lists, 1780.
Rutherford County Grantor Index.
Surry County Deed Books.
"Surry County, North Carolina, Will Abstracts," compiled by Jo White Linn, 1974.
"Tax Lists for Surry County, North Carolina, 1774 and 1785," compiled by Luther N. Byrd, 1947.
Wilkes County Deed Books.
Wilkes County Will Books.

Princeton University Library, Princeton, New Jersey
Uzal Johnson's Memorandum of Occunces [Occurrences] during the Campaigne [of] 1780. Thorne Boudinot Collection. Manuscripts Division. Department of Rare Books and Special Collections.

Private Collection
Newby, Fred B. "The Use of Maps by the British Army in the Carolinas, 1780–1781." Manuscript in possession of the editors.

Public Archives of Canada, Ottawa, Canada
Loyalist Regiment Muster Rolls, 1777–1783.

Rhodes House, Oxford, United Kingdom
North Papers, Transcripts of Documents Relating to Colonial Policy, Chiefly with Reference to the West Indies, 1670–1879.

Smith (George F.) Library of the Health Sciences, Newark, New Jersey
The Minute Book of the Essex County Medical Society for 1816–1865, University of Medicine and Dentistry of New Jersey.

South Carolina Department of Archives and History, Columbia
Accounts Audited of Claims Growing Out of the Revolution in South Carolina, 1775–1876.
Colonial Plat Books.
Cornwallis Papers, PRO 30/11, Microfilm from British Public Record Office.

Memorial Books.

Plat: Portion of a September 27, 1784, plat of the "Estate of Jacob Motte Esqr. called Mount Pleasant" surveyed by Joseph Purcell, contained in Charleston County, Court of Common Pleas, Petitions for Dower, 1791, No. 11a.

Records of the South Carolina Auditor and Accountant General, 1778–1788.

Records of the South Carolina Treasury, 1775–1780.

South Carolina Volumes from the New York Public Library Transcripts of American Loyalist Examinations and Decisions.

South Carolina Will Transcripts, 1782–1855.

State Plat Books.

Works Progress Administration, Historical Records Survey, South Carolina Genealogical Society alphabetical card file of Works Progress Administration cemetery inscriptions, microfiche.

South Carolina Historical Society, Charleston

Plat of Turkey Hill Plantation by Joseph Purcell, St. Peter's, Beaufort.

University of South Carolina, Thomas Cooper Library,
Map Department, Columbia

Petty, Julian J. South Carolina Gazetteer Alphabetical Card File.

PUBLISHED PRIMARY RECORDS

Asbury, Francis. *The Journal and Letters of Francis Asbury.* 3 vols. Edited by Elmer T. Clark. Nashville, Tenn.: Abingdon Press, 1958.

Bargar, Bradley. "Charles Town Loyalism in 1775: The Secret Reports of Alexander Innes." *South Carolina Historical Magazine* 63 (July 1962): 125–36.

Barnwell, Robert W., Jr., ed. "Reports on Loyalist Exiles from South Carolina, 1783." *Proceedings of the South Carolina Historical Association,* 1937, 34–46.

Bennett, William D., ed. *Orange County Records.* 16 vols. to date. Raleigh, N.C.: privately published by author, 1987–.

Bowling, Kenneth R., and Helen E. Veit, eds. *The Diary of William Maclay and Other Notes on Senate Debates.* Baltimore: Johns Hopkins University Press, 1972.

Brickell, John. "Observations on the Medical Treatment of General Washington in His [last] Illness." *Transactions of the College of Physicians of Philadelphia* 25 (1903): 90–94.

Cain, Robert J., ed. *Colonial Records of North Carolina [Second Series]: Records of the Executive Council, 1755–1775.* Raleigh: North Carolina Department of Cultural Resources, 1994.

Calendar of the General Otho Holland Williams Papers in the Maryland Historical Society. Baltimore: Maryland Historical Records Survey Project, 1940.

Campbell, Archibald. "Colonel Archibald Campbell's March from Savannah to Augusta, 1779." Edited by Doyce B. Nunis Jr. *Georgia Historical Quarterly* 45 (September 1961): 275–86.

————. *Journal of an Expedition against the Rebels of Georgia in North America under the Orders of Archibald Campbell Esquire, Lieut. Colol. of His Majesty's 71st Regimt., 1778.* Edited by Colin Campbell. Darien, Ga.: Ashantilly Press, 1981.

Candler, Allen D., ed. *Colonial Records of the State of Georgia.* 25 vols. 1904–1910. Reprint, New York: AMS Press, 1970.

Chesney, Alexander. "Memoir of Captain Alexander Chesney." In "The Battle of King's Mountain: As Seen by the British Officers," edited by Samuel C. Williams. *Tennessee Historical Magazine* 7 (April 1921): 51–66.

Clark, Murtie June, ed. *Loyalists in the Southern Campaign of the Revolutionary War.* 3 vols. Baltimore: Genealogical Publishing Co., 1981.

Clark, Walter, ed. *State Records of North Carolina.* Vols. 11–26. 1886–1907. Various publishers.

Clinton, Sir Henry. *The American Rebellion: Sir Henry Clinton's Narrative of His Campaigns, 1775–1782, with an Appendix of Original Documents.* Edited by William B. Willcox. New Haven, Conn.: Yale University Press, 1954.

————. "Sir Henry Clinton's 'Journal of the Siege of Charleston, 1780.'" Edited by William T. Bulger. *South Carolina Historical Magazine* 66 (July 1965): 147–74.

Columbia University Alumni Register, 1754–1931. New York: Columbia University Press, 1932.

Cooper, Thomas, and David J. McCord, eds. *Statutes at Large of South Carolina.* 10 vols. Columbia, S.C.: printed by A. S. Johnston, 1836–1841.

Cornwallis, Charles. *Correspondence of Charles, First Marquis Cornwallis.* Edited by Charles Ross. 3 vols. London: John Murray, 1859.

Dal Verme, Count Francesco. *Seeing America and Its Great Men: The Journal and Letters of Count Francesco dal Verme, 1783–1784.* Translated and edited by Elizabeth Cometti. Charlottesville: University of Virginia Press, 1969.

Davies, K. G., ed. *Documents of the American Revolution, 1770–1783.* 21 vols. Shannon: Irish University Press, 1972–1981.

DeBrahm, John Gerard William. *DeBrahm's Report of the General Survey in the Southern District of North America.* Edited by Louis DeVorsey Jr. Columbia: University of South Carolina Press, 1971.

Donkin, Robert. *Military Collections and Remarks.* New York: H. Gaine, 1777.

Elliot, Jonathan, ed. *The Debates in the Several State Conventions on the Adoption of the Federal Constitution as Recommended at Philadelphia in 1787. . . .* 5 vols. 1888. Reprint, New York: Ayer, 1987.

Ewald, Johann. *The Diary of the American War: A Hessian Journal; Captain Johann Ewald, Field Jager Corps.* Translated and edited by Joseph P. Tustin. New Haven, Conn.: Yale University Press, 1979.

Ferguson, Adam. *Biographical Sketch or Memoir of Lieutenant-Colonel Patrick Ferguson, Originally Intended for the British Encyclopaedia.* Edinburgh: John Moir, 1817.

Ferguson, Patrick. "An Officer Out of His Time: Correspondence of Major Patrick Ferguson, 1779–1780." Edited by Hugh F. Rankin. In *Sources of American Independence: Selected Manuscripts from the Collections of the William L. Clements Library,* edited by Howard H. Peckham. 2 vols. Chicago: University of Chicago Press, 1978.

Fries, Adelaide L., ed. *Records of the Moravians in North Carolina.* Vol. 4, *1780–1783.* Raleigh, N.C.: Edwards & Broughton, 1930.

Gerlach, Larry R., ed. *New Jersey in the American Revolution, 1763–1783: A Documentary History.* Trenton: New Jersey Historical Commission, 1975.

Gibbes, R. W., ed. *Documentary History of the American Revolution: Consisting of Letters and Papers Relating to the Contest for Liberty, Chiefly in South Carolina.* . . . 3 vols. 1853–1857. Reprint, Spartanburg, S.C.: Reprint Co., 1972.

Gray, Robert. "Colonel Robert Gray's Observations on the War in Carolina." *South Carolina Historical and Genealogical Magazine* 11 (July 1910): 139–50.

Greene, Nathanael. *The Papers of General Nathanael Greene.* Edited by Richard K. Showman, Dennis M. Conrad, and Roger N. Parks. 13 vols. to date. Chapel Hill: University of North Carolina Press, 1976–2005.

Hanger, George, 4th Baron Coleraine. *The Life, Adventures, and Opinions of Col. George Hanger Written by Himself.* 2 vols. London: J. Debrett, 1801.

Harris, Amelie. "Memoir." In *Loyalist Narratives from Upper Canada,* edited by James J. Talman, 109–48. 1946. Reprint, New York: Greenwood Press, 1969.

Hazard, Ebenezer. "A View of Coastal South Carolina in 1778: The Journal of Ebenezer Hazard." Edited by H. Roy Merrens. *South Carolina Historical Magazine* 73 (October 1972): 177–93.

Hemphill, William E., Wylma A. Wates, and R. Nicholas Olsberg, eds. *State Records of South Carolina: Journals of the General Assembly and House of Representatives, 1776–1780.* Columbia: University of South Carolina Press, 1970.

Hoffmann, Margaret M. *Colony of North Carolina: Abstracts of Land Patents, 1735–1775.* 2 vols. Weldon, N.C.: Roanoke News Co., 1982–1984.

Holcomb, Brent, comp. *Anson County North Carolina Deed Abstracts, 1749–1766: Abstracts of Wills and Estates, 1749–1795.* Baltimore: Genealogical Publishing Co., 1980.

———. *Deed Abstracts of Tryon, Lincoln and Rutherford Counties, North Carolina, 1769–1786: Tryon County Wills and Estates.* Easley, S.C.: Southern Historical Press, 1977.

———. *Marriages of Surry County, North Carolina, 1779–1868.* Baltimore: Genealogical Publishing Co., 1982.

———. *Newberry County, South Carolina: Minutes of the County Court, 1785–1798.* Easley, S.C.: Southern Historical Press, 1977.

———. *North Carolina Land Grants in South Carolina, 1745–1773.* Greenville, S.C.: A Press, 1980.

———. *Probate Records of South Carolina.* 3 vols. Easley, S.C.: Southern Historical Press, 1977–1979.

————. *1785 Tax List, Rutherford County, North Carolina*. Chapel Hill, N.C.: Holcomb, 1974.

————. *Tryon County, North Carolina, Minutes of the Court of Pleas and Quarter Sessions, 1769–1779*. Columbia, S.C.: SCMAR, 1994.

————. *Union County, South Carolina, Deed Abstracts*. 5 vols. to date. Columbia, S.C.: SCMAR, 1998–.

————. *Union County, South Carolina, Minutes of the County Court, 1785–1799*. Easley, S.C.: Southern Historical Press, 1979.

Hough, Franklin B., ed. *The Siege of Charleston by the British Fleet and Army under the Command of Admiral Arbuthnot and Sir Henry Clinton. . . .* 1867. Reprint, Spartanburg, S.C.: Reprint Co., 1975.

Jarvis, Stephen. "The Narrative of Colonel Stephen Jarvis." In *Loyalist Narratives from Upper Canada*, edited by James J. Talman, 149–272. 1946. Reprint, New York: Greenwood Press, 1969.

Jefferson, Thomas. *The Papers of Thomas Jefferson*, vol. 4, *1 October 1780 to 24 February 1781*. Edited by Julian P. Boyd. Princeton, N.J.: Princeton University Press, 1951.

Jervey, Elizabeth H., ed. "Death Notices from the *State Gazette of South-Carolina* of Charleston, South Carolina." *South Carolina Historical and Genealogical Magazine* 51 (July 1950): 24–28.

Johnson, Uzal. *Uzal Johnson, Loyalist Surgeon: A Revolutionary War Diary*. Edited by Bobby G. Moss. Blacksburg, S.C.: Scotia Hibernia Press, 2000.

Jones, Edward Alfred. *The Loyalists of New Jersey: Their Memorials, Petitions, Claims, etc., from English Records*. Boston: Gregg Press, 1972.

Kalm, Peter. *Peter Kalm's Travels in North America: The English Version of 1770*. Edited by Adolph B. Benson. 2 vols. New York: Wilson-Erickson, 1937.

Kinloch, Francis. "Letters of Francis Kinloch to Thomas Boone, 1782–1788." Edited by Felix Gilbert. *Journal of Southern History* 8 (February 1942): 87–105.

Laurens, Henry. *The Papers of Henry Laurens*. Edited by Philip M. Hamer, George C. Rogers Jr., David R. Chesnutt, and C. James Taylor. 16 vols. Columbia: University of South Carolina Press, 1968–2002.

McBee, Mary Wilson, comp. *Anson County, North Carolina, Abstracts of Early Records*. Baltimore: Genealogical Publishing Co., 1980.

Minutes of the Provincial Congress and the Council of Safety of the State of New Jersey, 1775–1776. Trenton, N.J.: Naar, Day & Naar, 1879.

Moore, Caroline T., and Agatha A. Simmons, eds. *Abstracts of the Wills of the State of South Carolina, 1760–1784*. Columbia, S.C.: R. L. Bryan, 1969.

Moultrie, William. "The Journal of William Moultrie While a Commissioner on the North and South Carolina Boundary Survey, 1772." Edited by Charles S. Davis. *Journal of Southern History* 8 (November 1942): 549–55.

————. *Memoirs of the American Revolution, So Far as It Related to the States of North and South Carolina, and Georgia. . . .* 2 vols. 1802. Reprint (2 vols. in 1), New York: New York Times and Arno Press, 1968.

Muhlenberg, Henry Melchior. *The Journals of Henry Melchior Muhlenberg.* Edited by Theodore G. Tappert and John W. Doberstein. 3 vols. Philadelphia: Evangelical Lutheran Ministerium of Pennsylvania and Adjacent States, 1942–1958.

Murray, James. *Letters from America, 1773 to 1780, Being the Letters of a Scots Officer, Sir James Murray, to His Home during the War of American Independence.* Edited by Eric Robson. Manchester, U.K.: Manchester University Press, 1951.

Nagle, Jacob. *A Diary of the Life of Jacob Nagle, Sailor, from the Year 1775 to 1841.* Edited by John C. Dann. New York: Weidenfield & Nicolson, 1988.

New York Public Library. *Calendar of the Emmet Collection of Manuscripts etc. Relating to American History.* New York: presented to the New York Public Library by John S. Kennedy, 1900.

Newsome, A. R., ed. "A British Orderly Book, 1780–1781, Part 4." *North Carolina Historical Review* 9 (October 1932): 366–92.

Peebles, John. *John Peebles' American War: The Diary of a Scottish Grenadier, 1776–1782.* Edited by Ira D. Gruber. Mechanicsburg, Pa.: Stackpole Books, 1998.

Powell, William S., James K. Huhta, and Thomas J. Farnham, eds. *The Regulators in North Carolina: A Documentary History, 1759–1776.* Raleigh, N.C.: State Department of Archives and History, 1971.

Pugh, Evan. *The Diaries of Evan Pugh, 1762–1801.* Translated by Horace F. Rudisill. Florence, S.C.: St. David's Society, 1993.

Ramsay, David. *The History of the Revolution of South Carolina, from a British Province to an Independent State.* 2 vols. Trenton, N.J.: Isaac Collins, 1785.

Redden, Alma Cheek, ed. *Abstracts of the Minutes of the Inferior Court of Pleas and Quarter Sessions of Orange County, North Carolina, 1777–1788.* Charlotte, N.C.: Artistic Letter Shop, 1966.

The Register Book for the Parish Prince Frederick Winyaw, Ann: Dom: 1713. 1916. Reprint, Easley, S.C.: Southern Historical Press, 1982.

Register, Jeannie H., ed. "Marriage and Death Notices from the *City Gazette.*" *South Carolina Historical and Genealogical Magazine* 27 (April 1926): 95–103.

Royal Commission on Historical Manuscripts. *Report on American Manuscripts in the Royal Institution of Great Britain.* 4 vols. London: His Majesty's Stationery Office, 1904–1909.

———. *Report on the Manuscripts of Mrs. Stopford-Sackville, of Drayton House, Northhamptonshire.* 2 vols. Boston: Gregg Press, 1972.

Russell, Peter. "The Siege of Charleston: Journal of Captain Peter Russell, December 25, 1779 to May 2, 1780." Edited by James Bain Jr. *American Historical Review* 4 (April 1899): 478–501.

Salley, Alexander S., Jr., ed. *Journal of the Commissioners of the Navy, October 9, 1776–March 1, 1779.* Columbia, S.C.: The State Co., 1912–1913.

Saunders, William L., ed. *Colonial Records of North Carolina.* 10 vols. 1886–1890. Reprint, Wilmington, N.C.: Broadfoot, 1993.

Simpson, James. "James Simpson's Reports on the Carolina Loyalists, 1779–1780."

Edited by Alan S. Brown. *Journal of Southern History* 21 (November 1955): 513–19.

Smith, Paul H., ed. *Letters of Delegates to Congress, 1774–1789*, vol. 16, *Sept. 1, 1780–Feb. 28, 1781.* Washington, D.C.: Library of Congress, 1989.

Smyth, J. F. D. *A Tour in the United States of America; Containing an Account of the Present Situation of That Country . . . .* 2 vols. Dublin: Price, Moncrieffe [etc.], 1784.

Stedman, Charles. *The History of the Origin, Progress, and Termination of the American War.* 2 vols. London: J. Murray, 1794.

Stevens, Michael E., ed. *Journals of the House of Representatives, 1789–1790.* State Records of South Carolina. Columbia: University of South Carolina Press, 1984.

Tarleton, Banastre. *A History of the Campaigns of 1780 and 1781, in the Southern Provinces of North America.* 1787. Reprint, Spartanburg, S.C.: Reprint Co., 1967.

Thompson, Theodora J., and Rosa S. Lumpkin, eds. *Journals of the House of Representatives, 1783–1784.* State Records of South Carolina. Columbia: University of South Carolina Press, 1977.

Tryon, William. *The Correspondence of William Tryon and Other Selected Papers.* Edited by William S. Powell. 2 vols. Raleigh: North Carolina Division of Archives and History, 1980–1981.

Turner, Daniel. "Letters and Papers of Dr. Daniel Turner: A Rhode Islander in South Georgia," part 1. Edited by Richard K. Murdoch. *Georgia Historical Quarterly* 53 (September 1969): 341–93.

Washington, George. *The Writings of George Washington from the Original Manuscript Sources, 1745–1799*, vol. 3, *Jan. 1770–Sept. 1775.* Edited by John C. Fitzpatrick. Washington, D.C.: Government Printing Office, 1931.

Webber, Mabel L., comp. "Extracts from the Journal of Mrs. Ann Manigault, 1754–1781." *South Carolina Historical and Genealogical Magazine* 20 (April 1919): 128–41.

———. "Inscriptions from the Church Yard of the Independent or Congregational Church at Wappetaw, Christ Church Parish." *South Carolina Historical and Genealogical Magazine* 25 (July 1924): 136–42.

———. "Marriage and Death Notices from *The City Gazette.*" *South Carolina Historical and Genealogical Magazine* 23 (October 1922): 205–12.

Webster, Irene. *Guilford County, North Carolina, Will Abstracts, 1771–1841.* Madison, N.C.: Irene Webster, 1979.

Weir, Robert M., ed. *The Letters of Freeman, Etc.: Essays on the Nonimportation Movement in South Carolina.* Columbia: University of South Carolina Press, 1977.

Winn, Richard. "General Richard Winn's Notes—1780." Edited by Samuel C. Williams. *South Carolina Historical and Genealogical Magazine* 43 (October 1942): 201–12.

NEWSPAPERS, PAMPHLETS, PERIODICALS, AND BROADSIDES

Early American Imprints, Series 1: Evans, 1639–1800. Readex Digital Collections.
Forest City (N.C.) This Week
Gazette of the State of Georgia
Gazette of the State of South Carolina
Gentleman's Magazine (London)
Names in South Carolina
New York Times
Newark Intelligencer
Pennsylvania Gazette
Rivington's Royal Gazette (New York)
South Carolina and American General Gazette
South Carolina Gazette

ATLASES, GAZETTEERS, AND MAPS

Collet, John. "A Compleat Map of North-Carolina from an Actual Survey." 1770.
DeLorme North Carolina Atlas and Gazetteer. 7th ed. Yarmouth, Maine: DeLorme, 2006.
DeLorme South Carolina Atlas and Gazeteer. Yarmouth, Maine: DeLorme, 1998.
Linder, Suzanne C. *Historical Atlas of the Rice Plantations of the ACE River Basin—1860.* Columbia: South Carolina Department of Archives and History, 1995.
Marshall, Douglas W., and Howard H. Peckham. *Campaigns of the American Revolution: An Atlas of Manuscript Maps.* Ann Arbor: University of Michigan Press, 1976.
Mills, Robert. *Mills' Atlas: Atlas of the State of South Carolina, 1825.* 1825. Reprint, Easley, S.C.: Southern Historical Press, 1980.
Mouzon, Henry. "Accurate Map of North and South Carolina." 1775.
Powell, William S., ed. *The North Carolina Gazetteer.* Chapel Hill: University of North Carolina Press, 1968.
Price, Jonathan, and John Strother. "This First Actual Survey of the State of North Carolina." 1808.
United States Geological Survey. 7.5 minute quadrangle map series. Pea Ridge, N.C., and Port Wentworth, Ga.
Urquhart, Frank J., et al. "A Plan of the Principal Part of Broad Street." In *A History of the City of Newark, New Jersey: Embracing Practically Two and a Half Centuries, 1666–1913.* 3 vols. New York: Lewis Historical Publishing Co., 1913.

BIBLIOGRAPHIES AND GUIDES

Arksey, Laura, Nancy Pries, and Marcia Reed. *American Diaries: An Annotated Bibliography of Published American Diaries and Journals.* 2 vols. Detroit, Mich.: Gale Research, 1983–1987.

Côté, Richard N., ed. *Local and Family History in South Carolina: A Bibliography.* Charleston: South Carolina Historical Society, 1981.

The Early South Carolina Newspapers ESCN Database Reports: A Quick Reference Guide to Local News and Advertisements Found in Early South Carolina Newspapers. Mt. Pleasant, S.C.: ESCN Database Reports, 1995–.

Gould, Christopher, and Richard P. Morgan. *South Carolina Imprints, 1731–1800: A Descriptive Bibliography.* Santa Barbara, Calif.: ABC–CLIO, 1985.

Guide to Research Materials in the North Carolina Archives: Section B, County Records. Raleigh, N.C.: Department of Cultural Resources, Division of Archives and History, Archives and Records Section, 1990.

Harper, Josephine L. *Guide to the Draper Manuscripts.* Madison: State Historical Society of Wisconsin, 1983.

Jones, H. G. *North Carolina History: An Annotated Bibliography.* Westport, Conn.: Greenwood Press, 1995.

Lesser, Charles H., comp. *Sources for the American Revolution at the South Carolina Department of Archives and History.* Columbia: South Carolina Department of Archives and History, 2000.

North Carolina State Archives. The Manuscripts and Archives Reference System [MARS online catalog].

South Carolina Department of Archives and History. Online Index.

SECONDARY ARTICLES AND BOOKS

Ahlstrom, John D. "Captain and Chef de Brigade William Tate: South Carolina Adventurer." *South Carolina Historical Magazine* 88 (October 1987): 183–91.

Anderson, Fred. *Crucible of War: The Seven Years' War and the Fate of Empire in British North America, 1754–1766.* New York: Alfred A. Knopf, 2000.

Anscombe, Francis C. *I Have Called You Friends: The Story of Quakerism in North Carolina.* Boston: Christopher Publishing House, 1959.

Atkinson, Joseph. *The History of Newark, New Jersey, Being a Narrative of Its Rise and Progress, from Its Settlement in May 1666, by Emigrants from Connecticut, to the Present Time.* Newark, N.J.: William B. Guild, 1878.

Avery, Sharon. "Place Names in Fairfield County." *Names in South Carolina* 30 (Winter 1983): 34–40.

Babits, Lawrence E. *A Devil of a Whipping: The Battle of Cowpens.* Chapel Hill: University of North Carolina Press, 1998.

Bailey, N. Louise, and Elizabeth I. Cooper. *Biographical Directory of the South Carolina House of Representatives,* vol. 3, *1775–1790.* Columbia: University of South Carolina Press, 1981.

Barefoot, Daniel W. *Touring South Carolina's Revolutionary War Sites.* Winston-Salem, N.C.: John F. Blair, 1999.

Bass, Robert D. *Gamecock: The Life and Campaigns of General Thomas Sumter.* New York: Holt, Rinehart and Winston, 1961.

———. *Ninety Six: The Struggle for the South Carolina Back Country.* Lexington, S.C.: Sandlapper Store, 1978.

———. *Swamp Fox: The Life and Campaigns of General Francis Marion.* Columbia, S.C.: Sandlapper Press, 1959.

Bassett, Victor H. *Voices from the Past.* Reprinted from the *Bulletin of the Georgia Medical Society.* Savannah, Ga., 1937.

Bell, Malcolm, Jr. *Major Butler's Legacy: Five Generations of a Slaveholding Family.* Athens: University of Georgia Press, 1987.

Bell, Whitfield J., Jr. "Medical Practice in Colonial America." In *Symposium on Colonial Medicine in Commemoration of the 350th Anniversary of the Settlement of Virginia,* 52–66. Williamsburg, Va.: Jamestown-Williamsburg-Yorktown Celebration Commission and the Virginia 350th Anniversary Commission, 1957.

Best, Geoffrey. *Humanity in Warfare.* New York: Columbia University Press, 1980.

Blackwelder, Ruth. *The Age of Orange: Political and Intellectual Leadership in North Carolina, 1752–1861.* Charlotte, N.C.: William Loftin, 1961.

Boatner, Mark M., III, *Encyclopedia of the American Revolution.* New York: David McKay, 1966.

———. *Landmarks of the American Revolution.* 2nd ed. Detroit, Mich.: Charles Scribner's Sons, 2006.

Borick, Carl P. *A Gallant Defense: The Siege of Charleston, 1780.* Columbia: University of South Carolina Press, 2003.

Boyd, George A. *Elias Boudinot: Patriot and Statesman, 1740–1821.* Princeton, N.J.: Princeton University Press, 1952.

Boyd, Julian P. "The Sheriff in Colonial North Carolina." *North Carolina Historical Review* 5 (April 1928): 151–80.

Brown, Richard M. *The South Carolina Regulators.* Cambridge, Mass.: Harvard University Press, 1963.

Brumwell, Stephen. *Redcoats: The British Soldier and War in the Americas, 1755–1763.* Cambridge: Cambridge University Press, 2002.

Bryan, Evelyn M. F. *Colleton County, South Carolina: A History of the First 160 Years, 1670–1830.* Jacksonville, Fla.: Florentine Press, 1993.

Buchanan, John. *The Road to Guilford Courthouse: The American Revolution in the Carolinas.* New York: John Wiley & Sons, 1997.

Bull, Elias B. "Community and Neighborhood Names in Berkeley County," part 2. *Names in South Carolina* 12 (Winter 1965): 32–39.

Bynum, William B., ed. *The Heritage of Rutherford County, North Carolina.* Winston-Salem, N.C.: Hunter, 1984.

Cann, Marvin L. *Ninety Six: A Historical Guide; Old Ninety Six in the South Carolina Backcountry, 1700–1781.* Troy, S.C.: Sleepy Creek Publishing, 1996.

Caruthers, Eli W. *Revolutionary Incidents; and Sketches of Character, Chiefly in the "Old North State."* Philadelphia: Hayes and Zell, 1854.

Cash, Philip. *Medical Men at the Siege of Boston, April, 1775–April, 1776: Problems of the Massachusetts and Continental Armies.* Philadelphia: American Philosophical Society, 1973.

Cashin, Edward J. *The King's Ranger: Thomas Brown and the American Revolution on the Southern Frontier.* Athens: University of Georgia Press, 1989.

Cassidy, Frederic G., ed. *Dictionary of American Regional English.* 4 vols. to date. Cambridge, Mass.: Harvard University Press, 1985–.

Chandler, J. W. Nelson. "Willtown, Black Mingo: The Rise and Fall of an Early Village in the South Carolina Lowcountry." *South Carolina Historical Magazine* 105 (April 2004): 107–34.

Chapman, John A. *History of Edgefield County from the Earliest Settlements to 1897.* 1897. Reprint, Spartanburg, S.C.: Reprint Co., 1980.

Chappell, Buford S. *The Winns of Fairfield County.* Columbia, S.C.: R. L. Bryan, 1975.

Charles, Allan D. *The Narrative History of Union County.* Spartanburg, S.C.: Reprint Co., 1987.

Cheney, John L., Jr., ed. *North Carolina Government, 1585–1974: A Narrative and Statistical History.* Raleigh: North Carolina Department of the Secretary of State, 1975.

Clowes, William L. *The Royal Navy: A History from the Earliest Times to the Present.* 7 vols. London: Sampson Low, Marston & Co. 1897–1903.

Cockayne, George Edward. *The Complete Peerage of England, Scotland, Ireland and the United Kingdom,* vol. 2, rev. ed. Edited by Vicary Gibbs. London: St. Catherine Press, 1912.

Coleman, Kenneth. *Colonial Georgia: A History.* Millwood, N.Y.: KTO Press, 1989.

Coleman, Kenneth, and Charles S. Gurr, eds. *Dictionary of Georgia Biography.* 2 vols. Athens: University of Georgia Press, 1983.

Conway, Stephen. *The War of American Independence, 1775–1783.* New York: St. Martin's Press, 1995.

Coon, Nelson. *Using Plants for Healing.* Emmaus, Pa.: Rodale, 1979.

Cowan, Thomas. "William Hill and the Aera Ironworks." *Journal of Early Southern Decorative Arts* 13 (November 1987): 1–32.

Cowen, David L. *Medicine and Health in New Jersey.* Princeton, N.J.: D. Van Nostrand, 1964.

Cross, J. Russell. *Historic Ramblin's through Berkeley.* Columbia, S.C.: R. L. Bryan, 1985.

Curtis, Edward E. *The Organization of the British Army in the American Revolution.* 1926. Reprint, Yorkshire, U.K..: E. P. Publishing, 1972.

DAR Patriot Index. Centennial Edition. 3 vols. Washington, D.C.: National Society of the Daughters of the American Revolution, 1994.

Davidson, Chalmers G. *Friend of the People: The Life of Dr. Peter Fayssoux of Charleston, South Carolina.* Columbia: Medical Association of South Carolina, 1950.

Davis, Curtis C. *Revolution's Godchild: The Birth, Death, and Regeneration of the Society of the Cincinnati in North Carolina*. Chapel Hill: University of North Carolina Press, 1976.

Davis, Mary K. "The Feather Bed Aristocracy: Abbeville District in the 1790s." *South Carolina Historical Magazine* 80 (April 1979): 136–55.

Davis, Robert Scott, Jr. "Colonel John Hamilton of the Royal North Carolina Regiment." *Southern Campaigns of the American Revolution* 3 (May 2006): 32–34. Available online at http://www.southerncampaign.org/newsletter/v3n5 .pdf (accessed August 3, 2010).

———. "Lord Montagu's Mission to South Carolina in 1781: American POWS for the King's Service in Jamaica." *South Carolina Historical Magazine* 84 (April 1983): 89–109.

———. "The Loyalist Trials at Ninety Six in 1779." *South Carolina Historical Magazine* 80 (April 1979): 172–81.

DeMond, Robert O. *The Loyalists in North Carolina during the American Revolution*. 1940. Reprint, Baltimore: Genealogical Publishing Co., 1979.

Draper, Lyman C. *King's Mountain and Its Heroes: History of the Battle of King's Mountain, October 7th, 1780, and the Events Which Led to It*. 1881. Reprint, Spartanburg, S.C.: Reprint Co., 1967.

Duncan, Louis C. *Medical Men in the American Revolution, 1775–1783*. 1931. Reprint, New York: Augustus M. Kelley, 1970.

Edgar, Walter B. *Partisans and Redcoats: The Southern Conflict That Turned the Tide of the American Revolution*. New York: William Morrow, 2001.

———. *South Carolina: A History*. Columbia: University of South Carolina Press, 1998.

———, ed. *The South Carolina Encyclopedia*. Columbia: University of South Carolina Press, 2006.

Edgar, Walter B., and N. Louise Bailey. *Biographical Directory of the South Carolina House of Representatives*, vol. 2, *The Commons House of Assembly, 1692–1775*. Columbia: University of South Carolina Press, 1977.

Ekirch, A. Roger. *"Poor Carolina": Politics and Society in Colonial North Carolina, 1729–1776*. Chapel Hill: University of North Carolina Press, 1981.

Evans, Oliver. *The Young Mill-Wright and Miller's Guide*. 9th ed. Philadelphia: Carey, Lea & Blanchard, 1836.

Farmer, John S., and W. E. Henley. *Slang and Its Analogues, Past and Present*. 7 vols. 1890. Reprint (7 vols. in 3), New York: Kraus Reprint Corp., 1965.

Feaster, William A. *A History of Union County*. Greenville, S.C.: A Press, 1977.

Fenn, Elizabeth A. *Pox Americana: The Great Smallpox Epidemic of 1775–82*. New York: Hill and Wang, 2001.

Ferguson, Adam. *Biographical Sketch or Memoir of Lieutenant-Colonel Patrick Ferguson: Originally Intended for the British Encyclopaedia*. Edinburgh: Printed by John Moir, 1817.

Ferguson, Clyde R. "Functions of the Partisan-Militia in the South during the American Revolution: An Interpretation." In *Revolutionary War in the South: Power, Conflict, and Leadership,* edited by W. Robert Higgins, 239–58. Durham, N.C.: Duke University Press, 1979.

Ford, Worthington C., comp. *British Officers Serving in the American Revolution, 1774–1783.* Brooklyn, N.Y.: Historical Printing Club, 1897.

Fraser, Walter J., Jr. *Patriots, Pistols, and Petticoats: "Poor Sinful Charles Town" during the American Revolution.* 2nd ed. Columbia: University of South Carolina Press, 1993.

———. *Savannah in the Old South.* Athens: University of Georgia Press, 2003.

Ganyard, Robert L. "Threat from the West: North Carolina and the Cherokee, 1776–1778." *North Carolina Historical Review* 45 (Winter 1968): 47–66.

Garraty, John A., and Mark C. Carnes, eds. *American National Biography.* 24 vols. and 2 supplements. New York: Oxford University Press, 1999–2005.

George, David P., Jr. "Ninety Six Decoded: Origins of a Community's Name." *South Carolina Historical Magazine* 92 (April 1991): 69–84.

Gill, Harold B., Jr. *The Apothecary in Colonial Virginia.* Charlottesville: University Press of Virginia, 1972.

Godbold, E. Stanley. *Christopher Gadsden and the American Revolution.* Knoxville: University of Tennessee Press, 1982.

Gordon, John W. *South Carolina and the American Revolution: A Battlefield History.* Columbia: University of South Carolina Press, 2003.

Gray, Henry. *Anatomy, Descriptive and Surgical.* 1858. New York: Gramercy Books, 1977.

Gray, Lewis C. *History of Agriculture in the Southern United States to 1860.* 2 vols. 1933. Reprint, Gloucester, Mass.: Peter Smith, 1958.

Gregg, Alexander. *History of the Old Cheraws.* 1867. Reprint, Spartanburg, S.C.: Reprint Co., 1982.

Gregorie, Anne King. *History of Sumter County, South Carolina.* Sumter, S.C.: Library Board of Sumter County, 1954.

———. *Thomas Sumter.* Columbia, S.C.: R. L. Bryan, 1931.

Griffin, Clarence W. *The History of Old Tryon and Rutherford Counties, North Carolina, 1730–1936.* 1937. Reprint, Spartanburg, S.C.: Reprint Co., 1977.

Gruber, Ira D. "Britain's Southern Strategy." In *The Revolutionary War in the South: Power, Conflict, and Leadership,* edited by W. Robert Higgins, 205–38. Durham, N.C.: Duke University Press, 1979.

Haller, Stephen E. *William Washington: Cavalryman of the Revolution.* Bowie, Md.: Heritage Books, 2001.

Halpenny, Francess G., ed. *Dictionary of Canadian Biography Online,* vol. 5, *1801–1820.* Toronto: University of Toronto Press, 1983.

Harrison, Mark. "Medicine and the Management of Modern Warfare." *Journal of the History of Science* 34 (December 1996): 379–410.

Hatcher, Patricia Law, ed. *Abstract of Graves of Revolutionary Patriots.* Dallas, Tex.: Pioneer Heritage Press, 1988.

Haw, James. "A Broken Compact: Insecurity, Union, and the Proposed Surrender of Charleston, 1779." *South Carolina Historical Magazine* 96 (January 1995): 30–53.

———. *John and Edward Rutledge of South Carolina.* Athens: University of Georgia Press, 1997.

Hay, Gertrude S., ed. *Roster of Soldiers from North Carolina in the American Revolution.* Durham: North Carolina Daughters of the American Revolution, 1932.

Hayes, Johnson J. *The Land of Wilkes.* Wilkesboro, N.C.: Wilkes County Historical Society, 1962.

Heitman, Francis B. *Historical Register of Officers of the Continental Army during the War of the Revolution, April 1775 to December 1783.* 1914. Reprint, Baltimore: Genealogical Publishing Co., 1982.

Higginbotham, Don. *Daniel Morgan, Revolutionary Rifleman.* Chapel Hill: University of North Carolina Press, 1961.

Higgins, W. Robert. "Charles Town Merchants and Factors Dealing in the External Negro Trade, 1735–1775." *South Carolina Historical Magazine* 65 (October 1964): 205–17.

Hill, Glenna See. "The Allaire Family of LaRochelle, France, and Westchester County, New York." *New York Genealogical and Biographical Record* 126 (January 1995): 55–59.

Hinshaw, William W. *Encyclopedia of American Quaker Genealogy,* vol. 1, *North Carolina.* Ann Arbor, Mich.: Edwards Brothers, 1936.

Holschlag, Stephanie L., Michael J. Rodeffer, and Marvin L. Cann. *Ninety Six: The Jail.* Ninety Six, S.C.: Star Fort Historical Commission, 1978.

Howe, Jonas. "Major Ferguson's Riflemen—the American Volunteers." *Acadiensis* 6 (October 1906): 237–46.

Jackson, Ronald V., ed. *North Carolina 1800 Census Index.* North Salt Lake, Utah: Accelerated Indexing Systems, 1974.

Jarvis, Julia. *Three Centuries of Robinsons: The Story of a Family.* Don Mills, Ontario: T. H. Best Printing Co., 1967.

Johnson, George Lloyd, Jr. *The Frontier in the Colonial South: South Carolina Backcountry, 1736–1800.* Westport, Conn.: Greenwood Press, 1997.

Johnson, Joseph. *Traditions and Reminiscences Chiefly of the American Revolution in the South.* 1851. Reprint, Spartanburg, S.C.: Reprint Co., 1972.

Johnson, Nexsen B. "Some Williamsburg County Names." *Names in South Carolina* 16 (Winter 1969): 36–40.

Jones, Daniel. *An Outline of English Phonetics.* 9th ed. London: Cambridge University Press, 1972.

Jones, Edward Alfred. *The Loyalists of New Jersey: Their Memorials, Petitions, Claims, etc., from English Records.* Boston: Gregg Press, 1972.

Jordan, Terry G. *Trails to Texas: Southern Roots of Western Cattle Ranching.* Lincoln: University of Nebraska Press, 1981.

Kars, Marjoleine. *Breaking Loose Together: The Regulator Rebellion in Pre-Revolutionary North Carolina.* Chapel Hill: University of North Carolina Press, 2002.

Katcher, Philip R. N. *Encyclopedia of British, Provincial, and German Army Units, 1775–1783.* Harrisburg, Pa.: Stackpole Books, 1973.

Kaufman, Matthew H. *Surgeons at War: Medical Arrangements for the Treatment of the Sick and Wounded in the British Army during the late 18th and 19th Centuries.* Westport, Conn.: Greenwood Press, 2001.

King, G. Wayne. *Rise Up So Early: A History of Florence County, South Carolina.* Spartanburg, S.C.: Reprint Co., 1981.

Klett, Joseph R., ed. *Genealogies of New Jersey Families from the Genealogical Magazine of New Jersey.* 2 vols. Baltimore: Genealogical Publishing Co., 1996.

Klingle, Philip. "Soldiers of Kings." *Journal of Long Island History* 12 (Spring 1976): 22–35.

Knight, Betsy. "Prisoner Exchange and Parole in the American Revolution." *William and Mary Quarterly* 48 (April 1991): 201–22.

Knight, Lucian, comp. *Georgia's Roster of the Revolution.* 1920. Reprint, Baltimore: Genealogical Publishing Co., 1967.

Krawczynski, Keith. *William Henry Drayton: South Carolina Revolutionary Patriot.* Baton Rouge: Louisiana State University Press, 2001.

Lambert, Robert S. *South Carolina Loyalists in the American Revolution.* Columbia: University of South Carolina Press, 1987.

Landrum, J. B. O. *The Colonial and Revolutionary History of Upper South Carolina.* 1897. Reprint, Spartanburg, S.C.: Reprint Co., 1977.

———. *History of Spartanburg County.* 1900. Reprint, Spartanburg, S.C.: Reprint Co., 1985.

Langdon, Barbara R. *South Carolina Marriages,* vol. 2, *1735–1885, Implied in South Carolina Law Reports.* Aiken, S.C.: Langdon & Langdon Genealogical Research, 1993.

Lawson, John. *A New Voyage to Carolina.* Edited by Hugh Lefler. Chapel Hill: University of North Carolina Press, 1967.

Lee, Charles. "Lands Granted by North Carolina below the 1772 Line: Validation of Titles." *South Carolina Historical Magazine* 69 (October 1968): 284–89.

Lefler, Hugh, and Paul Wager, eds. *Orange County, 1752–1952.* Chapel Hill, N.C.: Orange Printshop, 1953.

Leiby, Adrian C. *The Revolutionary War in the Hackensack Valley: The Jersey Dutch and the Neutral Ground, 1775–1783.* New Brunswick, N.J.: Rutgers University Press, 1962.

Lesesne, J. M., comp. "Marriage and Death Notices from the *Pendleton Messenger* of Pendleton, South Carolina." *South Carolina Historical and Genealogical Magazine* 47 (January 1946): 29–31.

Lewis, Walter H., and Memory P. F. Elvin-Lewis. *Medical Botany: Plants Affecting Man's Health.* New York: John Wiley & Sons, 1977.

Linder, Suzanne C. *Anglican Churches in Colonial South Carolina: Their History and Architecture.* Charleston, S.C.: Wyrick and Co., 2000.

Lipscomb, Terry W. "South Carolina Revolutionary Battles: Part 2." *Names in South Carolina* 21 (Winter 1974), 23–27.

———. "South Carolina Revolutionary Battles: Part 3." *Names in South Carolina* 22 (Winter 1975): 33–39.

———. "South Carolina Revolutionary Battles: Part 7." *Names in South Carolina* 26 (Winter 1979): 31–39.

———. "South Carolina Revolutionary Battles: Part 9." *Names in South Carolina* 28 (Winter 1981): 33–41.

Loring, Jessica Stevens. *Auldbrass: The Plantation Complex Designed by Frank Lloyd Wright: A Documented History of Its South Carolina Lands.* Greenville, S.C.: Southern Historical Press, 1992.

Lumpkin, Henry. *From Savannah to Yorktown: The American Revolution in the South.* Columbia: University of South Carolina Press, 1981.

Maas, David E. "The Massachusetts Loyalists and the Problem of Amnesty, 1775–1790." In *Loyalists and Community in North America,* edited by Robert M. Calhoon, Timothy M. Barnes, and George A. Rawlyk, 65–74. Westport, Conn.: Greenwood Press, 1994.

Martin, Joseph B., III. "A Guide to Presbyterian Ecclesiastical Names and Places in South Carolina, 1685–1985." *South Carolina Historical Magazine* 90 (January and April 1989): 4–212.

Massey, Gregory De Van. "The British Expedition to Wilmington, January–November, 1781." *North Carolina Historical Review* 66 (October 1989): 387–411.

———. *John Laurens and the American Revolution.* Columbia: University of South Carolina Press, 2000.

Mathews, Marty. *Forgotten Founder: The Life and Times of Charles Pinckney.* Columbia: University of South Carolina Press, 2004.

Mattern, David B. *Benjamin Lincoln and the American Revolution.* Columbia: University of South Carolina Press, 1995.

Matthew, H. C. G., and Brian Harrison, eds. *Oxford Dictionary of National Biography in Association with the British Academy: From the Earliest Times to the Year 2000.* 60 vols. Oxford: Oxford University Press, 2004.

Mays, Terry M. *Dictionary of the American Revolution.* Lanham, Md.: Scarecrow Press, 1999.

McCormick, Richard P. *Experiment in Independence: New Jersey in the Critical Period, 1781–1789.* New Brunswick, N.J.: Rutgers University Press, 1950.

McCowen, George S. *The British Occupation of Charleston, 1780–82.* Columbia: University of South Carolina Press, 1972.

McCrady, Edward. *The History of South Carolina in the Revolution, 1775–1780.* 1901. Reprint, New York: Russell & Russell, 1969.

————. *The History of South Carolina in the Revolution, 1780–1783.* 1902. Reprint, New York: Russell & Russell, 1969.

McIver, Petrona. "Early Taverns on the Georgetown Road." *Names in South Carolina* 14 (Winter 1967): 33–35.

————. "Some Towns and Settlements of Christ Church Parish." *Names in South Carolina* 13 (November 1966): 46–50.

————. "Wappetaw Congregational Church." *South Carolina Historical Magazine* 58 (January 1957): 34–47.

McMaster, Fitz Hugh. *A History of Fairfield County, South Carolina, from "Before the White Man Came" to 1942.* 1946. Reprint, Spartanburg, S.C.: Reprint Co., 1980.

Meriwether, James B. *The Expansion of South Carolina, 1729–1765.* Kingsport, Tenn.: Southern Publishers, 1940.

Merrell, James H. *The Indians' New World: Catawbas and Their Neighbors from European Contact through the Era of Removal.* Chapel Hill: University of North Carolina Press, 1989.

Merrens, H. Roy. *Colonial North Carolina in the Eighteenth Century: A Study in Historical Geography.* Chapel Hill: University of North Carolina Press, 1964.

Merrens, H. Roy, and George D. Terry. "Dying in Paradise: Malaria, Mortality, and the Perceptual Environment in Colonial South Carolina." *Journal of Southern History* 50 (October 1984): 533–50.

Messick, Hank. *King's Mountain: The Epic of the Blue Ridge "Mountain Men" in the American Revolution.* Boston: Little, Brown, 1976.

Milling, Chapman. *Red Carolinians.* Columbia: University of South Carolina Press, 1969.

Mills, Robert. *Statistics of South Carolina.* 1826. Reprint, Spartanburg, S.C.: Reprint Co., 1972.

Moore, John Hammond. *Columbia and Richland County: A South Carolina Community, 1740–1990.* Columbia: University of South Carolina Press, 1993.

Morgan, David T., and William J. Schmidt, *North Carolinians in the Continental Congress.* Winston-Salem, N.C.: John F. Blair, 1976.

Morgan, Edna Q. *John Adam Treutlen, Georgia's First Constitutional Governor: His Life, Real and Rumored.* Springfield, Ga.: Historic Effingham Society, 1998.

Moss, Bobby G. *The Loyalists in the Siege of Ninety-Six.* Blacksburg, S.C.: Scotia-Hibernia Press, 1999.

————. *The Patriots at Kings Mountain.* Blacksburg, S.C.: Scotia-Hibernia Press, 1990.

————. *The Patriots at the Battle of Cowpens.* Rev. ed. Blacksburg, S.C.: Scotia-Hibernia Press, 1985.

————. *Roster of the Loyalists in the Battle of Kings Mountain.* Blacksburg, S.C.: Scotia-Hibernia Press, 1998.

———. *Roster of South Carolina Patriots in the American Revolution.* Baltimore: Genealogical Publishing Co., 1983.

Nash, Francis. *Hillsboro, Colonial and Revolutionary.* 1903. Reprint, Chapel Hill, N.C.: Orange Printshop, 1953.

Nelson, Paul David. *General Horatio Gates: A Biography.* Baton Rouge: Louisiana State University Press, 1976.

O'Callaghan, E. B. *Names of Persons for Whom Marriage Licenses Were Issued by the Secretary of the Province of New York Previous to 1784.* Albany, N.Y.: Weed, Parsons & Co., 1860.

O'Donnell, James H., III. *Southern Indians in the American Revolution.* Knoxville: University of Tennessee Press, 1973.

On-Line Institute for Advanced Loyalist Studies. "Biographical Sketches on Infantry Officers of the British Legion, 1778–1782." Copyright by Donald J. Gara, New Jersey. Accessed online at http://www.royalprovincial.com/military/rhist/britlegn/blinf1.htm (accessed August 3, 2010).

Palmer, Gregory. *Biographical Sketches of Loyalists of the American Revolution.* Westport, Conn.: Meckler, 1984.

Peckham, Howard H., ed. *The Toll of Independence: Engagements and Battle Casualties of the American Revolution.* Chicago: University of Chicago Press, 1974.

Piecuch, Jim. "Massacre or Myth? Banastre Tarleton at the Waxhaws, May 29, 1780." *Southern Campaigns of the American Revolution* 1 (October 2004): 3–17. Available online at http://www.southerncampaign.org/newsletter/v1n2.pdf (accessed August 3, 2010).

Pope, Thomas H. *The History of Newberry County, South Carolina.* 2 vols. Columbia: University of South Carolina Press, 1973–1992.

Powell, William S., ed. *Dictionary of North Carolina Biography.* 6 vols. Chapel Hill: University of North Carolina Press, 1979–1996.

———. *North Carolina through Four Centuries.* Chapel Hill: University of North Carolina Press, 1989.

———. *When the Past Refused to Die: A History of Caswell County, North Carolina, 1777–1977.* Durham, N.C.: Moore, 1977.

Power, J. Tracy. "'The Virtue of Humanity Was Totally Forgot': Buford's Massacre, May 29, 1780." *South Carolina Historical Magazine* 93 (January 1992): 5–14.

Purcell, L. Edward. *Who Was Who in the American Revolution.* New York: Facts on File, 1993.

Purvis, Thomas L. Comment in "The Population of the United States, 1790: A Symposium." *William and Mary Quarterly* 41 (January 1984): 119–25.

Randolph County Historical Society. *Randolph County, 1779–1979.* Asheboro, N.C.: Randolph County Historical Society, 1980.

Rankin, Hugh F. *Francis Marion: The Swamp Fox.* New York: Thomas Y. Crowell, 1973.

———. *The North Carolina Continentals.* Chapel Hill: University of North Carolina Press, 1971.

Ranlet, Philip. "In the Hands of the British: The Treatment of American POWs During the War of Independence." *Historian* 62 (Summer 2000): 731–58.

Ratcliff, Clarence E., comp. *North Carolina Taxpayers, 1679–1790.* 2 vols. Baltimore: Genealogical Publishing Co., 1984–1987.

Raymond, W. O. "Roll of Officers of the British American or Loyalist Corps, 1775–1783." *Collections of the New Brunswick Historical Society* 5 (1904): 224–72.

Reiss, Oscar. *Medicine and the American Revolution: How Diseases and Their Treatments Affected the Colonial Army.* Jefferson, N.C.: McFarland, 1998.

Robertson, John. *The Scottish Enlightenment and the Militia Issue.* Edinburgh: John Donald, 1985.

Rogers, George C. *The History of Georgetown County, South Carolina.* Columbia: University of South Carolina Press, 1970.

Rowland, Lawrence S., Alex Moore, and George C. Rogers Jr. *The History of Beaufort County, South Carolina.* Columbia: University of South Carolina Press, 1996.

Sabine, Lorenzo. *Biographical Sketches of Loyalists of the American Revolution with an Historical Essay.* 2 vols. 1864. Reprint, Baltimore: Genealogical Publishing Co., 1979.

Salley, Alexander S., Jr., "Colonel Moses Thomson and Some of His Descendants." *South Carolina Historical and Genealogical Magazine* 3 (April 1902): 97–113.

———. *The History of Orangeburg County, South Carolina.* 1898. Reprint, Baltimore: Regional Publishing Co., 1969.

———, comp. *South Carolina Provincial Troops, Named in the Papers of the First Council of Safety of the Revolutionary Party in South Carolina, June–November 1775.* Baltimore: Genealogical Publishing Co., 1977.

Sappington, Roger A. "Dunker Beginnings in North Carolina in the Eighteenth Century." *North Carolina Historical Review* 46 (Summer 1969): 214–38.

———. "Two Eighteenth Century Congregations in North Carolina." *North Carolina Historical Review* 47 (April 1970): 176–204.

Scotti, Anthony J., Jr. *Brutal Virtue: The Myth and Reality of Banastre Tarleton.* 1995. Reprint, Bowie, Md.: Heritage Books, 2002.

Searcy, Martha C. *The Georgia-Florida Contest in the American Revolution, 1776–1778.* University: University of Alabama Press, 1985.

Selby, John E. *A Chronology of Virginia and the War of Independence, 1763–1783.* Charlottesville: University Press of Virginia, 1973.

———. *The Revolution in Virginia, 1775–1783.* Williamsburg, Va.: Colonial Williamsburg Foundation, 1988.

Selesky, Harold E., ed. *Encyclopedia of the American Revolution.* 2nd ed. 2 vols. Detroit: Charles Scribner's Sons, 2006. [A revised and expanded version of Mark M. Boatner's *Encyclopedia of the American Revolution,* published in 1966.]

Shaw, William H. *History of Essex and Hudson Counties, New Jersey.* 2 vols. Philadelphia: Everts and Peck, 1884.

Sherrill, William L. *Annals of Lincoln County, North Carolina.* 1937. Reprint, Baltimore: Regional Publishing Co., 1967, 1972.

Smith, Henry A. M. "Goose Creek." *South Carolina Historical and Genealogical Magazine* 29 (January 1928): 1–25.

———. "The Town of Dorchester, in South Carolina—a Sketch of Its History." *South Carolina Historical and Genealogical Magazine* 6 (April 1905): 62–95.

Smith, Paul H. "The American Loyalists: Notes on Their Organization and Numerical Strength." *William and Mary Quarterly* 25 (April 1968): 259–77.

———. *Loyalists and Redcoats: A Study in British Revolutionary Policy.* Chapel Hill: University of North Carolina Press, 1964.

———. "New Jersey Loyalists and the British 'Provincial' Corps in the War for Independence." *New Jersey History* 87 (Summer 1969): 69–78.

Starr, J. Barton. *Tories, Dons, and Rebels: The American Revolution in British West Florida.* Gainesville: University Press of Florida, 1976.

Stewart, Mart. "'Whether Wast, Deodand, or Stray': Cattle, Culture, and the Environment in Early Georgia." *Agricultural History* 65 (Summer 1991): 1–28.

Stockard, Sallie W. *History of Guilford County, North Carolina.* Knoxville, Tenn.: Gaut-Ogden Co., 1902.

Stryker, William S. *"The New Jersey Volunteers" (Loyalists) in the Revolutionary War.* Trenton, N.J.: Naar, Day & Naar, 1887.

Swanton, John R. *Indians of the Southeastern United States.* 1946. Reprint, Washington, D.C.: Smithsonian Institution Press, 1979.

Terry, George D. "Eighteenth Century Plantation Names in Upper St. John's, Berkeley." *Names in South Carolina* 26 (Winter 1979): 15–19.

Thomson, Thomas. Letter from Thomas Thomson to James Chitwood. *St. Louis Genealogical Society Quarterly* 12 (Summer 1979): 102.

Thorp, Daniel B. *The Moravian Community in Colonial North Carolina: Pluralism on the Southern Frontier.* Knoxville: University of Tennessee Press, 1989.

Tilley, John A. *The British Navy and the American Revolution.* Columbia: University of South Carolina Press, 1987.

Treacy, M. F. *Prelude to Yorktown: The Southern Campaign of Nathanael Greene, 1780–1781.* Chapel Hill: University of North Carolina Press, 1963.

Troxler, Carole. "Refuge, Resistance, and Reward: The Southern Loyalists' Claim on East Florida." *Journal of Southern History* 55 (November 1989): 563–96.

U.S. Congress. *Biographical Directory of the United States Congress, 1774–2005.* Washington, D.C.: Government Printing Office, 2005.

Updike, Ethel S. *Tate Families of the South.* Salt Lake City, Utah: Hobby Press, 1971.

Valentine, Alan C. *Lord George Germain.* Oxford: Clarendon Press, 1962.

Waddell, Eugene, comp. *Indians of the South Carolina Lowcountry, 1562–1751.* Spartanburg, S.C.: Reprint Co., 1980.

Wait, Jane Wofford, ed. *The History of the Wofford Family.* 1928. Reprint, Spartanburg, S.C.: Reprint Co., 1993.

Wallace, David D. *The History of South Carolina.* 4 vols. New York: American Historical Society, 1934.

Ward, Christopher. *The War of the Revolution.* Edited by John R. Alden. 2 vols. New York: Macmillan, 1952.

Ward, Henry M. *Charles Scott and the "Spirit of '76."* Charlottesville: University of Virginia Press, 1988.

Waring, Joseph Ioor. *A History of Medicine in South Carolina, 1670–1825.* Charleston: South Carolina Medical Association, 1964.

Watterson, John S. *Thomas Burke, Restless Revolutionary.* Washington, D.C.: University Press of America, 1980.

Weir, Robert M. *Colonial South Carolina: A History.* Columbia: University of South Carolina Press, 1997.

Whitlow, Jeannine D., ed. *Heritage of Caswell County, North Carolina.* Yanceyville, N.C.: Hunter, 1985.

Wicker, Tom. "Turning Point in the Wilderness." *Military History Quarterly* 11 (Fall 1998): 62–71.

Wickwire, Franklin B., and Mary Wickwire. *Cornwallis: The American Adventure.* Boston: Houghton Mifflin, 1970.

Willcox, William B. *Portrait of a General: Sir Henry Clinton in the War of Independence.* New York: Knopf, 1964.

Wilson, Robert C. *Drugs and Pharmacy in the Life of Georgia, 1733–1959.* Atlanta, Ga.: Foote and Davies, 1959.

Wilson, T. E. "Names in Darlington County." *Names in South Carolina* 3 (Winter 1956): 8–9.

Work Projects Administration. Workers of the Writers' Program of the Work Projects Administration in South Carolina. *South Carolina: A Guide to the Palmetto State.* 1941. Reprint, Columbia: University of South Carolina Press, 1988.

Work Projects Administration for the State of North Carolina. Federal Writers' Project of the Federal Works Agency. *North Carolina: The WPA Guide to the Old North State.* Columbia: University of South Carolina Press, 1988.

Works Progress Administration of Georgia. Federal Writers' Project. Savannah Unit. "Causton's Bluff, Deptford, Brewton Hill: Three Allied Plantations," part 2. *Georgia Historical Quarterly* 23 (June 1939): 122–47.

Wright, Esther C. *The Loyalists of New Brunswick.* Hantsport, N.S.: Lancelot Press, 1955.

Wright, J. Leitch. *Florida in the American Revolution.* Gainesville: University Press of Florida, 1975.

Wright, Robert K. *The Continental Army.* Washington, D.C.: U.S. Army Center of Military History, 1984.

Yearbook, City of Charleston, South Carolina. 1893 and 1897.

DISSERTATIONS AND THESES

Coker, Kathy R. "The Punishment of Revolutionary War Loyalists in South Carolina." Ph.D. diss., University of South Carolina, 1987.

Hill, James R., III. "An Exercise in Futility: The Pre-Revolutionary Career and Influence of Loyalist James Simpson." Master's thesis, University of South Carolina, 1992.

Lane, George W. "The Middletons of Eighteenth-Century South Carolina: A Colonial Dynasty, 1678–1787." Ph.D. diss., Emory University, 1990.

Londahl-Smidt, Donald M. "After Eutaw Springs: The Last Campaign in South Carolina." Master's thesis, University of Delaware, 1972.

Ryan, Dennis P. "Six Towns: Continuity and Change in Revolutionary New Jersey, 1770–1792." Ph.D. diss., New York University, 1974.

Stadelman, Bonnie S. "The Amusements of the American Soldiers during the Revolution." Ph.D. diss., Tulane University, 1969.

Terry, George D. "'Champaign Country': A Social History of an Eighteenth Century Lowcountry Parish in South Carolina, St. John's Berkeley County." Ph.D. diss., University of South Carolina, 1981.

Troxler, Carole. "The Migration of Carolina and Georgia Loyalists to Nova Scotia and New Brunswick." Ph.D. diss., University of North Carolina, 1974.

Index

Note: Because militia service was so common among the individuals identified, the editors have not indexed references to such service in the notes.

About the Editors

A graduate of the University of South Carolina Honors College and Duke University Law School, WADE S. KOLB III is the former executive editor of the *Duke Journal of Constitutional Law and Public Policy.* He now serves as a clerk for the Honorable Ed Carnes, U.S. Court of Appeals for the Eleventh Circuit.

ROBERT M. WEIR is a distinguished professor emeritus of history at the University of South Carolina and the author of *Colonial South Carolina: A History* and *The Last of American Freemen: Studies in the Political Culture of the Colonial and Revolutionary South.* Weir has been honored for his scholarship by the American Antiquarian Society, the Southeastern Society for the Study of the Eighteenth Century, and *William and Mary Quarterly.*